Dartmouth College

THE CAMPUS GUIDE

Dartmouth College

AN ARCHITECTURAL TOUR BY

Scott Meacham

WITH PHOTOGRAPHS BY

Joseph Mehling

PRINCETON ARCHITECTURAL PRESS

NEW YORK

Published by
Princeton Architectural Press
37 East Seventh Street
New York, New York 10003

For a free catalog of books, call 1.800.722.6657.
Visit our web site at www.papress.com.

Series Editor: Nancy Eklund Later
Editor: Lauren Nelson Packard
Designer: Arnoud Verhaeghe

Special thanks to: Nettie Aljian, Sara Bader, Dorothy Ball,
Nicola Bednarek, Janet Behning, Becca Casbon, Penny (Yuen Pik) Chu,
Russell Fernandez, Pete Fitzpatrick, Wendy Fuller, Clare Jacobson,
John King, Mark Lamster, Linda Lee, Laurie Manfra, Katharine Myers,
Jennifer Thompson, Paul Wagner, Joseph Weston, and Deb Wood of
Princeton Architectural Press —Kevin C. Lippert, publisher

Library of Congress Cataloging-in-Publication Data

Meacham, Scott.
   Dartmouth College : an architectural tour / by Scott Meacham ; with
photographs by Joseph Mehling.—1st ed.
      p. cm —(The campus guide)
   Includes bibliographical references and index.
   ISBN 978-1-56898-348-6 (alk. paper)
   1. Dartmouth College—Guidebooks. 2. Dartmouth College—
Buildings. 3. Dartmouth College—History. I. Mehling, Joseph. II.
Title.
   LD1439.M43 2008
   378.742'3—dc22
                          2007048648

CONTENTS

HOW TO USE THIS BOOK

This guide is intended for visitors, alumni, and students who want an insider's look at the most historic and interesting buildings on the campus of Dartmouth College and around the town of Hanover, from the colonial Green to Charles Moore's Hood Museum and beyond.

After an introductory history of the campus, the book is divided into eight Walks covering the major precincts of the campus and the town. Each Walk begins with an aerial map and short essay about that area, followed by a collection of profiles of the constituent buildings. The entry for each building includes information about designers and dates as well as the historical and architectural characteristics of the building; most entries are illustrated with photographs. The third Walk, which covers athletic facilities, ranges from a specific part of campus to the school's more distant properties, including the Moosilauke Ravine Lodge and the Second College Grant.

Visitors are welcome to tour the Dartmouth campus:
To arrange a tour, please contact the campus Admissions Office at 603.646.2875. For more information on Dartmouth, please visit www.dartmouth.edu.

FOREWORD

Dartmouth College is a place of strong community and vibrant individuality. In a time of increasing homogenization, it has maintained a unique culture and campus in which shared purpose is sustained by individual exploration. It strikes me that this duality is sustained by two other dynamic balances that have informed the college from its inception: the balance between building and nature and the relationship between college and town.

While mandated by a royal Charter in 1769, the planning and construction of the early campus was uniquely American in its energy and practicality. The choice of Hanover was due in part to its proximity to the Connecticut River and to military roads. Under Reverend Wheelock's direction a common green was cleared in a primal act of taming what he called the "horrid wilderness." The original college plan, attributed to townsman Jonathan Freeman, sited the green along the compass cardinal points.Most critically, it platted the adjoining parcels as a mix of college and town uses so that the life of a growing New England village could support the life of the college.

From the beginning, the buildings of Dartmouth have expressed the ethos of their New England roots. They are unpretentious, well crafted and Platonic in their austere geometry. They are built with the wisdom and eloquence of the carpenter and mason: taut and solid against the elements. They have strong unpretentious exteriors that protect a rich interior life. They stand as individuals around the green and yet aggregate to define streets, paths, and common spaces.

Yet for all their strength, they never overwhelm the natural landscape. Buildings suggest ensembles, yet paths and spaces flow around them. Buildings may link but do not form enclosed quadrangles in the manner of Oxford, Cambridge, and their Ivy League successors.

The natural landscape of mountains and valley roll close upon the central campus. The topography and movement of the campus reflect in microcosm that of the valley and regional landforms. Even in the core campus the landscape maintains an unmannered character composed of simple lawns, paths, and trees.

Successive campus plans and buildings have respected the balance of architecture and landscape and the symbiosis of town and college. This has provided a framework for harmonious growth while allowing for creativity and change. Buildings have come in diverse expressions from Colonial to Georgian, Gothic, Romanesque, and on to various interpretations of contextual contemporary. Their variety and richness have only added to the shared experience of place, even as the increasing diversity of the college community has brought greater depth and maturity to its life.

For over two hundred and thirty years Dartmouth College has maintained its physical and cultural ethos. It is a place of quiet exteriors and lively interiors; a place where individuals test and temper themselves by interacting with the natural world; a place where community is strong but not constricting. Its buildings and landscape unite to express but not limit the spirit of its place and community.

Buzz Yudell
Principal, Moore Ruble Yudell Architects & Planners

A History of Dartmouth's Campus

In his 1932 poem *Build Soil*, Robert Frost advised:

> Don't join too many gangs. Join few if any.
> Join the United States and join the family—
> But not much in between unless a college.[1]

A collegiate community really does lie somewhere between the scale of a house and a nation, and it needs a permanent place to inhabit—a place apart, an academic precinct that becomes a setting for learning, a backdrop for living, and a stage for the collective rituals that express the institution's own identity. In serving these functions, Dartmouth's campus in Hanover, New Hampshire, is meant to be a coherent and distinct ensemble of mostly Classical buildings and spaces full of interesting variety and not lacking in artistry. As the remotest and northernmost of America's colonial colleges, and the only one not established in a town, Dartmouth claims to have operated longer without interruption than any institution of higher learning in the United States.

Dartmouth's campus of about 270 acres has grown up as a simple, largely rectilinear, arrangement of closely-spaced buildings at the center of town. The oldest buildings line three sides of the Dartmouth Green, while double rows of buildings on the long sides of the space hemmed in by the hills of College Park and the ravines of the Dartmouth Cemetery. Lying neatly to the south of the Green is the business district of the Town of Hanover itself. The college arts center forms the interface between the two worlds on the Green's south side. Opposite is the college library, its clock tower the hub of academic axes extending to the north and west toward Dartmouth's three professional schools. These axes frame a residential neighborhood that the school developed on former farmland during the 1890s; another farm southeast of the Green became an athletic park around the same time. The Connecticut River marks the western border of the college, the town, and the state, and is lined by a high, forested bank that has accumulated a bridge, a set of boathouses, and a landscaped auto road leading up to the center of campus.

Much of the crispness and bracing austerity of Dartmouth's grounds derives from its avoidance of some of the popular tropes of campus architecture, such things as Gothic spires, enclosed quadrangles, domed

Reconstruction of southeast corner of the Green in 1775 by Aldren Watson (1964), showing Wheelock's Mansion House in upper right opposite the College on the other side of the street. Left of the College is the Hall, with the Log Hut opposite.

buildings, or extensive colonnades. Dartmouth has very little outdoor sculpture and has never put a statue of the founder or anyone else on a pedestal. The campus lacks "college gates" or much in the way of walls or substantial decorative plantings. These absences might be a result of the winter climate, an early religiously-based disdain for frippery, or just a traditional New Hampshire frugality. Whatever its basis, benefactor Joel Parker summed it up in 1867, when he allowed that some limited shrubbery might have to be planted in the College Park, stating nevertheless that "if the intention is to make a College Park…it appears to me that the main article should be trees—many of them trees which will grow to a large size—and finally make a grand old woods."[2] This is not a campus for hedges or flowerbeds, it is a landscape of horizontal grass and vertical elms, of simple gravel paths and dark pine woods.

The school's founder was the ambitious Rev. Eleazar Wheelock, a Congregational minister of the Great Awakening who was ordained not long after he graduated from Yale College in 1733. He soon opened a college-preparatory Latin School in what is now part of Columbia, Connecticut. In its nearly thirty-five years of operation, the school's best-known graduate was Samson Occom, a Mohegan from Connecticut. Occom arrived as a student at Wheelock's school in 1743 and spent four years there with funding from London's Society for the Propagation of the Gospel in Foreign Parts. Occom went on to establish a successful school for the Montauks on Long Island, to be ordained as a minister, and to serve as a missionary among Native Americans. From Occom's academic success, Wheelock drew the idea of establishing a charity school to train Indian youth as missionaries.

The first students of Wheelock's second school began their studies in 1754, arriving in groups of two or more to preserve their native languages. The institution that became known as Moor's School would last for nearly a century in Columbia and then in Hanover, educating both boys and girls, Native as well as English. One of its pupils from 1761 to 1763 was Hayendanegea (Joseph Brant), who became a Mohawk leader and British Army captain during the Revolution. During the early 1760s, Wheelock decided to move Moor's School to some province that would grant him a charter and take him closer to the Canadian tribes from which he hoped to draw students.

After Wheelock initially proposed a multi-town evangelical-educational settlement scheme of an unworkably utopian scale, he put forth a reduced plan for moving Moor's School that intrigued several London officials. New Hampshire Governor Benning Wentworth offered 500 acres in 1763, and in 1766 Wheelock sent Samson Occom and fellow minister Nathaniel Whitaker on a preaching tour of Britain to raise funds. Benning Wentworth's governorship and his position as Surveyor General of the King's Woods in North America went to his nephew John Wentworth, who would become the college's chief patron. He reiterated his uncle's offer and promised to grant a charter.

The British fundraising trip, which lasted more than two years, was a huge success. Crowds thronged to hear Occom preach, and King George III gave £200 to the relocation project. The two fund-raising preachers met in London with William Legge, the second earl of Dartmouth and an ongoing supporter of Moor's School, who gave £50 and agreed to head the Board of Trust that would manage the growing fund. Wheelock continued to plot something grander than a simple relocation of his charity school, and during 1768 he established a collegiate department within Moor's School to educate students who would receive their degrees from Yale and Princeton. By January of 1769, Wheelock was speaking of something he called "Dartmouth College."

Eleazar Wheelock drafted the charter that Wentworth granted in the name of the King during December of 1769. The charter not only reestablished the preparatory academy but added a college for the education "in all liberal Arts and Sciences" of "Indian youth…and also of English Youth and any others."[3] The last such royal charter in the thirteen colonies, the instrument empowered to the new college to grant degrees "as are usually granted in either of the Universities" of Oxford and Cambridge

The Green and Dartmouth Hall as engraved by Josiah Dunham and published in Massachusetts Magazine (February 1793). Flanking Dartmouth Hall are Kinsman Commons on the left and the Chapel on the right.

"or any other College in our Realm of Great Britain," a far cry from the expected missionary academy for tribal children.[4] Naming the school after Lord Dartmouth did not appease the London Board of Trust, which protested the way Wheelock was using its appropriations.

Like the charters of many towns before it, the charter of the college was a settlement device. Wentworth's grant required the school to provide 60 to 80 settlers within five years, a task typically left to the shareholders of a township, and the governor hoped that Dartmouth would "have the Government of the Town" itself rather than simply move into some existing settlement.[5] The charter empowered a board of trustees in America to make laws, a power that President Wheelock intended to use "to keep out bad Inhabitants, prevent Licentiousness, regulate Taverns & Retailers of strong drink, prevent the corruption of the Students by evil minded persons, Incourage & Support divine Ordinances, &c &c."[6] The college's pseudo-civic origin explains why, as an institution of learning, it would nevertheless lay out a New England town green at the center of its own village.

The place Wheelock selected to plant his school was the corner of the six-square mile Township of Hanover, "a New Plantation" chartered in 1761 and still existing largely on paper. The shareholders of both Hanover and the neighboring Lebanon supplemented the Governor's land grant to create a single block of 3,300 uninhabited acres where the college was to establish not just a school but a civil society. Wheelock called his remote site a "horrid wilderness," and the nearest settlement was a single house more than two miles away.

Wheelock gathered dozens of workers, including four slaves he owned (apparently Caesar, Archelaus, Lavinia, and Chloe) and began to build the college during August of 1770. "I made a hutt of loggs about eighteen feet square, without stone, brick, glass or nail, and with thirty, forty, and sometimes fifty labourers, appointed to their respective departments, I betook myself to a campaign," he wrote.[7] Using funds from the English trust, Wheelock's laborers soon built a college building and a cluster of outbuildings near what is now the corner of College and Wheelock Streets. The workers cleared the forest around the buildings; the campus was beginning.

The Log Hut that Wheelock mentioned (1770; demolished 1782) stood on the slope of the hill, near where Reed Hall now stands. Workers erected a proper two-level academic building called the College (1770–1772; demolished 1791), which stood on the Green and presented its eighty-foot front facade toward College Street. The basic clapboard-sheathed building stood atop a shallow stone foundation. It featured a stair for each of its two front entrances, creating a separate entry layout that was typical at English and American colleges of the time. Inside the building were students' rooms, a library, and an "academy" room for Moor's Charity School. Finally, a one-level frame storehouse (1770; demolished 1789) stood to the north of the College, its gable end facing College Street. After a few years it became the Hall—a single room used as both a religious meetinghouse and college dining hall that became known during 1774 for "the Badness and slovenly Dressing" of its food. Marked with a belfry, the Hall also served as the capitol building for the regional government, with Revolutionary Committees of Safety meeting there during 1776 and agitators founding the College Party there during 1778—they renamed the village "Dresden" and made it part of Vermont for several years after 1781.

Although the College and the Hall framed a rear yard, a space that Professor Frederick Chase's 1891 history described as an "incipient quadrangle," the real face of the buildings seems to have been on the other side, facing College Street and the president's house. The beginnings of a formal row along the street implied a future extension to the north in the same pattern of alternating long and short facades. At the time, Yale had recently placed a long academic building next to the narrow end of its chapel, leaving room for a third building that would arrive later to create an influential A-B-A pattern.

Dartmouth Row and Wheelock's Mansion House as depicted in an 1835 Currier print.

Trekking overland from Connecticut, nearly thirty students of Moor's School and its collegiate department arrived to continue their schooling in Hanover during the fall of 1770. Two of the party, Abraham and Daniel Simon, were Narragansett Indians, and the group included Eleazar's wife Mary and two of the family's slaves, Exeter and Peggy. Four of the students had completed most of their college studies, and Dartmouth held its first commencement in 1771. There were seven degree-granting institutions in North America, four of them having sprung up since Wheelock started his Latin School. Opening Dartmouth Hall on the hill in 1791 allowed the school to clear the original buildings from the Green, and flanked by a contemporary chapel and dining hall, the row of buildings formed a complete college. At the same time, Moor's Charity School built its frame building on the other side of the Green; the place had matured.

Beginning during the late eighteenth century, one of the main influences on the design of Dartmouth's campus was the essential tension that exists between the ideals of the college and the university. Dartmouth established a medical school in 1796, and by the early nineteenth century was using the words "College" and "University" in its name interchangeably, albeit without much meaning attached to the difference. In 1815, John Wheelock, the son of the founder, asked the state legislature to put him back in charge of the college after the trustees ousted him from the presidency he had inherited in 1779. The legislature did more; in 1816 it refashioned the school as a state-run "Dartmouth University." Seeing its chance to strike a blow for Jeffersonian Republicanism the legislature required university officers to swear an oath to the state and established fines for anyone serving as a college officer. The university broke the locks on the doors of Dartmouth Hall and began holding its classes there during 1817. The university ostensibly added graduate colleges of theology and law, and the college lost its suit in the state supreme court, apparently doomed.

The college continued operating throughout its two-year period of tribulations. It held classes in professors' houses and rented a local assembly room for its chapel exercises. Its students crossed paths with those of the university on the Green. The college's lawsuit reached the United States Supreme Court during 1818. Daniel Webster gave his peroration before Chief Justice Marshall, as others later recalled part of it:

> Sir, you may destroy this little institution; it is weak; it is in your
> hands! I know it is one of the lesser lights in the literary horizon
> of our country. You may put it out: but if you do, you must carry
> through your work! You must extinguish, one after another, all
> those great lights of science, which, for more than a century,
> have thrown radiance over the land! It is, sir, as I have said, a
> small college, and yet there are those that love it.[8]

The court found in favor of the college: although the government had granted the charter, it could no longer control the institution, because the charter was protected from state interference by the same constitutional provision that guarded private contracts. The milestone of constitutional law eventually would shelter the modern commercial corporation from the whims of the state, but at Dartmouth, the result was immediate and utterly practical. The news reached Hanover early in 1819, the college took back its buildings, and cannons boomed. Later, the case would be used to deliver another message: whatever its relation to the state, this "small college" would not be a university.

The school ended its long recovery from the case with a pair of new buildings designed by architect Ammi Burnham Young of the nearby town of Lebanon. He designed all six of the buildings that the college and Moor's Charity School erected or altered during the three decades at the middle of the nineteenth century. At the conclusion of his Dartmouth work, Young became the Architect of the Treasury, head of the federal government's design office and the author of thirty bold granite customhouses in the nation's ports. His restrained Greek Revival forms were appropriate for the Dartmouth of the time, which was not a fancy place—its students were largely from rural New England towns and, according to the stereotype, were studying to become preachers and teachers. In many ways, Dartmouth

Dartmouth Row as depicted in a watercolor of about 1840 attributed to Ann Frances Ray in the collection of the Hood Museum of Art.

was a traditional denominational college, all charcoal and candlelight, with Classical recitations and hard wooden benches.

Dartmouth's collegiate pendulum began one of its several swings toward the university as Young's tenure as architect ended. Dartmouth picked up a second undergraduate college in 1852, after a retired Boston commission merchant named Abiel Chandler, a native of Walpole, New Hampshire, left a gift to establish the Chandler School of Science and the Arts. Like Harvard's Lawrence Scientific School (1847) and Yale's Sheffield Scientific School (1854), the Chandler School introduced technological subjects such as engineering and architecture, which were still too practical and pedestrian for the literary college. The new school moved into the second building of Moor's Charity School (Ammi Burnham Young, 1837), just above the present Parkhurst Hall. Dartmouth opened its third undergraduate college in 1868, after requesting and receiving the state's new land-grant college. The state took advantage of the educational infrastructure already in place in Hanover, and Dartmouth received funding. Dartmouth split the cost of two brick buildings for the school, expanding its existing roster of six buildings (the Medical and Chandler Schools also occupied one building each). Dartmouth opened its second professional school soon after, in 1871 creating a postgraduate engineering school with a gift from General Sylvanus Thayer. The goals of expanding the frontiers of knowledge and training professionals after their graduation from college were beginning to compete with Dartmouth's traditional aim of fostering undergraduate learning.

The college-university conflict reached an awkward peak under president Samuel Colcord Bartlett, a Congregational minister and graduate of 1836 who imposed an utter traditionalism upon taking office in 1877. Because he could not do away with the associated schools, he ignored them, focusing on the literary college as an old-fashioned molder of character. He prevented the Chandler School from raising its standards to those of Dartmouth, and he famously insulted the career prospects of the agricultural students at their commencement. Bartlett's backward-looking curriculum and autocratic style made him controversial among many alumni, and in 1881 the trustees held courtroom-style hearings in one of the country's first public accountings by a president for his educational practice, according to historian Marilyn Tobias. President Bartlett managed to stay on, overseeing the construction of the only academic building in a nearly fifty-year period (Wilson Hall, the library) and remained as a popular professor after resigning in 1892.

The most important period in the history of Dartmouth's campus since its establishment was that of Bartlett's successor, the reformative William Jewett Tucker. A progressive of the class of 1861 who subscribed to the theory of evolution and was punished for religious heterodoxy at Andover Theological Seminary, Tucker swung Dartmouth's pendulum away from the apparent model of the university by practically refounding the institution as a modern college, albeit a large one. Tucker saw the Chandler School merge with the literary college and the state school decamp for Durham, both moves that began just prior to his arrival. Tucker invented new traditions to emphasize spirited institutional loyalty and the free mixing of students from all social classes. He wove into Dartmouth's fabric several aspects of the modern university, adopting a business model that described freshmen as raw materials and capitalized the school's history. He expanded enrollment and invested heavily in rent-producing dormitories. He helped introduce widespread elective courses, a physics laboratory for faculty research, and the country's first graduate school of business. At a time when rank was tied closely to enrollment, Tucker's effort was so successful that it turned Dartmouth into something like the nation's college—a school that was large in size and yet could offer a spirited alternative to the fragmented research institution.

The task of establishing a new architectural identity as Dartmouth multiplied the size of its campus at the turn of the century fell to the New York architect Charles Alonzo Rich, a member of the Chandler class of 1875 who was known for his exuberant and evocative shingle-style country houses. After the college consulted with landscape architect Charles Eliot of Olmsted, Olmsted & Eliot, Rich planned an expansion campaign. His initial buildings flirted with an American Renaissance style reminiscent

*The Green's north end in 1912, showing (from left) the Vestry and College Church, the
Choate and Lord Houses with the Butterfield Museum behind and Webster Hall.*

of Columbia or New York University, but he and the trustees soon settled
on a broadly "Colonial" mode that was seen as the proper one for this
colonial institution. The two dozen buildings of Tucker and his successor,
Ernest Fox Nichols, expanded the campus beyond the Green in several
novel forms: three-building ensembles imitating Dartmouth Row, three-
sided Beaux-Arts quadrangles, residential avenues, and a scenic auto road.
Tastemaking art professor Homer Eaton Keyes served as Dartmouth's
aesthetic conscience during much of this time, assuming many presidential
powers in 1913 as business manager and later proposing that the college
institute the position of official college architect, as well as proposing the
person who should take the job.

If Tucker made Dartmouth into what it is today, the big interwar
presidency of Ernest Martin Hopkins refined the large college and tweaked
its relationship with the university form. Under the avuncular and straight-
shooting Hopkins, practical education and citizenship came to the fore:
the school declined to receive state tuition grants, to maintain the famous
Dartmouth Eye Institute, or to let the football team play in the 1938 Rose
Bowl. This attitude fit with the 1920s heyday of American collegiate life,
as women rode the train up from the Seven Sisters colleges to watch ski-
jumping in the Vale of Tempe during Winter Carnival, and alumni

came to football games in raccoon coats. Dartmouth's campus experienced its own architectural heyday, providing an idealized backdrop for the collegiate experience through a new policy that required its resident architect to design almost everything. After commissioning a master plan from John Russell Pope, the college turned Jens Fredrick Larson loose on the campus in 1919.

Larson apprenticed to designers in Boston, but he must have gained much of his planning insight while serving as a Royal Flying Corps pilot on the Western Front. Confident, charming to clients, and never without a pipe, Larson established a firm with Harry Artemas Wells, the college's superintendent of buildings and grounds. Larson's long campaign at Dartmouth helped implant a conventional Georgian style among the two or three standard options available for any new college building in the nation. As the architectural advisor to the Association of American Colleges, Larson became an authority on the question of what it meant to design a campus, and he cowrote with Archie MacInnes Palmer the first treatise specifically on planning a college (rather than a university). Over more than twenty years at Dartmouth, his master plans centered a unified and harmonious campus on the Baker Library complex, which he designed at the head of the Green.

With the internationalist president John Sloan Dickey looking outward and favoring abstract Modernism, the school replaced Larson after World War II with the Boston designer Nelson Wilmarth Aldrich. As consulting architect, Aldrich designed some buildings himself and helped select outside designers for the others, ending the one-designer policy and damping its intended harmony. Although the firm of Margaret K. Hunter and Edgar Hayes Hunter ('38) had been placing flat-roofed glass boxes for modern living on local hillsides since immediately after the war, Dartmouth did not welcome Modernism until Campbell & Aldrich designed the Choate Road dormitories of the mid-1950s. Those were peripheral buildings, and Modernism was not controversial until Aldrich and his cousin Nelson Rockefeller, the head of the building committee for the long-awaited arts center, asked Wallace Harrison to design the building at the south end of the Green. The Hopkins Center opened in 1962, the effects of its somewhat disjunctive form then and now moderated by its massive utility. The college would show an uncharacteristic affinity for large and anonymous research buildings in the Medical School complex it built at the north end of campus, adjacent to the town's nineteenth-century hospital.

Traditionally collegiate forms, even when used to mask functions characteristic of a university, reemerged after the school selected New York architect Lo-Yi Chan as its master planner in 1980. A graduate of 1954, Chan had grown up in Hanover prior to college and would make a point of fitting new works respectfully into the existing campus. Both Charles Moore's Hood Museum and Chan's own Rockefeller Center epitomize this policy, and both buildings, notably, are attached to historic buildings rather than standing alone. Dormitory construction boomed during the early twenty-first century, with an emphasis on reinforcing the college's sense of community, partially in reaction to the effects of the schedule of year-round operation adopted with coeducation in 1972, which can require students to shuttle on and off campus frequently. The construction of two schoolwide dining halls cemented the reemphasis on the undergraduate experience, and the construction boom at the turn of the century is marked by infill on vacant lots rather than an expansion of the bounds of the campus.

Dartmouth continues to conduct its anxious and productive conversation about the dangers of universitization, reflecting a tension that flows through the institution with enough vehemence to shape its campus. The school's official mission is pointedly that of an undergraduate liberal arts college that incorporates the best features of the university, creating an unclassifiable blend that routinely causes national surveys to put it into a category of its own. This conflict has given the institution an outsized personality, with Chicago professor James Weber Linn describing it as "the great American college; vivid; the one Rubens in our collection."[9] Dartmouth's wooded residential campus, containing architectural variety within a cogent and harmonious whole, depends on the institution's ability to learn from its minor excesses, testing architectural decisions for their effect on the lives of students. The result is an ongoing experiment in the wilderness, a place that remains special in the lives of those who are connected with it, a true college campus.

1. Robert Frost, "Build Soil" (reading, Columbia University, New York, May 31, 1932), printed in *A Further Range* (New York: Harry Holt and Co., 1936), 95.

2. Joel Parker to Asa Dodge Smith (October 19, 1867), Ms. 867569, Dartmouth College Archives.

3. Charter of Dartmouth College (granted December 13, 1769).

4. Ibid.

5. John Wentworth to Eleazar Wheelock (January 29, 1770), Ms. 770129.2, Dartmouth College Archives.

6. Eleazar Wheelock to William Smith (December 30, 1773), Ms. 773680, Dartmouth College Archives.

7. Eleazar Wheelock, *A Continuation of the Narrative of the Indian Charity-School, in Lebanon, in Connecticut: From the Year 1768, to the Incorporation of it with Dartmouth-College, and Removal and Settlement of it in Hanover, in the Province of New-Hampshire, 1771* (1771).

8. Daniel Webster (peroration March 10, 1818), from notes by Chauncey A Goodrich quoted by Goodrich in letter to Rufus Choate (November 25, 1852), as reprinted in John C. Sterling, ed., *Daniel Webster and a Small College* (Hanover, N.H.: Dartmouth Publications, 1965), opp. 42.

9. James Weber Linn, "Dartmouth from Without," *Dartmouth Alumni Magazine* 24, no. 4 (January 1932), 237.

WALK ONE: THE GREEN

TUCK MALL

DARTMOUTH CEMETERY

8

7

6

5

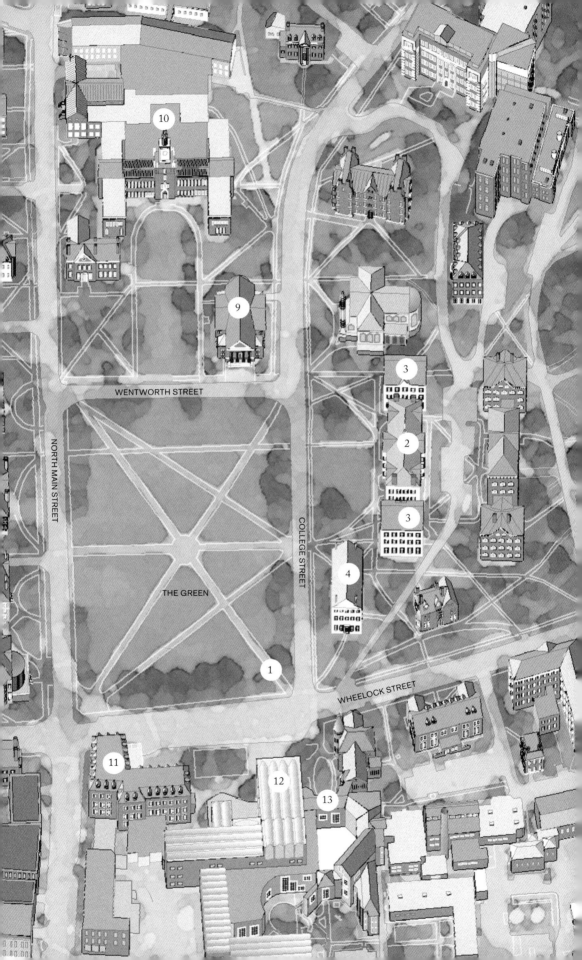

WENTWORTH STREET

NORTH MAIN STREET

COLLEGE STREET

THE GREEN

WHEELOCK STREET

The Heart of the College

College buildings line the four sides of the Green. Each side matured during a different period, and each retains its own quirks and varying degrees of completeness. The four basic Classical buildings of Dartmouth Row on the east are the oldest surviving buildings built by the college; where a fifth member of the row was meant to stand is the Romanesque Rollins Chapel, obviously a half-century too late. Dartmouth Row has a central axis, but it lies significantly north of the Green's center-line, creating an asymmetrical arrangement. After initially parceling out the other three sides of the Green to individuals during the eighteenth century, the school began reacquiring all of the surrounding plots during the 1880s. A bank on the west side that sold its building to the college in 1913 was the last commercial enterprise on the Green and, in place of the bank and its neighbors, the school built the row of replacement mansions between 1901 and 1915. Those buildings now contain office and student-life functions, as does the diminutive and disjunctively white-pained Blunt Alumni Center, the only one-time house still facing the Green.

On the north side of the Green is the C-shaped library complex of the late 1920s, a composition that belatedly carried on the spirit of a thirty-year-old City Beautiful development plan. The only surviving original building of that plan is Webster Hall of 1907, and it has been marooned on the street since a 1931 fire destroyed its counterpart on the quadrangle, an eighteenth-century church. The school moved dormitory rooms and the business and engineering schools away from the Green during the early twentieth century, recreating the Green as a monoculture of undergraduate academic functions. The south side is the newest. The somewhat alien Hopkins Center floats next to the slightly later college-owned Inn. Now, although the buildings around the Green make the place appear some-what less like a town than in the past, they also give visitors who step onto the Green the sense of being in the college rather than just facing toward it.

1. The Dartmouth Green
Jonathan Freeman, 1771–72; 1836; 1873; 1893

The Dartmouth Green is a remarkably large rectilinear space of about seven and a half acres that serves as the heart, the symbol, and the main point of transit for Dartmouth. As Dartmouth's original site, the Green is the oldest surviving work of landscape architecture at the college. The Green is a serviceable and strictly pragmatic place that enjoys hard use as a pseudo-civic zone, a communal living room, and a stage for institutional traditions. Neither a college quad nor a Beaux-Arts plaza, the Dartmouth Green is one of the country's great campus spaces.

Sled races on the Green during Winter Carnival

The Green uniquely adopts the form of a New England town common, the same kind of space that hundreds of English colonial towns built in North America using forms they inherited from feudal conventions of land ownership and shared grazing. Jonathan Freeman, a farmer and surveyor who was the first permanent settler in Hanover township just six years earlier, laid out the street plan of the collegiate village during 1771. Freeman centered his town plan around a conventional common that encompassed the two main college buildings within its bounds.

Wheelock's crew finished felling the white pines that were thick on the Green during 1772, and no description of the school's founding omits mention of the trees' astonishing height: workers measured one tree at 270 feet tall, or roughly 40 feet taller than Baker Tower stands today. The Green remained covered in stumps, however. Yale president Timothy Dwight wrote after a 1797 visit that the space was "covered with lively verdure," and until about 1820, the school required each graduating class to remove one stump. Some accounts place the last stump at 1836.

The school established itself on one side of its Green and put the village on the other three, with the college trustees exercising their town-making powers by granting plots of land around the Green to useful settlers: a carpenter and a mason on the west side, a pair of tutors on the north, and a physician-apothecary on the south. The taverner who held the charter office of College Steward received a corner site on the south side of the Green, where an inn still operates. Wheelock built an executive Mansion House on the east side of the Green, in front of the college buildings on the hill of the early 1790s. The most important local road traveled diagonally across the Green, from southwest to northeast.

Although the broader Hanover Township agreed to let the college govern its surrounding village as an independent collegiate town, New Hampshire's provincial assembly turned down several requests for town status during the early 1770s. Wheelock complained of the town's "arbitrary power and control" during a college-town dispute over smallpox quarantines in 1776 and threatened to move the school to New York. The collegiate village seceded from Hanover and New Hampshire off and on during the six years following 1777, but the idea of a collegiate government never found its chance. The only physical legacy of Dartmouth's period of civic hope for a true collegiate government.

The school formally prohibited further structures atop the Green in 1827, and the place remains free of permanent buildings. The school has declined to pave any of the shifting Versailles-like gravel paths that cross the Green. Nor has it covered the surface with trees or monuments, or blocked any of the surrounding streets that are essential to marking the borders of the space. To Dartmouth's credit, two of these streets still lack curbing or sidewalks alongside the Green, preserving the elemental character of the space as a rectilinear clearing.

The Green was the site of some contention between the overlapping camps of Dartmothians and Hanoverians during the nineteenth century. Townspeople frequently used the space as if it were a town common, pasturing their cows there overnight, although the school prohibited it. Students occasionally rounded up the cattle and drove them to a guarded pen behind Dartmouth Hall, or into the basement of the building itself, or all the way to Vermont. Such actions sometimes led to the throwing of brickbats and the gathering of armed mobs on both sides, but not to widespread violence.

The school's fence of 1835 blocked travelers from using the diagonal road across the Green, causing angry townspeople to demolish the fence. The school and a few citizens then erected a more substantial barrier of square granite posts and wooden rails the following year, creating an iconic two-rail fence that would feature in countless photographs and the memories of thousands of graduates over the next sixty years. It was students, in turn, who would burn a part of the fence during 1873, after the town straightened Wheelock Street by moving the Green's southeast corner thirty feet northward; the students later learned that the town had permission and paid for the damage. The town's final attempt to assert authority was a bandstand that local merchant Dorrance B. Currier generously started building on the Green's southwest corner. The college asked Currier to stop, and students put the grandstand to the torch.

Occurrences that take place at Dartmouth often take place on the Green, from Revolutionary meetings of the local Committee of Safety to the antiwar rallies of the 1960s, from the cannon-shot that commemorated Napoleon's 1814 defeat to the shantytown that protested Apartheid during the 1980s. The Green is naturally the site of Commencement, although students of the nineteenth century seemed to value the Green mainly as an athletic field, using it for intramural games of cricket by 1793 and the primitive proto-soccer called Old Division Football by 1820. Adding a small grandstand to the Green's northwest corner created an official baseball diamond for the school's first intercollegiate sporting event, a baseball game of 1866. Intercollegiate meets in track athletics (1875) and rugby (1881) followed, and the tennis association laid out courts on the Green's west side in 1884.

For all its carefully-preserved New England asceticism, the Green features a few annual and perennial landmarks. By the late twentieth century, the ascendant lord of the local trees undoubtedly was the Hiker's Elm, which holds down the southwest corner of the Green and towers over the most important intersection in town. The tree bears the blaze of the Appalachian Trail, guiding "through-hikers" up from the river and through town to the east along a part of the seventy-mile stretch of the Trail that the Dartmouth Outing Club maintains. The disjunctive row of maples lining the Green's south side dates to a gift of 1969, before disease-resistant elms were available; the Hurricane of 1938 and the arrival of Dutch Elm Disease in 1950 destroyed many of the fountain elms that lined Hanover's streets. The best landmarks on the Green might be the ephemeral monuments of ritual in its center, such as the Winter Carnival sculpture and the tall bonfire of untreated Eastern Larch railroad ties that the entering class builds each fall. The bonfire is the latest in a long tradition of frequent conflagrations that merged during the 1940s with the speeches and songs of Dartmouth Night, an indoor event created in 1895, producing a fall spectacle that involves a rousing rhetorical prelude and a roaring inferno.

The Green's main landmark is the Senior Fence, which stands at the southwest corner. Cows were scarce enough by 1893 that the school could demolish the original fence, but students wanted to maintain a place for seniors to sing, carve canes, and watch passers-by. The first Senior Fence went up in 1897 on College Street, where there was not much to see. The school moved the fence in 1900 to the Green's busy southwest corner and eventually extended it to two parallel rows

Dartmouth Hall

about one hundred feet long. Although the daily and annual rituals that students created around the fence faded following World War II, the importance of the fence as a landscape feature grew. The school rotated one of the fencerows ninety degrees in 2003 in order to channel heavy foot traffic away from nearby tree roots, and in its latest position the fence forms a balanced frame for the Hiker's Elm. From some angles, it even provides a vista of a formal and bounded Green not seen in more than a century.

2. Dartmouth Hall

Charles Alonzo Rich, 1904–1906; Jens Fredrick Larson, 1935–36

The original Dartmouth Hall was part of Eleazar Wheelock's plan from the time he established the school in 1770. Before he even moved to Hanover, Wheelock notified the English trustees of his ideas for a three-story hall. The ostensible modesty of Wheelock's proposal for a building "in the most plain, decent, and cheapest Manner, after the dorick Order" was belied somewhat by his desire to erect a building 200 feet long and 50 feet wide, built of brick.

Several designers lent their opinions as to how this gigantic building should look. William Gamble's Georgian design of 1771 proposed a "Common Hall" on the ground floor and a Butler's Office and buttery in the basement of a stone building. Governor John Wentworth sketched his own design to inspire his friend Peter Harrison, perhaps the leading architect in the Colonies, but Harrison did not create a plan. Wheelock preferred a New York carpenter named Comfort Sever, who had been an unofficial consultant since 1768. Sever provided a design in 1772 that was probably the one Wheelock selected, and requests went to the English trustees to send glass, nails, paint, locks, and hinges. The following year saw the Provincial Assembly appropriate £500 for construction, and during 1774, Wheelock persuaded the college trustees to have laborers begin digging a foundation on the hill east of the Green.

Most of the workers left the construction site during 1775, with the Revolution escalating. Worse, Wheelock used up all of the English fund. The board signed off from London: "We can say nothing respecting your new proposed building, or the carrying on [of] the schools in [the] future, except that you have our best wishes[.]" Wheelock died in 1779, leaving his presidency to his son John and much of his land to the college.

The building would rise, slowly, after John Wheelock returned from his service as a Lieutenant Colonel in the Continental Army. It followed a new and slightly smaller design, probably by master carpenter John Sprague. It retained the tripartite form with its focus on a central gabled pavilion, resembling not only Sever's plan but the standard Georgian institutional building, as found in James Gibbs's design

Dartmouth Hall's gable recalls the building's predecessor.

for King's College, Cambridge (1724–30) and in its American heirs, including Nassau Hall at Princeton (1755–57), Harvard Hall in Cambridge (1764), University Hall in Providence (1770), and countless city halls, prisons, asylums, hospitals, and jails in the colonies. Construction began in earnest in 1784, and the new state government allowed the college to fund the work with the conventional means of a lottery, which was not a success.

Dartmouth Hall was gigantic, almost uniquely large for a timber structure at 175 feet long and 52 feet deep. Its timbers of oak or pine from Etna were 15 inches on a side, some of them measuring 75 feet long in finished form. Workers spent ten days raising the frame during 1786, and they had put up enough of the walls that Commencement could take place inside in 1787–when the *New Haven Gazette* called the building "perfectly agreeable to the most refined taste of modern architecture." The finishing work finally concluded in 1791. The original cupola lasted about fifty years before it was replaced with the iconic design that later builders would replicate. Workers finished the building with whitewash.

Dartmouth Hall was the college, and it contained the library, the museum, the dormitory rooms, and the recitation rooms where classes took place. The only functions outside were the Chapel to the east (1790) and the sometimes privately run Kinsman Commons to the west (1791). Nathan Smith's two-year-old Medical School moved into Dartmouth Hall during 1799 and built its own miniature version up College Street in 1811. Each of the student literary societies, the Social Friends (1783) and the United Fraternity (1786), obtained a library room above one of the building's flanking entrances. Architect Ammi Young remodeled the building's interior completely in 1829, focusing the building around a central double-height chapel on the ground level. Dormitory rooms left gradually, making way for classrooms on the ground level by 1886 and on the second level by 1895. The rooms of the third level, known as "Bed Bug Alley," retained their dormitory function for the whole life of Dartmouth Hall.

Although the *New York Times* wrote in 1871 that "[o]ne is struck, on entering the place, at the contrast between the reputation of the College and the appearance of its buildings," attitudes changed during the late nineteenth century. Students came to revere the building as a connection to Colonial Dartmouth, praising its supposed antiquity in poetic terms. Only the school's administrators recognized that the building was a firetrap. One master plan that Charles Rich created around 1893 suggested demolishing the building, grafting a forty-foot chapel addition to its rear, or preserving it as a relic on a new site. Instead, the school merely carried out a modest Lamb & Rich remodeling in 1895, installing electric lighting and steam heating. President Tucker created the Dartmouth Night celebration in 1895 specifically as something to do in Dartmouth Hall's Old Chapel, with ex-president Bartlett starting off the first event by appealing for the preservation of the building. The Old Chapel also would host the last event ever to take place in the building, an evening meeting of the Baseball Association in 1904.

The original Dartmouth Hall caught fire early on a February morning in 1904. The main photograph of the conflagration depicts the windows at the rear of the building exploding from the heat, with deep snow on the ground. The fire shocked the alumni into acting collectively as they never had before. As the building burned, President Tucker telephoned trustee Melvin Ohio Adams, a Boston attorney. He was on the scene within hours and called a meeting of the Boston alumni two days hence, writing, "this is not an invitation, but a summons." The loss of the physical connection to the school's origins became a practical motivation. As Bartlett Tower had replaced the fragile Old Pine in masonry, the new Dartmouth Hall would manufacture a new connection to history, and the Boston alumni voted that in the replacement, "[s]entiment will be preserved as much as possible by utilizing foundation stones, windows, and other things which have been saved from the fire." The school decided to use brick construction to recreate the old frame building.

The replacement Dartmouth Hall still stands. Although it has ceded some iconographic responsibility to Baker Library, it remains the symbol of the college, a visible connection between the present and the past whose fidelity to its Colonial predecessor testifies to its builders' devotion to the Dartmouth of their own experience. Instead of being cordoned off for administrative functions, Dartmouth Hall is an active home of classrooms and offices, housing several foreign language departments and one of the school's main auditoriums. The building remains a part of the experience of every student.

The architect started by designing the 1904 replacement by projecting an old photograph of the original building onto a screen and tracing its outlines. The job of laying the cornerstone fell to William Heneage Legge, who was a freemason, a former Member of Parliament, the sixth Earl of Dartmouth, and the ideal image of an English lord in an American's eyes. He obligingly sat through several costumed historical tableaux and said that he wished to be thought of "as one of the old boys."

The new Dartmouth Hall diverges from its prototype in form, materials, and detailing. Slightly larger than the old building, it exaggerates the original's graduation in the size of the window openings. Most important, the new building is built of brick with a steel frame. It abandoned the original trio of cross-corridors and longitudinal hall in favor of a more efficient I-shaped circulation system, and the replacement originally substituted a small one-level Doric auditorium for the Old Chapel. The building's finishes and furnishings were a fantasy on the Colonial, incorporating "old-fashioned" brass door handles and long communal desks made from single birch planks.

The main relics of the old building in the new are the surviving window frames that flank the central pavilion above plaques cast from the bronze of the ruined college bell. A red oak corner post of the old hall became the speaker's podium in the auditorium, while the lock in the central door and the granite steps to the side entrances also came from the original hall. The resulting building, nearly indistinguishable from its predecessor in photographs, continues to preside over the Green and to symbolize the college itself.

The building that alumni cheered in 1906 is not entirely the one that stands today, since a fire of 1935 destroyed the cupola and damaged the upper levels. In response, the school gutted the building and rebuilt the interior with concrete floors and steel stairs. The two-level auditorium in the style of the Old Chapel returned, this time starting from the basement (105 Dartmouth). The most visible exterior change was minor, the introduction of small copper gables, carrying the years 1904 and 1935 in relief, flanking the central gable, where the builders placed the year 1784.

3. Wentworth and Thornton Halls

Wentworth Hall
Ammi Burnham Young, 1828–29; Charles Alonzo Rich, 1912
Thornton Hall
Ammi Burnham Young, 1828–29; Larson & Wells, 1924

Wentworth and Thornton Halls are companions to Dartmouth Hall, flanking it on the north and south. Although the two subsidiaries turn their narrower gable ends to the College Yard, in some ways they are more pretentious than the main building that originally stood between them. Both halls are built of brick to the designs of a recognized architect, and each carries the name of one of the most important pre-Revolutionary benefactors of the college.

Whether to create a row of buildings or to enclose a quadrangle was one of the main design questions that faced Ammi Young in designing Wentworth and Thornton. The irregular frame buildings that flanked Dartmouth Hall at the time hinting at a formal frame for the College Yard. The college archives preserve a Young design for a modified open quad here, with Wentworth and Thornton standing forward and presenting their main entrances inward. Instead, Young adopted a less-insular and less-limiting row, holding all three buildings to the same facade plane with all entrances to the front to create a Palladian A-B-A pattern. This form is related but not identical to the often-cited precedent of Yale Row, which adopted a B-A-B rhythm whose central building presented its narrow end, not its long side, to the viewer.

Young built Wentworth and Thornton to be practically identical in their Greek-Revival brick simplicity. They exude sturdiness, with their shallow-pitched roofs and gabled pediments, each window opening topped by a substantial splayed lintel of granite.

Dartmouth named the northern building for Sir John Wentworth eight years after he died, having been made a baronet. The personal and official gifts of the Royal Governor of the Province of New Hampshire had made him the essential patron of the college and were especially notable because he was an Anglican supporting a dissenter institution. While Wentworth was obtaining the school's charter, he politely rebuffed Eleazar Wheelock's offer to name the institution Wentworth College. Wentworth managed to attend the first Commencement in 1771 traveling overland in a convoy that included an ox for roasting, a barrel of rum, and sixty Portsmouth gentlemen. Popular with provincial citizens and credited with delaying the Revolution in New Hampshire, he fled the province during 1775. He became Lieutenant-governor of Nova Scotia in 1791, and in 1802 obtained a charter for the existing King's College there (1789).

A fire during the spring of 1911 prompted the school to gut Wentworth Hall

Wentworth Hall

Thornton Hall

and insert a steel skeleton supporting concrete floor plates and a new skylit central stair. The architect rotated the corridors ninety degrees to allow for lecture halls, which replaced the previous dormitory rooms. Workers reinstalled the original granite entrance details below a new gable in the side facade. The architect applied iron plates to the exposed roof trusses to make them look, as he wrote, "like the old-fashioned truss-work of our daddies." Cast-iron numerals went up on the front gable to indicate the years of construction and reconstruction, and since then, Wentworth Hall has continued to play its role as a generic campus "background building" that now houses offices, including those of the Deans of the Faculty and of Graduate Studies.

Thornton Hall carries the name of John Thornton, a wealthy London merchant in the Russian trade and an eccentric promoter of religious causes. He became the treasurer of the fund raised for Moor's School in England, opening subscription books at a dozen London banks to encourage donations from those who heard Occom and Whitaker preaching from 1766 to 1768. What made John Thornton unique was that, although he was as dismayed as the other trustees by Wheelock's establishment of the college ("I am afraid there is too much worldly wisdom in this charter," he wrote), he nevertheless continued to donate his own funds after the English fund ran out. Thornton was Wheelock's main source of personal income from then until the revolution and sent more than £1,000 in total.

Thornton Hall, like its counterpart, became an old, unpopular dormitory within twenty-five years. Dark, cold, dirty, and insect-ridden, it housed some students who felt no compunction against raising chickens in their rooms. Some rooms were allegedly unrentable, inspiring students to room with families in town. The school started installing recitation rooms in 1871 and moved in the Thayer School of Engineering during 1874. Although Thornton's eventual remaking was less radical than that of Wentworth Hall, it still required a gutting during the 1920s for a steel and concrete interior of offices and classrooms.

Dartmouth Row took many years to reach its iconic form of a line of white buildings on a hill, a group that Hugh Morrison called in 1952 "perhaps the finest group of early college buildings in the country" outside of Jefferson's campus for the University of Virginia. Wentworth and Thornton remained unpainted red brick for their first few decades, finally receiving a whitewashing around 1859, the better to match the white-painted Dartmouth Hall. A yellow wash covered the halls in 1868 for the College Centennial, reiterated in 1898 in a hue described as "Colonial yellow" (or "real Dutch yellow"). Finally, both buildings were painted white in 1912.

4. Reed Hall
Ammi Burnham Young, 1839–40; Jens Fredrick Larson, 1931–32

The college trustees decided during 1838 to "erect two college buildings on the range north and south of the present buildings," following an innovative campus master plan by Ammi Burnham Young. Instead of extending the flat row to the north or south, the design added an original element of depth and enclosure. It sited the proposed halls well ahead of the existing facade line, turning them inward to frame the College Yard in front of Dartmouth Hall. Although the school would not be able to build both buildings, it was able to build the southern building of the pair after receiving a bequest from former trustee William Reed, a businessman of Marblehead, Massachusetts. Ammi Young again served as architect, with brother Dyer as the building contractor and brother Ira, the astronomy professor, overseeing the work for the college. The expensive result of their work is a chaste but fashionable Greek temple.

Reed was the school's most fully-developed building in stylistic terms, showing more sophistication and better proportions than its neighbors, exhibiting Doric corner pilasters and a proper entablature, as well as a strong graduation in

Reed Hall

story heights. The building started in yellow, apparently wore white during the second half of the nineteenth century, and alternated once more before becoming permanently white around 1912.

Reed was built to house specialized rooms for many of the bulky institutional functions that no longer fit in Dartmouth Hall. On the first level were the College Museum, the school's picture gallery, and a tiered lecture hall called the Philosophy Room. A set of science laboratories filled out the floor, including the physics lab where Dr. Gilman Frost and Frank Austin would perform the country's first clinical X-ray during 1896. The library, housed in medieval-plan alcove stacks, filled the entire second level. The space actually contained three separate libraries at first, those of the two literary societies and that of the college. (The societies consolidated their libraries during 1874 and join with the College Library later.) Reed's third level was built as a dormitory, and the student rooms expanded downward into the second level (1885) and the first (1904). The building's radical remaking took place during the early 1930s, when the school gutted it for the standard steel frame supporting poured concrete floor plates. Although the building lost half of its eight original chimneys, the architect wrote that "its architectural charm was retained" by preserving its brick shell around the dozens of new offices and classrooms.

5. The Collis Center

Charles Alonzo Rich, 1901; Banwell Architects, 1979; Tony Atkin & Associates, 1993–94

The Collis Center

The heavily rhetorical College Hall and its attached Commons dining hall, now known collectively as the Collis Center, were essential to President William Jewett Tucker's transformation of the traditional and outdated classical college into an institution that was fully modern and even smacked of the university—what many called the "New Dartmouth." This building was meant to maintain an atmosphere of democracy and unity among students despite the higher enrollments, specialized courses, professional schools, and increasingly fragmentary social cliques. To inhabit this place of old-fashioned communal dining and hearty porch-sitting, the school created two new institutions: an eating club called the Dartmouth Dining Association (now Dartmouth Dining Services) and a fraternity called the College Club, now defunct.

Lacking experience with a dining hall since the demolition of Kinsman Commons during the 1820s, the trustees studied dining halls at other schools in 1897. They likely looked at the only modern student union in the country, Houston Hall at the University of Pennsylvania (1895), a building that took the important step of placing a social club alongside the dining program. Dartmouth would add a third use, a set of dormitory rooms for students or visiting alumni, and it would make all three functions visible in the final structure of its own student union.

At the northwest corner of Wheelock and Main Streets stood the mansarded Balch Mansion (1871), by then a down-at-heel commercial building. After a fire in

February of 1900 severely damaged the mansion, the college chose its site for the union over the site initially proposed at the south end of the Green. Workers rushed to complete College Hall in time for the Centennial of Daniel Webster's graduation in 1901, and they left the old mansion's original granite steps in place to serve the new building; they also substituted wood for stone in the building's corner quoin. College Hall emerged as a flat-roofed three-level brick clubhouse with the frame ell of the dining commons attached at the rear.

College Hall's idiosyncratic thirty-foot-wide semicircular entrance portico, with its giant-scale fluted Ionic columns, symbolized the social club that occupied the ground level of the building. The architect asked, "[w]hy not the grand large porch— the building was rather a club center, a place where the boys could meet instead of straddling their fence[.]" The egalitarian College Club behind the columns was an all-school fraternity that accepted any dues-paying student, thereby combating the perceived tendency of fraternities to squelch the emergence of a natural "aristocracy of ability." The Club had its own oak-paneled Club Room with a leather-cushioned "hearty welcome" bay window; its Reading Room occupied the front of the building with a smaller fireplace; and the Trophy Room, now a café serving area, featured glass cases full of trophy baseballs and a mounted moose head. Despite its superior digs, the club would struggle until it collapsed in 1925.

The side-gabled Commons ell, sheathed in white-painted clapboard siding, originally had its own exterior entrance where it met College Hall. Beneath the hammerbeam roof of Commons are a carved oak chimneypiece and mantle flanked by doors to the original serving room, where student waiters gathered food sent up from a basement kitchen. A dinnertime orchestra played from the mezzanine that originally occupied the opposite end of the room, helping Commons compete directly against the eating clubs that had existed ephemerally in houses around town since the 1770s.

In a private eating club, a student commissary would pool the members' weekly fees, buy ingredients, hire the cook, rent the dining room, and seek new members. With wide variations in quality according to their members' wealth, the clubs generally were accused of discouraging safe food, good nutrition, and refined manners. When Commons opened, the school gave exclusive rental rights to a new student-run eating club formed for this purpose called the Dartmouth Dining Association (DDA). The school later boosted the club by requiring all freshmen to eat in Commons during 1919, but the DDA did not vanquish the town eating clubs until it opened Thayer Dining Hall in 1937.

Finally, rooms for about forty students—or returning alumni—filled the two upper levels of College Hall, reached by the side entrance on Wheelock Street. The disturbing noise of downstairs social events and the Inn's competition for alumni made the rooms less successful than hoped, and after a wartime pause, the

Outing Club Trips conclude at Robinson Hall.

dormitory use ended in 1957. This was the last dormitory on the Green.

A late-1970s reworking gave the Commons its own one-level brick entrance pavilion and installed a dimly lit mezzanine around the interior of the dining room, rechristened "Collis Commonground," while a café kitchen crammed into the former servery. The project was a gift of Charles A. Collis ('37), a Taunton, Massachusetts, housewares retailer, and was only a prelude to the remodeling of the same spaces that he and his wife Ellen would provide fifteen years later. Commons returned to its original form, a curving, two-level entrance pavilion infilled the crook of the ell, and a three-level glass-roofed atrium lit a broad stair to the basement between College Hall and Commons. With the letters on the portico changed from "College" to "Collis" and a café occupying the old club rooms, the building continues to uphold its mandate of welcoming all students.

6. Robinson Hall

Charles Alonzo Rich, 1913–14; Facilities Planning Office (FPO), 1995–96

The size and specialization of Dartmouth's new gymnasium confirmed a fear among many that athletics had come to dominate student life at Dartmouth. Historian Wilder D. Quint wrote of the concern that "prowess on the gridiron, or on the track, or the diamond has created a species of hero-worship not always healthful to the

Robinson Hall landing with the donor's portrait

other and certainly no less valuable activities of a student body." Vermonter Wallace
Fullam Robinson, whose brother was a graduate of 1855, was convinced that the
survival of the college's sense of democracy required a new building exclusively for
student organizations, something to "afford a just balance of intellectual and artistic
expression as against bodily prowess and muscular skill."

Wallace Robinson was the vice president of the remarkable United Shoe
Machinery Corporation, a monopoly producer of the equipment that shoe factories
required. The U.S.M.C. was the subject of a nearly constant series of federal
Sherman Antitrust Act suits between 1911 and 1971, but it also advertised itself

as a champion of progressive workers' programs at its massive turn-of-the-century plant in Beverly, Massachusetts, where it provided a clubhouse with a bowling alley, a theater, and a reading room adorned with the mounted heads of moose and elk (1910). For the building that Wallace Robinson donated to Dartmouth, he prohibited use by any group unless it was nonathletic and "the qualification for membership is proved ability only."

Students filled out architectural suggestion forms, Professor Keyes laid out a floor plan, and Walter Wanger, a dynamo of dramatics in the class of 1919 who was effectively establishing modern dramatics at the college, advised on Robinson Hall's Little Theater. Historian Henry B. Williams credits Wanger with convincing the donor to substitute a proper theater for a planned "small audience hall for impromptu dramatics." The Little Theater that came to occupy the ell of Robinson Hall would be the home of dramatics at the college for nearly half a century. (As a Hollywood director, Wanger would use Robinson Hall as a main setting of his unsuccessful 1939 film *Winter Carnival*.)

The bulky three-level Robinson Hall terminates in a shallow-pitched hipped roof originally studded with tall brick chimneys. Although an unexpected Renaissance arch frowns broadly across the center of the building's facade, supported on the chunky brackets typical of Rich, the theme of most of Robinson's exterior is smoothness. The building's Classicism is largely stripped of traditional ornament. Its reduced corner pilasters lie flush with the facade planes and lack either bases or capitals. Even the flat-arched limestone portal that is tacked onto the front facade evokes Mayan architecture as much as that of Rome. The pair of lion's heads decorating the porch are the work of the Massachusetts sculptor (and Dartmouth parent) Timothy John McAuliffe, who had earlier carved a lion's-head fountain in marble for College Hall. Below the limestone band that marks the building's third level stands a Palladian window, its flanking limestone shields replaced by windows during the early 1920s.

The interior of Robinson Hall embodied many of Wallace Robinson's ideas. The cruciform-plan entrance hall has shrunk with the expansion of the Dartmouth Outing Club beyond its original allotment of rooms. The student paper, the annual *Aegis*, and *The Jack-O-Lantern* ("Jollity Is the Goal of Wit") also were among the building's initial occupants, and a newly invented Nonathletic Council policed the qualifications of each organization seeking space. The Council also helped invent The Arts, a group of upperclassmen and faculty that aimed "[t]o stimulate undergraduate interest in cultural activities" and from its prime suite of purpose-built club rooms on the second level. The band and other musical clubs got practice rooms with felt-filled walls on the third level. The focus of Robinson, however, was the Little Theater in the ell. The theater lobby on the second level is reached by a formal stair and originally opened onto the flat-floored 350-seat theater. With Broadway theater-design experience, the architect decorated the Little Theater in a white Colonial style that would suit a variety of activities. Soon after the Little

Theater opened, it presented exhibitions of the artists' colony in Cornish, south of Hanover, and hosted Robert Frost speaking on New Sounds in Poetry.

Robinson has remained an extremely busy place, although the proportion of the dozens of student organizations that it can hold continues to shrink. The Arts did not survive World War II, and other groups took its library and flanking rooms. The college radio station moved from its radio shack atop Wilder Hall to become the main occupant of Robinson's third level. The Outing Club's Environmental Studies Division, which started in 1970 with a library in the Titcomb Room, became a permanent and full-fledged college academic program during 1974. The Little Theater faded into obscurity when the Hopkins Center opened, and the school filled it with two levels of student offices during the mid-1990s. That project added a new entrance facade to the rear of the building, a plain, flat-roofed limestone porch with a character even more engagingly funerary than that of the front entrance. This is the main door for the basement headquarters of the Ski Team—in apparent contravention of Wallace Robinson's original nonathletic condition, the country's first college ski team traditionally operates under the auspices of the Outing Club that created it, rather than under the school's athletic department.

7. McNutt Hall

Charles Alonzo Rich, 1903–1904; Larson & Wells, 1920; 1930

Edward Tuck ('62) was a banker, philanthropist, and adopted Frenchman who joined a New York bank soon after Lincoln appointed him vice-consul to Paris. Within a decade of retiring in 1881, he settled permanently in Paris. The careers of college graduates were shifting from law, teaching, or the ministry to business affairs, and in 1899 Tuck suggested to President Tucker, his one-time college roommate, that he would endow a new graduate department. Tuck donated stock in the Great Northern Railroad as a memorial to his father, trustee Amos Tuck ('35).

Dartmouth's trustees established the Amos Tuck School of Administration and Finance during January of 1900, creating the first graduate school of business in the country. Although college seniors taking the right electives could complete the new business program in a year, Edward Tuck focused his new school specifically on the two-year program for those who had already graduated from college. In 1901, Walter Blair ('00) became the first American to receive a master's degree in business administration. As if to settle in their own minds what a third professional school would mean to the college, the trustees stated, according to the student paper, that they "are convinced that they are acting in direct accordance with the traditions of Dartmouth" in establishing a business school. The Tuck School had a little campus facing the Green, starting with two dormitories in college-owned houses, and during 1901, Edward Tuck sent more railroad stock to help the school

McNutt Hall, with Inuksuk *(Peter Irnig, 2007)*

erect an American Renaissance building on its property.

The rusticated ground level of Tuck Hall originally underpinned a temple front: four monumental pilasters with stylized Ionic capitals supporting a stepped, parapetted gable. With skylights lighting the third-level commercial museum and its displays of industrial raw materials and sample advertisements, the walls of the building's attic story could remain blank, articulated with a row of limestone panels. The building's rear ell contained a business library above a sloping 250-seat lecture hall.

Not long after the school moved in, Edward Tuck agreed to a request for a major remodeling of Tuck Hall. The project Georgianized Tuck Hall with multiple-paned windows and a triangular pedimented gable that was meant to refer to Dartmouth Hall. Removing the pilasters exposed the original quoining behind them, and moving the museum to the basement allowed new window openings to light the top level. Within the next decade, a rail bearing the initials "TH" would be installed to guard the new second-level French doors, and those letters remain the only outward sign that this was the first building erected for a graduate business school.

With the completion of Edward Tuck's new complex on Tuck Mall in 1930, the business school sold its original building to the college. Dartmouth renamed the hall for Randolph McNutt ('71), who had left an unrestricted bequest, and had workers carve the initial "M" into the escutcheon at the center of the building's pediment. In 1940, Professor George Stibitz would use a teletype terminal in one of the building's classrooms to operate a Complex Number Calculator at Bell Labs in New York, the first remote operation of a binary computer. The classrooms later were divided as permanent spaces for the Admissions Office and related departments, but the building's original black cast-iron columns and the broad central stair that dominates its interior still suggest the optimism of McNutt Hall's origins.

8. Parkhurst Hall
Charles Alonzo Rich, 1910–1911; Larson & Wells, 1924

The influence of new management science and the growth of Dartmouth's administration beyond just a president during the early 1890s created the need for an administration building. President Tucker occupied his predecessor's office on the second floor of Wilson Hall, but in 1898 he moved with the Dean and the Inspector of Buildings to President Nathan Lord's old house at the head of the Green. Tucker hoped to build a permanent headquarters next door, including an apsidal space where the faculty could hold their meetings. The expected building finally opened a decade late as Webster Hall, absent any administrative spaces, and Tucker began asking donors for a new Nathan Lord administrative building. The plea soon would be met by Lewis Parkhurst ('78), a partner in the schoolbook publishing firm of Ginn & Co.

Lewis Parkhurst was interested in building: he helped set up Hanover's first rugby goalpost on the Green during his junior year, led local building committees at home in Winchester, Massachusetts, advised Hanover's planners on the workings of Winchester's reservoir while passing through on a bookselling tour, and oversaw the construction of Ginn's large Athenaeum Press in Cambridge during the late 1890s. His nomination to Dartmouth's board of trustees in 1908 came four years after his son, Wilder Lewis Parkhurst of the class of 1907, had died of complications from an appendectomy. Lewis and Emma Wilder Parkhurst decided to fund and oversee the construction of an administration building as a memorial to

Parkhurst Hall and the Parkhurst Elm

their son.

   Supervising the ongoing project, Lewis Parkhurst met with the architect and helped select the site west of the Green. The pressing design question was not stylistic but scale-related: the school wanted the building to compete with the imposing, pilastered Tuck Hall next door, while Lewis Parkhurst preferred a modest or even domestic building topped by a side-gabled roof. A compromise produced a two-and-a-half level building that is smaller than its neighbor but large enough to contain space for administrative expansion. Giant-scale brick pilasters divide Parkhurst Hall's front facade into irregular bays, while Greek Doric columns in antis support a large limestone lintel above the entrance portal carved with the word ADMINISTRATION. The building's two spiky iron lamps follow Renaissance prototypes that the architect had seen at the Palazzo Strozzi in Florence. Inside, a Guastavino-vaulted vestibule leads to a marble and bronze entry hall, lighted by a skylight that originally featured a giant representation of the College Seal.

   The domestic geography of the previous administration building seems to have

LEFT: *Skylight, Parkhurst Hall*
RIGHT: *Detail of Parkhurst Hall window*

influenced the initial layout of Parkhurst Hall. The building also contained novel rooms such as spaces for the trustees and for the treasurer, who moved from an office three doors down where he and his predecessors had worked for sixty years. Lewis Parkhurst helped design the treasurer's three-ton vault, and with President Nichols he plotted the building's one grand room, a parliamentary chamber that originally filled the upper stories of the building's rear ell. The Faculty Hall featured English Oak paneling lit by tall windows. The faculty took only a decade to outgrow the tiered benches for 150 people, causing the school to lengthen the building by a modest single bay. After outgrowing the hall again, the faculty left it to become two levels of offices. This was the building that students occupied during 1969 after the faculty voted to phase out R.O.T.C. over time instead of immediately, an occupation that ended when state troopers of New Hampshire and Vermont removed the building's front door and took the fifty-six students to jail in buses. The building continues to represent and house college leadership, and although Lewis Parkhurst wanted the hall to be called simply the Administration Building, it has gradually come to be known as Parkhurst Hall.

9. Webster Hall

Charles Alonzo Rich, 1901, 1906–1907
Rauner Special Collections Library
Venturi, Scott Brown & Associates, 1997–98

Between planning Webster Hall during the early 1890s and finally completing it nearly fifteen years later, the school shifted the building's ostensible purpose away from that of presenting inspirational college history through an elaborate and impractical domed shrine and toward that of housing a relatively simple auditorium. The initial designs for an "Alumni or Memorial Hall" placed the building at the heart of the Beaux-Arts quadrangle that the school proposed for the block north of the Green, joined to subsidiary classroom buildings by colonnades. The domed, marble-walled temple of college worthies would have contained a lofty chamber dedicated to the school's century-old pantheon of portraits and busts, which was then located in Wilson Hall's Portrait Gallery. The ground level was to contain the college's minimal administrative offices, also moving from Wilson. Such a building would have looked much like Stanford White's contemporary design for the Gould Library at New York University, a monumental Roman temple with sweeping colonnades built to house the Hall of Fame of Great Americans.

With unexpected funding on hand for the Butterfield Museum (1898–99), Dartmouth gave that building the central site and shunted Memorial Hall to the front corner of the Quadrangle, where it would form a gateway with the existing College Church. The school modified Memorial Hall's rhetorical purpose to fit the fundraising centennial of Daniel Webster's graduation in 1901, reshaping it as "Webster Hall"–a domeless building featuring a rusticated ground level for administrators and a practical auditorium above. The Webster Centennial was the biggest celebration Hanover had ever seen, with a torchlight procession of alumni dressed in "Websterian costume" of blue coats and tall hats, floats displaying scenes from college history, and Dartmouth Night on the Green with a bonfire. The fundraising failed to push the hall beyond its foundation, and only after Dartmouth Hall's destruction in 1904 kindled "a spirit of practical loyalty," as trustee Henry Hilton put it, could the school finally finish Webster Hall. The last in the series of designs required a foundation ten feet longer than the one the school already had built, and the building dropped all of the proposed functions except that of an auditorium. Nevertheless, the building rose as a monumental red-brick Roman temple.

Webster Hall's four giant-scale Corinthian columns of limestone create the only masonry temple front at the college. Montgomery Schuyler termed Webster "one of the most impressive, inside and out, of college auditoriums," and the building

OPPOSITE: *Webster Hall*

predicted the design of the architect's larger John M. Green Hall at Smith College (1909–10). The cruciform basilica plan of the 1,700-seat auditorium helps the building's interior create an attitude of worship, even though the most religious elements of the design had fallen away: from the marble-tiled vestibule, a visitor emerges into a flat-floored chamber framed by full-height Corinthian pilasters. Novel constellations of electric light bulbs sparkle down from deep ceiling coffers. The focus of the auditorium originally was just beyond the crossing, where a pilastered triumphal arch screened a coffered, semidomed apse. Here, Professor Keyes arranged the school's portrait collection for maximum rhetorical effect and, as President Tucker put it, to "bring out our illustrious dead into daily fellowship with the living, to quicken within us the sense of a common inheritance and of a common duty." Founders, presidents, and counsel in the Dartmouth College Case inhabited the building's apse, flanking Daniel Webster's mahogany office desk. Other portraits were grouped by theme on subsidiary walls in the transepts, and Tucker discussed the possibility of installing a sixty-foot historical painting along the rear of the apse. Notable is the absence of much mention of the Civil War. Even the massive bronze memorial doors designed by Rich and sculpted by Melzar Hunt Mosman were a memorial to the class of 1841 rather than to the war dead in general. Not until 1914 did the two bronze memorial plaques in the vestibule list those who died on both sides of the Civil War, as well as those who served the U.S. from the class of 1863.

For several decades, Webster Hall provided an ennobling setting for Commencement and Dartmouth Night as well as countless concerts and lectures. After the Hopkins Center made the building redundant, workers partitioned the areas beneath the balcony into storage spaces, art studios, and rehearsal rooms, including a space in which the dance company Pilobolus formed during 1971. Removing the floor seats during 1987 made the hall more useful for rock concerts and presidential campaign speeches, and the school's installation of the 1978 Diana M. and Bruce V. Rauner Library would give Webster Hall its second existence.

A restrained renovation combined with the insertion of a Modernist building-within-a-building recreated Webster Hall as a monumental reading room for the school's special collections library. A calm cube of glass containing the book stacks, its four levels regulated by an aluminum-clad concrete grid, extends forward from the apse. The balconies became study spaces named for the class of 1965, and a new tunnel to Baker contained further book storage. The project also reiterated the old pantheon idea in the south balcony, where portraits of the college's most recent presidents hang along with those of other notables, including architect Charles Rich ('75). As the home of the college archives, Webster Hall might serve the building's original didactic purpose even better and more thoughtfully than it did as a templelike auditorium.

10. Baker Library

*Jens Fredrick Larson, 1926–28, 1941–42; W. Brooke Fleck, 1957–58;
Fleck & Lewis Architects, 1967; Venturi, Scott Brown & Associates,
2000–2002*

Baker Memorial Library did nothing to dispel the image of Dartmouth in the 1920s
as a straightforward, traditional place—and the school has benefited ever since.
Baker stands at the center of the head of the Green and employs the tallest tower
in town to proclaim its role as the intellectual and physical heart of the institution.
The red-brick pile goes beyond the symbolic, expressing a pre-Depression
confidence in higher education and a bold certainty in the collegiate form at any
scale. Intended as neither a scholar's workshop nor a storage facility, Baker is an
undergraduate research library in the form of an English country house, supplying
everything that students will find useful for a liberal education—from open stacks to
comfortable armchairs to memorializations of students of the past.

Within a quarter-century of Wilson Hall's opening as a library, enrollment rose
by a factor of five and the collection of books grew by tens of thousands. President
Tucker began consulting with Henry Vincent Hubbard, a landscape architect with
the Olmsted Brothers, regarding sites for a new library. Around 1912, Tucker asked
Charles Rich to sketch a design for a building north of the Green, and the architect
offered a proposal based partly on the medieval library at Cambridge University.
The 1916 predictions of a "Tucker Library" were too soon, however, and the
trustees decided not to build unless they could do so on a grand scale—a million-
dollar building rather than an incremental improvement. Otto Eggers's evocative
rendering of a library in John Russell Pope's 1922 master plan foreshadowed
Baker's essential form, and college architect Jens Larson designed Baker Library
shortly thereafter. The trustees finally move ahead during 1925.

George Fisher Baker, Jr., was a founder of the First National Bank of New
York and a colleague of Edward Tuck. He was also a nephew, friend, and heir of
Fisher Ames Baker ('59), who was a lieutenant colonel in the 18th Massachusetts
Volunteers during the Civil War and later a New York attorney. George Baker told
of walking from Troy, New York, to attend his uncle's graduation, and his uncle's
death in 1919 prompted him to propose a memorial. President Hopkins suggested
that only a gift of a certain scale would be worthy of Fisher Baker, or, for that matter,
of George Baker, the eventual donor of the Harvard Business School campus and
Baker Field at Columbia University. Baker responded with a gift of the building and
later with an endowment for the expansion of its collection.

Baker is an H-shaped building focused on the central tower attached to its front
facade. The main gabled cross-range contains a single long formal room on each

level, while the more utilitarian subsidiary arms contain reading rooms and offices, also presenting secondary entrances to the east and west that align with the tower. By embracing Baker Lawn, the wings are a belated realization of the Quadrangle plan of 1893, although the creation of the lawn itself required the school to demolish the Butterfield Museum, originally meant as the quad's centerpiece. The demolition of the young natural history museum became a textbook example of the situation in which the procurement of "[a] development plan, which would have visioned the future, would have avoided this loss," according to architects Charles Klauder and Herbert Wise in their early book on campus design.

The square-planned brick Baker Tower with its frame steeple is a literal imitation of William Strickland's 1828 addition to Independence Hall in Philadelphia, a symbol of American liberty that was a natural formal source for the library of a liberal arts college during the Colonial Revival. The tower also makes a supremely functional campus signpost, and for the architect, the appeal seems to have been aesthetic as much as symbolic: Larson applied all or part of the Independence Hall tower to such projects as an unbuilt remodeling of the 1850s main building at Wabash College in Crawfordsville, Indiana, an unbuilt twenty-story skyscraper designed for the Chicago Tribune Tower competition (1922), Fuld Hall of the Institute for Advanced Study in Princeton, New Jersey, (1938–39), and the Bertrand Library of Bucknell University in Lewisburg, Pennsylvania (1950–51). Baker Tower was the largest such tower that Larson completed, and its aptness would influence academic buildings by other authors up to the Second World War. It became Dartmouth's most prominent landmark and a constant competitor with Dartmouth Hall for the role of chief architectural symbol of the college. Within the tower is a set of bells that President Hopkins meant create a properly collegiate atmosphere, programmed first by a patented paper-roll system and from 1979 by student-run computer automation.

At the ground level Baker's main range encloses the broad double-height corridor of its Catalog Room, with the library's stacks forming an ell behind the room. Subordinate spaces within the wings include Hough's Room, an intensely decorated chamber that originally housed the college archives. The heart of Baker is the Tower Room, a double-height timber-ceilinged alcove library that occupies much of the building's second level. It was meant to exude a clubby atmosphere, and students continue to read or nod off in the room's carefully-retained high-winged armchairs, looking out over the Green through an arcade of tall window openings.

Given the stalwart Georgian mode in which Baker operates, the major space in its basement level provides something of a shock. The Mexican muralist Jose Clemente Orozco, a visiting assistant professor of art, painted a fresco titled *The Epic of American Civilization* on the bare walls of the long Reserve Corridor that forms much of Baker's basement. To the left of the book delivery desk he

OPPOSITE: *Baker Library*

LEFT: *Detail of* The Pre-Columbian Age, *panel 6 in Jose Clemente Orozco's Baker Library Fresco.* RIGHT: *A clock face inside Baker Tower*

painted seven panels depicting the coming of Quetzalcoatl, including the brightly colored "Ancient Human Sacrifice." To the right of the desk are seven more panels depicting colonization and the arrival of modernity including the "Gods of the Modern World" with its chilling warning against the creation of dead knowledge for its own sake—a depiction of a demonic professor delivering a mortarboarded infant skeleton. Lewis Mumford described the frescoes as "[n]ot decoration, not gentility, not Georgian correctness," and alumni generally were outraged. Although President Hopkins did not find the frescoes appealing either, he stuck to what he had promised Orozco and to his belief that any idea worth calling "dangerous" was worth debating openly. The frescoes prompted a reaction in the form of the strained heartiness of the 1937–39 murals in the Hovey Grill of Thayer Dining Hall, by illustrator Walter Beach Humphrey ('14). Hopkins advised his successor to avoid having anything to do with murals.

Much more than Webster Hall had done, Baker became a repository of memory. A shrapnel-riddled scrap of canvas from an ambulance driven by Richard Nelville Hall ('15) occupies the west lobby of the Reserve Corridor, part of a memorial to Hall, the first American Field Service member killed in World War I. Edward Tuck gave the main bronze relief sculpted by Louis Aimé Lejeune in 1920. The tiny Woodward Room, in a mezzanine overlooking the Catalogue Room, contains some books from the school's original library and recalls founding librarian Bezaleel Woodward. A late arrival is a barrel-vaulted Senior Fellows' seminar room in the library's southwest wing, a memorial to Carroll Paul ('03), Thayer School (Th) ('04) (Jens Fredrick Larson, 1938).

The library could seat about half of the school's two thousand students when it opened, and it required a typical number of enlargements over the years. A utilitarian stack expansion of 1941 joined the arms of the building together at the rear, creating courtyards that were infilled during the late 1950s. The vast Berry Library addition put a new range beyond the 1941 stacks; immediately afterward, largely as the result of a gift from George Baker's eponymous grandson, the school renovated Baker itself. Venturi's design used glass to announce the Kiewit Computation Center outside the Tower Room as well as other new insertions, but his firm's work on the old building itself was conservative. The renovation revived several original interior details and expanded the Reserve Corridor behind the murals, part of a larger effort to ensure that the library's architectural stature continued to comport with its role as the beloved intellectual heart of Dartmouth. Baker Tower remains the tallest landmark around, and the building's sights, sounds, and smells are inevitably affixed in the memories of the college's graduates.

11. The Hanover Inn

William Benjamin Tabler, 1966–67
The McNutt Addition
Larson & Wells, 1923

The first inn of the town held down this site after Wheelock granted the corner parcel in about 1780 to the College Steward, General Ebenezer Brewster, for a tavern. The Inn Corner has remained a center of visiting and eating through a succession of buildings since that time. Brewster's Tavern lasted about twenty-five years before son Colonel Amos Brewster replaced it in brick with the imposing Greek-Revival Dartmouth Hotel. After the great Main Street fire of 1887, the college bought the hotel's ruins and had Lambert Packard design a heavily-porched stick-style resort in brick called the Wheelock Hotel (1888–89), establishing the hostelry as a college venture. A 1902 remodeling by Charles Alonzo Rich made the pile more Dutch Colonial, as the school renamed the building the Hanover Inn. By 1919, the site was theoretically slated for a block-wide Inn worthy of Baker Library, and Jens Larson made a first step in that direction by replacing the Inn's frame annex with a red brick addition funded by Randolph McNutt ('71), which still stands. The wrecking ball did not swing on the main block of the hotel until 1966.

The architects of the present inn were more used to designing giant Modernist Hiltons in San Francisco, Washington, and Pittsburgh, but here they created a four-level Colonial Revival building that responds sympathetically to its subsidiary wing, which predates it. For all its bulk and severity, the inn is a contextual building that manages to enclose a large number of guest rooms without too obviously dominating Main Street. The inn remains the most ambitious hotel in the region,

The Hanover Inn, including 1923 addition at left

and its restaurants help supply the catering arm of Dartmouth Dining Services: with an enclosed connection to Alumni Hall, mementoes salvaged from the precursor building, and newer plaques added frequently, the Hanover Inn is perpetually in demand as a reunion headquarters.

12. The Hopkins Center

Harrison & Abramowitz with Campbell & Aldrich, 1959–62;
Moore Grover Harper, 1984

The last major building built on the Green, the Hopkins Center for the Creative and Performing Arts is the most important Modernist building in town and carries out the unique function of housing a pioneering American arts center, an integrated, multidisciplinary institution that has been a vibrant regional hub of all forms of creativity for decades. Most of all, the Hop has had an immense effect on the tenor of life at Dartmouth, representing (along with coeducation) the biggest change in student life during the seventy-five years that followed the opening of Baker Library. President Hopkins predicted at the opening of the Center that bears his name that it "will in the course of events, I am certain, become the heart and soul of Dartmouth," and it has come close to doing that. Beloved for its familiarity, iconically stylish in its late-fifties Modernism, and above all, a useful and astonishingly well-used place.

The Hopkins Center

The school tried for decades to establish a student union or auditorium complex at the south end of the Green. A 1929 student-life committee shelved the previous plan for a block-wide Hanover Inn and proposed a vast domed student union called Dartmouth House. The union died during the Depression, and by 1937 the idea was to build a New Webster Hall—a theater and opera-house meant to mirror the old Webster and justified in large part by the self-imposed requirement that it always have one room large enough to hold all of its students. By now, the Dartmouth Players were offering five full-length plays a year, the Experimental Theater was presenting another five, and the popular Interfraternity Play Contest produced another twenty one-act plays, far too many for the Little Theatre in Robinson or for Webster Hall's awkward space.

Jens Larson designed a gigantic New Webster Hall during 1939. Dressed in the stripped classical mode of a New Deal Post Office, the building was similar in plan to today's Hopkins Center, although it would have had a much greater audience capacity. It was meant to recast Hanover as a national center for theater, with a summer drama festival to draw New Yorkers. The war intervened, and Larson redesigned the center during 1945 and 1946. This proposal, named for the just-retired president Ernest Martin Hopkins, added a music building, an art building, and a crafts workshop to replace the workshops in Bissell Hall, the old gym that still stood on the site. The Korean War halted planning again, although the faculty continued to push the arts center onward.

All of the pieces required to make an arts center finally came together in 1955, as Nelson Aldrich Rockefeller ('30) became the head of the building committee. For years he had operated in a powerful team of patron and designer with the New

York architect Wallace Kirkland Harrison, his cousin by marriage. The school's consulting architect, Nelson Wilmarth Aldrich, also a Rockefeller cousin, worked with Harrison to design the center, and John D. Rockefeller started off the project with a million dollars in honor of President Hopkins.

The Hopkins Center was the fourth of a series of large Manhattan-like theater complexes that Harrison designed for Rockefeller family members. One was Manhattan's Rockefeller Center itself, originally a Metropolitan Opera project for which architect William T. Aldrich recommended him as designer. Second was an imitation Rockefeller Center that Harrison designed for a site that John D. Rockefeller later gave to the United Nations. Harrison then directed the planning of the trio of connected U.N. buildings that ushered large-scale International Style Modernism into New York in 1952. Third was a new opera house for the Met at Lincoln Center that was in many ways a twin to the contemporary design for the Hopkins Center. At one point, Harrison even proposed that a windowless office tower form a backdrop to the opera house, much as the Hop's blank-walled fly loft stands behind its theater entrance.

Harrison's office came out with two successive designs for the Hopkins Center. The first became public in a cheerful watercolor perspective rendering by Paul Sample, a member of the faculty building committee and the school's artist in residence. The proposal was similar in plan to the executed second version, but its forms were considerably more angular. A cross-gabled roof topped its theater loft, and the theater itself had a rather grim flat roof. The *Alumni Magazine* put the rendering on its cover in May of 1957, and alumni were furious. Although the buildings already on the Green were varied, they were also largely harmonious in their use of Classical forms, and the Hop would be an anomaly.

Harrison went back and altered the design to suit alumni, improving it in the process. This second design is the one that was built, and its novel feature was a roof form comprising a series of long concrete barrel vaults arranged in a row. The ends of the vaults formed an arcade at the front of the main theater that became the symbol for the entire complex. By the spring of 1958, Harrison was putting a variation of the Hopkins Center's barrel vault atop his ongoing schemes for the Metropolitan Opera. On paper, both buildings now had a sloping, multivaulted roof with a five-bay arcade, although the Met's design soon would diverge.

The Hopkins Center's four programmatic elements are arranged to form a rectilinear G-shape. At the top was the main event, the Moore Theatre, its glazed arcade presenting a large marquee to the Green. The theater held the audience of one of the interfraternity plays of the time, about 450 people. Harrison gave the theater a wraparound balcony like those he had seen in eighteenth-century court theaters of Europe, as historian Victoria Newhouse has noted. Above the theater is the high-ceilinged Top of the Hop, a hip but generally underused lounge that was a counterpart to the Top of the Met restaurant. Below the theater is the Warner

OPPOSITE: *The stair to the Top of the Hop*

Bentley Theater, a black-box or arena theater. The second element in the Center is the perpendicular block of Alumni Hall, which strives to contain the busy and cramped ground-level student mail center known as the Hinman Boxes. Third is a one-level studio block with a saw-toothed roof that stretches south from Alumni Hall, lined on one side by a snack bar that Charles Moore would expand into the Courtyard Café. In the basement is a warren of printmaking studios and the Student Workshops, run by professional instructors in woodworking and jewelry-making.

The final element of the complex, the 900-seat Spaulding Auditorium (it was calibrated to hold a class year) stands on Lebanon Street. The auditorium is full of the tones and textures of the period, from the water-struck bricks of the walls, their soft irregularities emphasized by sharp downlighting, to the heaven of overlapping polychromatic rectangles that floats below the roof. Vertical wood slats line Spaulding's stage, a reference to Harrison's treatment of the meeting chambers of the United Nations. Beneath Spaulding are the rehearsal rooms and offices of performing groups.

Three goals informed the school's attempt to combine wildly varied functions into a single small-town arts center. First, the Hop was to be not just a group of distinct buildings but a connected "city of the arts." In plan, it is not so much a city as a superblock development like Lincoln Center, and it required Dartmouth to close College Street and demolish more than a half-dozen frame buildings as well as the historic Bissell Gymnasium. Typologically, the Hop is neither town nor campus but resembles an industrial building, with its saw-toothed roof, blank-walled brick silos, and concrete vaults, giving it a kinship with the small industrial zone next door. Functionally, the Hop is often compared to a customs checkpoint: if the college is one country and the town another, then the Hop is the border crossing, and it does manage to form a transition that architect William Rawn called "one of the most seamless connections between city and campus" of any college.

The Hop undoubtedly succeeds at its second goal of fostering interaction among a variety of disciplines. The planners arranged the complex to emphasize the relations between the arts, hoping that practitioners might inspire one another in a positive cross-pollination. One writer described the center as a place "where all the arts could mingle and impinge," while Warner Bentley, the first director of the center, wrote that "[i]n the Hopkins Center we cannot escape each other, even if we should want to."

The unique third aspect of the Hop is the way it embraced a procollegiate and antispecializing ideal, welcoming all students, including the non-artistic "sidewalk superintendent." All agreed that any liberally educated student needs exposure to the doing and viewing of art, especially modern art, as a part of daily life. Therefore the architect placed exhibit spaces in the corridors and lined the studios with as much glass as possible, to let passers-by watch their classmates rehearse plays, build sets, craft objects in metal, or practice musical instruments. (Frank Stella said that the place was "designed for the public, not for the people who use it," and the school eventually covered most of the glass.) *Progressive Architecture* commented that the "[m]ethods by which the entire student body will be either required to visit this lively place or lured to it are most resourceful," a polite comment on the fact that the school used the snack bar as an enticement, the centralized mailboxes as a prod, and the mandatory all-class lectures in Spaulding as a requirement to enter the building.

The Hop's quirks include Harrison's placement of the least-used component at the front of the complex, turning the theater lobby into the main entrance of the whole center. Meanwhile, an ostensibly minor side entrance tucked behind the sunken Zahm Garden turns out to be the best way for half the campus to reach the busy Hinman Boxes. The weakness in the street line created by recessing half of the center's front facade has prompted almost every architect who has looked at the complex to suggest a front addition. The passage of time, however, has combined with a renewed appreciation for the optimistic forms of mid-century Modernism to lessen the building's stylistic difference from its neighbors, and the Hop has no problems that some judicious alterations cannot fix. The Hop is undeniably one of the essential touchstones of Dartmouth student life, and its influence on the college has rightly been described as immeasurable.

13. The Hood Museum
Moore Grover Harper, 1982–85

To remedy the dearth of gallery space in the Hopkins Center, New England dairy operator and trustee Harvey P. Hood ('18) gave Dartmouth a new museum in 1978. The school selected architect Charles Moore, whose civic-minded interest in urban space, skill at conversing in historical styles, and wittily humane spirit made him perhaps the ideal architect to handle the difficult site alongside the Hopkins Center.

Having established Moore Ruble Yudell in California, Charles Moore was consulting with his Connecticut firm at the time of the commission, and one early drawing of the Hood records the architect toying with new names for the group that would become Centerbrook Associates. The firm established an office in one of the Hop's studios during 1981, and, using a favorite community-input technique, Charles Moore and Chadwick Floyd invited students to critique a half-dozen proposed building sites near the Hop. "Then we designed—or rather I designed—a different building for each of the six sites. They were all very tight, very difficult to fit. Our boys then worked like absolute fiends and built a model for each of the six designs. They were all *very* different," wrote Moore. The two popular schemes for a museum facing the Green canceled each other out, and nearly a dozen more designs for the awkward and sloping site adjacent to the Hopkins Center followed. The result was a recessed archipelago of brick volumes that connects to the arts

Churchill P. Lathrop Gallery, Hood Museum, including Orange and Lilac over Ivory *(Mark Rothko, 1953) and* Hombre Colgado Pie *(Juan Munoz, 2001)*

center by a pair of bridges, framing a series of outdoor rooms.

For its entrance, the museum presents a somber gateway of concrete, a layered stage-set. Behind is a copper-clad bridge to walk under, and then an entrance ramp that curves around the Bedford Courtyard and its untitled abstract figure in bronze (Joel Shapiro, 1989–90). Passing through the court and beyond a second bridge one finds the tail end of the museum and the earlier courtyard of the Hopkins Center, along with *X-Delta* (Mark di Suvero, 1970). To travel the casual path through the portals and their irregular courts is to experience a spatial journey that is unique on this campus of rectilinear C-shaped quadrangles.

The museum borrows its simple planes from the mill, enlivening the edges with a few glazed bands, green-painted cornices, and a copper-domed finial. The entrance pavilion's multicolored interior is framed in bright roof beams set on exaggerated corbels and leads directly to the museum's high twentieth-century gallery. Down a monumental side stair, its torchieres held by anthropomorphic three-fingered brackets, one finds a traditional series of small in-line galleries meant to recall an eighteenth-century cabinet of curiosities or the long gallery of an English country house. The galleries focus on the dramatically lit Nineveh Slabs, a set of stone reliefs that antiquarian Austin Hazen Wright excavated from the ancient tomb of King Ashurnasirpal in Numrud, Assyria, during the mid-nineteenth century. In the basement is a cinema favored by film classes, reached by an informal stair that manages to recall Michelangelo's entrance to the Laurentian Library in the Vatican.

What Charles Moore created is a building that is original without being insensitive, frivolous yet sincere, a backdrop for an inspiring and revelatory visit to a collegiate teaching museum. The building has its problems: its entrance is obscure, and its bridges tend to shed snow onto the pathway. Nevertheless, the award-winning Hood Museum is Hanover's most acclaimed building in many decades and the most seriously fanciful building Dartmouth has ever built.

Hood Museum entrance through the Bedford Courtyard

COLLEGE STREET

THE GREEN

COLLEGE PARK

NORTH PARK STREET

SOUTH PARK STREET

WHEELOCK STREET

CROSBY STREET

15
16
17
18
18
19
20
21
22
22
22
23
24
24
24
24
24
24
24
25
25

The Old State College

East Wheelock Street was Dartmouth's first avenue of expansion beyond its sextet of permanent buildings on College Street. From 1854 to 1895, Wheelock Street was the only place for new academic buildings, half of which belonged to the campus of the state's land-grant college. The Morrill Act (1862) gave the state of New Hampshire 150,000 acres of federal land in the west to support a new college that would teach practical subjects. As other states did, New Hampshire gave the proceeds of its land sale to an existing colonial college. Dartmouth agreed that the small New Hampshire College of Agriculture and the Mechanic Arts (1868) would be an independent institution associated with Dartmouth and headed by Dartmouth's president. With different goals and admissions requirements, the two schools inevitably experienced some friction: according to President Bartlett, the agricultural students were suitable "for highway surveyors, selectmen, and perhaps, members of the legislature." The advent of this third undergraduate college nevertheless created something like a university at Dartmouth, and students began selecting a representative university nine for intercollegiate baseball and a university crew for rowing events.

Dartmouth and the state split the cost of building Culver Hall (Edward Dow, 1869–71; demolished 1929), a chemistry building on the hill facing Crosby Street. Its namesakes were the Lyme businessman General David Culver and his wife, who left money to Dartmouth to establish the state college. The main dormitory of N.H.C. was Conant Hall, now Hallgarten Hall. To the west of Conant stood Allen Hall, a frame dormitory (1872; demolished 1919), while to the east lay the state farm. Across Park Street lay the farm's complex of barns and silos, a house for the farm manager, and the state's agricultural experiment station.

In contrast, Dartmouth built fairly little during this time. It built Wilson Hall facing College Street (it had to lease the rear of the site from N.H.C.) and it finally made its first step eastward with Bartlett Hall during the early 1890s.

The decision of N.H.C. to leave Hanover spared Dartmouth the challenge of remaining a "small college" while still trying to coordinate multiple undergraduate institutions. Landscape architect Charles Eliot designed a campus for N.H.C. on donated land in Durham, about one hundred miles from Hanover, and when the original buildings by architects Dow & Randlett were ready in 1892, the state sold most of its Hanover property to Dartmouth. (The state college would become the University of New Hampshire in 1923.) Dartmouth took over operation of the N.H.C. eating club, expanded its chemistry department into the other half of Culver Hall, and let its alumni build a grandstand and sports park on the front field of the state farm. Also during 1892, the college absorbed the Chandler Scientific Department and brought in William Jewett Tucker as president, ending the small bloom of the apparent university and creating a unified and centralized institution on which to base the next decade of large-college reform. Tucker would manage deftly to erase the appearance of a modern university even as he incorporated many of its benefits.

14. Wilson Hall

Samuel J.F. Thayer, 1884–85; 1928–29; Moore Grover Harper, 1984

Wilson Hall finial

Wilson Hall is the fraternal twin of Rollins Chapel, a library building dedicated on the same day. Each building moved an important function from Dartmouth Row to another site on College Street. Although General Thayer had offered a new library building in 1867, the college was unable to meet the conditions of his will and had to leave the collection in Reed Hall. Only after Edward Rollins conditioned his 1883 chapel gift on the school obtaining funds for a library did the school finally erect a freestanding library building, Wilson Hall.

George Francis Wilson, an industrialist-inventor of East Providence, Rhode Island, produced enough baking powder in his Rumford Chemical Works to fund a variety of philanthropic bequests, including Wilson Hall at Brown University (Gould & Angell, 1890–91). Wilson's attorney, Halsey J. Boardman ('58), suggested he also give a building at Dartmouth. The donor's only condition was that "a block of Cumberland Granite bearing in plain letters the word 'Wilson'" span the building's entrance.[1]

Boston architect Samuel J. F. Thayer, designer of the Providence City Hall, gave Wilson Hall the conventional library form of the time, much like that of Henry Hobson Richardson's Ames Free Library in North Easton, Massachusetts (1878–79), and his larger Billings Library at the University of Vermont (1883–86). The design for this building, with its finely-carved sandstone trim, made each function visible: the building's Syrian-arched entrance originally led to a book delivery hall, flanked by an octagonal reading room on the north and a wing for the four levels of closed cast-iron stacks on the south. The building's stair tower and its conical cap stand picturesquely alongside the entrance. In the iron-trussed and skylit attic above the stacks was the public "Picture Gallery," crowded with portraits. Trustee and former governor Benjamin Franklin Prescott ('56) was the chief collector behind a late-nineteenth century expansion of the portrait collection and was a member of the building committees of Rollins and Wilson.

Wilson Hall proved invaluable. While using the library as a freshman during 1892, Robert Frost read Richard Hovey's poem *Seaward* and was inspired to begin his career. "I always hope they won't tear that down," Frost said of Wilson Hall in 1958, "because under that arch I went into my idea of publishing something."[2] As all library buildings do, however, Wilson Hall started on its way to inadequacy the moment it opened. By 1905, books were taking over offices and the attic, as the portrait gallery moved to Webster Hall. The librarians asked for a tunnel to the Bissell Gymnasium and a new reading room there. Instead, the school waited.

After Baker Library opened, the college used income from the Second College Grant to remodel Wilson for the College Museum and the Anthropology Department, both refugees from the demolished Butterfield Museum. Wilson became increasingly unappealing, and the crammed natural history collection, having started out in 1772 as a cabinet of curiosities containing some "curious elephant bones" (mammoth fossils), had difficulty keeping up with modern museological practice. The lifelike mounted fawn and the Sanborn collection of stuffed fish were visited less frequently. The collection reached its high point in 1940 with the creation of the Robert Ripley Room, housing artifacts donated from the collection of *Ripley's Believe It–Or Not!* The room closed in 1961, and the connection to the Hood Museum in 1984 led to a major housecleaning.

Hopkins Center administrators and functions related to film and television occupied the former library after Charles Moore's colorful remodeling, which centered around a baffling drum in the former book-delivery hall. Many of the natural history specimens went to academic departments or across the river to the Montshire Museum of Science (Childs Bertram Tseckares, 1989; 2002); Wilson started on its third career, still one of the most distinctive buildings on campus.

15. Bartlett Hall
Lambert Packard, 1890–91; 1963

Although the picturesque arrangement and Romanesque styling of the red brick and brownstone Bartlett Hall regularly send the building out of favor, the inertia of its granite foundation has kept it standing on its outcrop overlooking East Wheelock Street. The well-fortified clubhouse is an example of a national building boom that occurred during the 1880s, when local Young Men's Christian Associations strove to make their clubhouses appealing to potential converts. A speaker at a national convention of 1887 stated that the location for such a building "can be selected more on the principles which govern the location of a handsome

Bartlett Hall

residence, or a social or political club house of the best class, than on those which govern the location of a mercantile house." The entrance was to be the main feature a passer-by would see, and a number of contemporary Y.M.C.A. buildings, including Boston's of 1883, would adopt the convivial and clubby stepped gable that was unique in Hanover when it appeared on Bartlett Hall.

Bartlett Hall answered a request from Dartmouth's Y.M.C.A. Dedicated to converting fellow students and local residents through evangelical mass meetings, revivals, and carefully honed small-group recruiting sessions, Dartmouth's nonsectarian Protestant student club had used a succession of monikers since it began in 1801 as the Society Religiosii. The most important donation to the building came from the prime mover on the building committee, trustee Henry Fairbanks ('53). An inventor and the vice president of his father's scale-making enterprise of E.&T. Fairbanks & Co. in St. Johnsbury, Vermont, Henry Fairbanks was also a Professor of Natural Philosophy and Natural History and had built an 1864 mansion on his large Hanover property, later known as the Hitchcock Estate. An 1857 graduate of Andover Theological Seminary, the conservative Fairbanks was a fervent writer of religious tracts and headed the New Hampshire Y.M.C.A. He donated a new clubhouse to the Y.M.C.A. of St. Johnsbury (1883–85), designed

Lounge addition, New Hampshire Hall

by the family architect, Lambert Packard, and he brought Packard to this project.

A specifically nonfraternity clubhouse, Bartlett Hall represents a precursor to the school's student union. The association sought to make the building the center of social life and offered rooms to all student organizations. Rental bedrooms for ten men in the attic helped defray operating costs. At the Association's request, the trustees named the building during 1893 after the recently retired President Bartlett, who had been the head fundraiser.

Bartlett Hall has spent most of its existence housing groups other than the Y.M.C.A., which moved to College Hall within a decade to be at the center of student life. The music department occupied the hall before the Hopkins Center opened, followed later by language departments. The college added a utilitarian concrete bridge behind the building to connect its second level with the hillside. Bartlett Hall's decorative window depicting John the Baptist (John Ballantyne & Sons, installed 1893) naturally predates the ground-level restroom in which it now is located.

16. New Hampshire Hall

Charles Alonzo Rich, 1907–1908; Charles G. Hilgenhurst Associates, 1985; 2008–2009

With limestone embellishments hinting at the gables of Boston's Fanieul Hall (1742), the concrete-floored, steel-framed dormitory is one of a dozen such buildings erected almost annually to house ever-increasing enrollments. The school's largest dormitory when it opened, New Hamp features a C-shaped plan focused on a flat-roofed entrance portico of tripled Tuscan columns. One of the most elaborate examples of the mid-1980s program to expand dormitory social facilities is the two-level ell that projects from the rear of the building.

New Hampshire Hall's name recognizes the generosity of the state government. Although the Dartmouth College Case confirmed that the state did not control the college, it did not mean that the state was not among Dartmouth's largest benefactors. The land on which the campus stands was largely a gift of the Province, as filtered through the shrewd personal charity of Governor Wentworth. The state gave several income-producing townships between 1789 and 1807. Siting the federal land-grant college where this building stands also would benefit Dartmouth, especially when the state donated its half-interest in Culver Hall upon the school's departure. Fairly regular legislative appropriations began during the late nineteenth century, peaking at $20,000 by 1904, although President Hopkins declined the gifts after 1920 to avoid developing a dependence. As the state's first college and a celebrant in its woods and rivers, Dartmouth maintains a special relationship with New Hampshire that is memorialized by this dormitory.

Hallgarten Hall

17. Hallgarten Hall

Edward Dow, 1873–74; partially demolished 1925

Only Hallgarten remains as a built reminder of the twenty-five-year presence of
the state school in Hanover. When New Hampshire College of Agriculture and
the Mechanic Arts (N.H.C.) erected this building as a substitute for the town's
boarding houses, farmer John Conant of Jaffrey, the school's largest benefactor at
the time, covered some of the cost. The bulk of the funding came from legislative
appropriations. The school bought a building site adjacent to its farm and laid out
Crosby Street between the two. Only the rear ell stands today; the original cross-
gabled brick building known as Conant Hall stood three and a half levels high
atop a T-shaped footprint, presenting a tripartite front facade to Wheelock Street.
Flattened arcading attached to the building's wall planes supported prominent
paired roof brackets, allowing the imposing Victorian building to house an optimistic
post-Civil War institution.

The dormitory and "boarding establishment" in Conant's ground level were open to all students, including those of Dartmouth, and was the closest thing to a dining hall in Hanover. The state school contracted out the club's operation to a local couple who had experience running a private eating club, and they supplied about 135 students with moderately priced meals prepared in the kitchen ell. The farm across the street provided the club with some of the produce it required, although the hope that it would break even did not work out.

When New Hampshire College moved to Dow & Randlett's campus in Durham during 1892, it sold Conant to Dartmouth. A benefactor of eight years earlier, Julius Hallgarten became the building's new namesake, although Dartmouth maintained the original combination of functions for nearly a decade. The dormitory commanded the lowest rents and was unpopular enough to earn the nickname "Hellgate," and the college demolished the building's main block a few years after Topliff rose in front of it, leaving the three-by-three-bay ell that still stands. Following shorter-term uses, the school remodeled the standing remnant during 1989 into the Bregman Electronic Music Studio. The school's Electroacoustic Music Program operates on the fringes of the performing arts center at an institution that strives to involve itself in computing: the department's founders during the mid-1970s invented the Dartmouth Digital Synthesizer, later known as the Synclavier.

18. The Heating Plant and the Store House
Lamb & Rich with Richard D. Kimball Co., 1898; Larson & Wells, 1923; 1940; 1958
The Store House
Harry Artemas Wells, 1916
McKenzie Hall, 1931

Dartmouth's hardest-working building is a battered chapel of steam that has served as the chief node in an energy-broadcasting network for more than a century. The Heating Plant south of Wheelock Street continues to be ruled by expedience and remains the only significant building on campus to be known by its function alone.

During the early 1890s, a unified push for urban-scale civic improvements produced a joint College-Village reservoir in the hills northeast of Hanover as well as this central heating plant. Although a consultant predicted that winter weather would sap the heat from the underground mains, the arrival of Benjamin Ames Kimball ('54) on the board of trustees in 1895 led to a solution. Kimball was a banker, a politician, and president of the Concord & Montreal Railroad, an expert in locomotive engineering, and the builder of a striking stone house in Gilford called Kimball's Castle (1897–99). He and his collaborators at Dartmouth devised a cheap method of suspending iron steam lines within conventional earthenware sewer pipes, insulating them with ground cork to make the plant cost-effective.

Placing the plant well back from East Wheelock Street established a southern boundary for the campus while also maintaining the traditional industrial use of the area. The plant occupied part of the footprint of the private College Gas Works with its brick retort and Gothic stack (Ezekiel Dimond, 1872, mid-1880s; demolished 1898).

Two functionally distinct parts made up the original heating plant: the main one-level Romanesque boilerhouse and a blank-walled coal pocket adjoining it to the west. The dark, squat strength of the plant's round arches would not have looked out of place at an urban lager brewery, signaling the presence of power and production. Engineer Richard Kimball's interior, with its high iron-trussed roof, originally contained a battery of four 125-horsepower horizontal boilers fed by firemen shoveling in eight-hour shifts. Several times a day, horse-drawn wagons would bring coal from the Boston & Maine coal trestle across the river in Lewiston to dump the fuel through the roof of the coal pocket on College Street. The steam went out to the campus, and the coal smoke left by the stack that originally stood behind the building, a brick tower with the elaborated iron cap that *The Dartmouth* called "a most pleasing land-mark of the town."

A pair of dynamos occupied the plant's empty east room in 1904 to supply electric lights on campus, also connecting to the power plant in White River Junction in order to let the school buy and sell power. Jens Larson's second level Georgianized the building in 1923 but nevertheless recreated the original pediment and roof forms. Other architectural changes have resulted from the shift to oil (late 1920s), the shift to 110-volt AC (1940), the substitution of a plainer replacement stack (1958), and the installation of a pair of oil tanks in the rear (1991). Finally, the school ensured the plant's future utility during the mid-1990s when it connected the plant to a large new steam tunnel running to the chiller plant at the opposite end of the campus. A crew largely made up of Navy veterans continues to run the plant's boilers constantly, generating almost half of the school's electricity and heating about one hundred buildings, or cooling a number of them.

Next to the Heating Plant stands the Store House, a flat-roofed brick mill building that occupies the site of the state school's 1887 frame machine shop for reaching the "mechanic arts." The Store House turns the corner onto Crosby Street, producing an unexpectedly superb campus building: human-scaled and carefully detailed, with large windows and multiple entrances among its rhythmic bays, adopting an efficient and space-saving urban footprint behind the softening of a grassy verge and tall elms. Designer Harry Artemas Wells ('10), Th ('11), described as having "a streak of obstinacy in hanging on to work (and to an opinion)," was the school's Superintendent of Buildings and Grounds at the time and later would form architecture firms with Jens Fredrick Larson (1919–26) and Archer E. Hudson (1926–32).[3] Wells's design for the Store House rejected the

The Heating Plant

idea of erecting a combined storehouse-and-grandstand across Crosby Street, which was an idea that had been proposed by the Thayer alumni working at the engineering firm of Lockwood, Greene & Co.

McKenzie Hall, the small building between the Heating Plant and the Store House, began as a pasteurization plant. Although state law did not require pasteurization during the early 1930s, an alumnus working with a dairy equipment supplier seems to have planted doubts among administrators about the safety (or public-relations risk) of the unpasteurized milk the school was buying from dairies in Norwich and Hanover. This site was close to high-pressure steam lines, refrigeration, and truck parking. After state dairy regulations made the building redundant, it became the headquarters of those who maintained Dartmouth's buildings and grounds. Since the eighteenth century, the school had appointed a professor as an inspector of buildings. Alexander Anderson McKenzie ('91), Th ('96), an engineer who had left the Chandler School during his junior year to work on the proposed Nicaragua Canal, was the first professional to hold

Topliff Hall, Wheelock Street entrance

the office, and he was elevated to the school's first superintendent of buildings in 1898. The distinctive department known since 1994 as the Department of Facilities, Operations, and Management has a broad variety of responsibilities that traditionally includes the management of the college flags on the Green, trucking snow from Occom Pond for the Carnival sculpture, if needed, delivering the timbers for the Dartmouth Night bonfire each fall, and skillfully whisking away the charred debris of that inferno
by dawn.

19. Topliff Hall

Larson & Wells, 1919–20; Charles G. Hilgenhurst Associates, 1986

Topliff symbolizes the unpredictable growth that wracked Dartmouth before the school introduced one of the nation's first modern admissions systems. The giant dormitory is the first building of an interwar building boom that would stretch on for two decades and seems made for a different institution: its capacity of between 158 and 180 students makes it still the largest dormitory at Dartmouth.

Through the late nineteenth century, colleges were not "selective" in today's sense of the word, meaning that they did not regularly turn away qualified students. As the nation's public schools matured and the expanding commercial class made higher education less of a niche service, enrollments rose across the country. Dartmouth in particular grew inordinately popular, which President Tucker attributed to the school's modernization, its emphasis on its history, and its ability to benefit from the recruiting activities of alumni. Administrators began to await the annual announcement of freshman numbers with trepidation, since growing classes required new dormitories. The trustees committed to housing everyone, since the idea of barring qualified students for lack of beds seemed "undemocratic." A 1905 resolution offered "no effort to restrain the normal increase of students or general growth of the College," and an extension of that idea in 1911 admitted even qualified students for whom the school could provide no dormitory space. Enlarging the college to meet the demand became something of a national duty. Enrollment boomed after World War I, and the school decided to build Topliff Hall.

To reduce the barracks-like effect of Topliff Hall's great bulk, Larson divided each main facade of the L-shaped building into the standard tripartite Dartmouth Hall form. This preference for local models over an apparently generic prewar Classicism also involved the skillful deployment of granite basement trim, a bracketed white cornice, and a broadly hipped, copper-clad roof. The building is not unattractive for its size, and Topliff's superb siting on the corner of Wheelock and Crosby Streets—screened by elms and post-game crowds—makes it another archetypical dormitory in a campus without a standard dormitory type. The school named the building for Manchester attorney Elijah Miller Topliff, a native of Hanover Center who showed little interest in the college after graduating in 1852 but would leave it his entire estate upon his death in 1911.

The opening of Topliff Hall marked the end of an era. If uncontrolled enrollments warranted this building before 1920, incoming students overwhelmed the school in 1921 when an article about the Dartmouth Outing Club appeared in *National Geographic* magazine. "Ski-ing over the New Hampshire Hills," by club founder Fred Harris ('11), featured photographs of ski-jumpers performing aerial maneuvers that could not have been better calculated to recruit young men across the country.

Middle Fayerweather Hall

Applications reportedly jumped 318 percent, and President Hopkins, who had previously disparaged admissions caps, helped convince the trustees to start the Selective Process of admissions during 1921. Unlike any college in the country (but following NYU's University College by about two years), Dartmouth began turning away qualified applicants for reasons over which the applicants had little control. Other schools condemned the move but soon imitated it.

The initial basis for selection was geography, with President Hopkins later explaining that "an undergraduate gets a considerable part of his education from association with his fellows, and that the more broadly representative your undergraduate group, why, the better your educational process." Like the formal and informal systems in place in other schools, however, the Selective Process also could be used to turn away Jewish applicants. Although administrators stated that they saw no need to follow other schools in formally capping Jewish enrollment, the Selective Process came under criticism as being anti-Semitic within five years of its inception. In 1933, the college also added common but unsavory application questions regarding "religious background" and "racial inheritance," a bias that would take several years to remove. Thus the new process that permitted Dartmouth to avoid building any more dormitories the size of Topliff Hall also forced it to make uncomfortable decisions about which individuals it would welcome into its academic community, and why.

20. Fayerweather Row

Middle Fayerweather Hall
Charles Alonzo Rich, 1899–1900; Charles G. Hilgenhurst Associates, 1985–86
North and South Fayerweather Halls
Charles Alonzo Rich, 1906–1907

The tanneries of Fayerweather & Ladew, the nation's largest suppliers of industrial leather for machine belts and the like, provided Daniel Burton Fayerweather with about three million dollars to give away on his death in 1892. After several lawsuits, the money flowed without restriction to Fayerweather's list of forty-six colleges and hospitals. Many of the institutions, including Amherst, Columbia, Wesleyan, Williams, Yale, and the University of Virginia, would name a building after Fayerweather. Dartmouth did as well, after using the gift to pay off crucial debts. President Tucker wrote that "[n]o fund of many times its value, if it had been restricted in its uses, could have served equal purpose at this juncture in the development of the College." Fayerweather Hall occupies the backyard of Dartmouth Hall, which had been the site of nearly 120 years' worth of outhouses known variously as "the Temple of Cloacina," "the Little College," or "Old Number 10," a building that still was known to the students of 1900.

Built of redder brick than most buildings on campus, Fayerweather Hall deploys granite and terra cotta trim, most notably in the large cartouche of terra cotta in the central gable, which features a book with laurels above the word "Fayerweather." The flattened arcade applied to the hall's central pavilion was an innovation as well. In plan and massing, however, Fayerweather Hall was unique for the degree to which it imitated a historic prototype on the campus. It adopted the tripartite form of the eighteenth-century Dartmouth Hall, employing a pair of brick firewalls to separate the building into three sections. Each entry housing only about eight men per stair landing, following an English vertical-circulation form that administrators praised for creating a secluded and "homelike" atmosphere. Fayerweather Hall was the largest dormitory at the time by almost fifty percent, and it featured some of the most expensive rooms, although the span of rents it made available was broad enough to place its average room in the bottom quarter of Dartmouth's luxury index.

The "staircase" circulation model went without imitation at Dartmouth, and it failed to survive even in this building. Workers punched through the firewalls and closed Fayerweather Hall's subsidiary entrances in 1929. Preparing for the boom of the G.I. Bill following World War II, the college adapted Fayerweather Hall for women and their student husbands by installing kitchenette suites in 1945. That improvement must have seemed wasteful or inappropriate once the married students moved out, and the school removed the kitchens just two years later. The next wave of student-living reform, of the 1980s, created a pair of flat-roofed basement connectors to join the three buildings of Fayerweather Row through kitchens and social rooms.

The two subsidiary companions to what became known as Middle Fayerweather Hall were the first buildings on campus to imitate the simple A-B-A arrangement of Dartmouth Row. Erecting these bookends provided a substantial amount of housing without creating a large and uncollegiate barracks. South Fayerweather is the larger of the two and has an exposed stone-clad basement that overlooks Wheelock Street. After a fire gutted the building completely in 1910, the replacement interior reduced the number of old-fashioned sleeping alcoves in favor of full-fledged two-room suites, making the building more luxurious and expensive. North Fayerweather did not follow until the school installed concrete stairwells in 1935 and an entire replacement interior in 1960.

21. Ripley, Woodward, and Smith Halls
Jens Fredrick Larson, 1930

Woodward Hall

The trio of connected dormitories known as RipWoodSmith is unusual on this campus for its unitary C-shaped form, which combines with the slate-sheathed gambrel roofs to bring to mind Harvard's collegiate houses more than anything in Hanover. The group's doorways open "upon a common lawn," as the architect described it, while the door accessing Ripley's programming-staff apartment was inserted during the year 2000.

The group's site well back from Wheelock Street created a significant incursion into College Park. After the trustees initially announced that a single building would occupy the site in honor of founding trustee Benjamin Pomeroy, they soon named each part of the group for one of the original tutors at the college: Sylvanus Ripley ('71), Bezaleel Woodward, and John Smith ('73). (The charter office of tutor, roughly equivalent to an instructor today, lasted through the late nineteenth century.)

22. Societies on East Wheelock Street

The Sphinx Tomb (William M. Butterfield, 1904–1905) is a technological achievement and stylistic oddity that continues to serve its original function as the meeting hall of the Sphinx senior society. Dartmouth students formed a variety of ephemeral class societies during the mid-nineteenth century, often focusing on freshmen, who were prohibited from joining fraternities. Permanent senior societies began in 1885, when fourteen juniors formed the Sphinx, a local group that seems to have styled itself after secretive New Orleans clubs such as Ye Mystick Krewe of Comus (1857), itself a joking imitation of an English social club. Each Krewe of seniors in the Sphinx continues to tap a group of juniors during Winter Carnival Weekend, which is the time when the six or so other senior societies at the school select their own delegations. Sphinx has become more secretive than in the days when it published members' names in the annual *Aegis*, and, like several other societies, it hides its roster until commencement, when graduating members carry identifying canes.

In building the first freestanding senior society building in Hanover, the Sphinx followed the practice of fraternities of the mid-nineteenth-century, constructing a hall for meetings without including any living space. The prolific architect William Butterfield of Manchester, New Hampshire, initially designed a Romanesque hall of rusticated stone but he soon came back with a cheaper and more apposite design derived from Egyptian prototypes. The Temple of Dendur, which would move from Egypt to the Metropolitan Museum of Art during the 1960s, was a common model for mausolea during the nineteenth century; adopting it as a model here made the Sphinx Tomb the state's most thoroughly Egyptian revival building. It also is apparently the region's first building built entirely of poured-in-place reinforced concrete, and historian Christopher Closs notes that society alumnus Morton Charles Tuttle ('97), a concrete expert and general manager of the Boston contractors Aberthaw Construction, was the moving force behind the building's construction and its unusual methods. The building was the first in town to be listed on the National Register of Historic Places.

The original windowless main block of the Sphinx stands atop a basement on a rocky outcrop overlooking East Wheelock Street. A deep cove molding of stamped metal marks the building's cornice and its flat roof, while reedy moldings of cast stone mark the corners of its battered walls of unfinished concrete. A pair of massive palm columns frames the tomb's monumental entrance porch and its

Alpha Delta house

The Sphinx Tomb

handleless wooden door. Larson & Wells added the sympathetic one-level rear addition (1925–26) having proposed a more elaborate three-level design in 1923. An Egyptian Revival interior lit by a large hipped skylight of colored glass allegedly reposes inside the building, installed after a 1931 fire to the designs of Wells & Hudson and decorator Robert S. Chase of the office of R. Clipston Sturgis.

Adjacent to the Sphinx stands Alpha Delta (1920–22), a brick house that was first planned in 1916. It led a wave of Roaring Twenties fraternity construction. Rarely has so conventional a building replaced one of such interest, the spooky brick Venetian temple that the Alpha Delta Phi chapter (1846) built to face the street in 1872. Grander and more formally homogeneous than the frame dwellings most contemporaries occupy, this Georgian house faces in the direction of the Green. The house was the setting for the free-wheeling experiences that Chris Miller ('65) described in short stories and the screenplay he cowrote for the 1978 film *National Lampoon*'s *Animal House*. Continuing to serve the fraternity as a local organization (1969), the house and its Tuscan Doric portico became a semiofficial platform from which candidates address the nation's youth in the presidential primaries: "To paraphrase the movie, it's time to start voting heavily," said Senator Bob Dole during the 1996 campaign.

The fraternity with the Greco-Beowulvian name of Chi Heorot originated as Chi Phi in 1897 and leased the mansarded house then on this site in 1903. This long hip-roofed brick replacement (Wells & Hudson, 1927–28) shares a shallow-C-shaped footprint with the Sigma Nu house but places its front entrance eccentrically in the western pavilion, creating an unclassically even number of facade openings. Chi Phi did not last unchanged as an organization, since it broke with the national group in 1968 as Chi Phi Heorot, rejoining it temporarily during

Chi Heorot house

the early 1980s before going local again and transferring its building to the college.

The clapboard house at 23 East Wheelock (1915; FPO, 2005) originally was the house of college electrician Roy J. Raymond, and by the early 1950s it housed a small crowd of renters. Under college ownership, the house became the headquarters of Amarna in 1993. The group takes its name from Akhenaten's ancient Egyptian capital city of Tel El-Amarna. Amarna follows the basic model of a fraternity while offering full membership to any student. About eleven Amarnites live in the house.

Kappa Kappa Gamma (1842; 1925; FPO, 1991; Fleck and Lewis, 2002) is the finely-detailed side-gabled house with the prominent cornice brackets. Its site at 24 East Wheelock Street is a long way from where the house started. Abigail Dewey, the widow of farmer William A. Dewey, built the house on College Street near the future entrance to Baker Library, where the house became the home base of mathematics and astronomy professor James Willis Patterson ('48). His service in Congress during the 1860s and 1870s prompted the trustees to bar professors from holding any governmental office more distracting than a local position. The college acquired the house from widow Sarah Wilder Patterson in 1908 and lent it to the Graduate Club before dragging the building's main block to its current site on the south side of Wheelock in 1925. The building's various ells became parts of other houses in this neighborhood. The school rented the house to professors and officers until the sorority moved in a few years after students founded it in 1978.

The James S. Brown House next door (1812; 1903; 1927) also originated near Baker's east entrance, where it housed professors and became a rooming house and official dormitory (Elm House) before the college moved it to 26 East Wheelock Street as a faculty rental.

23. The East Wheelock Cluster
Andres, Morton, and Zimmerman Halls and Brace Commons
Herbert S. Newman Associates, 1985–87
McCulloch Hall
Atkin Olshin Lawson-Bell Architects, 1999–2000
Frost House, 1897

The "cluster" scheme of the early 1980s grouped the school's formerly independent dormitories into administrative units with new lounges, kitchens, and live-in programming directors. The goal was to promote a sense of community during an era when the flexible quarterly enrollment system, the D-Plan, seemed to produce the side effect of some social fragmentation. The East Wheelock Cluster, as the first new dormitory group in about twenty-five years, is the first cluster to be built from scratch. The original four-building group included a purpose-built office for the programming head and a largely freestanding social space that was unusual for its great size; a dozen years passed before the school finally built the fifth dormitory planned for the group.

Several years into its operation, the East Wheelock Cluster became the only Dartmouth example of a national revival of the romantic late-1920s educational movement that promoted a "collegiate way of living" as Oxford and Cambridge were thought to practice it. Dartmouth had long been committed to the idea that learning also takes place outside the classroom, and had tried, in experiments such as the Choates, to house faculty among students. Under a new Dean in 1996, a "residential college" came into existence within Dartmouth, as faculty moved into Frost House on the small quadrangle; workers expanded the kitchen and snack bar for more frequent meal service; and administrators created recruiting brochures to let Dartmouth students know that they would have to apply to join. The basement seminar room of McCulloch Hall would supply the missing element, a space for teaching, and regular academic classes could take place in a Dartmouth dormitory for the first time in more than a century. The cluster even began to colonize nearby faculty apartments, bringing its undergraduate membership to about 325 students by the turn of the century, a population that equals that of Dartmouth College

Zimmerman and Morton Halls, with pyramid marking entrance to Brace Commons

in 1869 or the typical Oxford college of today. The experiment was a success, although it was not an overwhelming one. By East Wheelock's tenth anniversary, the school was content to see it simply as one residential option among several and had no plans to try it anywhere else.

The cluster's U-shaped figure recalls the footprints of nearby dormitories, and it owes something to the collegiate experience at Yale, where its architects designed numerous projects from the firm's office alongside a New Haven residential college. Each of the three dormitories comprises a pair of brick wings joined by a glassy gabled entrance pavilion. Andres and Zimmerman bend that basic form into mirror-image ell shapes on staggered sites well back from the street. Morton Hall aligns its constituent elements in a row instead, turning its side gable to the street and holding down one side of the cluster's simply-landscaped forecourt. At the head of this forecourt is the one-level Brace Commons, a half-recessed social room that joins A to Z. Its roof is an unusual paved plaza, and its entrance is marked by a unique and adventurous pyramidal-roofed pergola. These buildings are post-modern in their peppy quotation of traditional architectural forms and materials, from their green-painted doors to their copper-clad roofs, and in their non-archeological inexactness: they substitute squares and right triangles for the attenuated proportions of the Georgian Revival, giving prominence to wall dormers and diamond-shaped openings. The buildings carry the names of trustees F. William Andres ('29), Charles J. Zimmerman ('23), William H. Morton ('32), and

McCulloch Hall

Lloyd D. Brace ('25).

The interior-block McCulloch Hall is more obscure than its predecessors. It includes a stacked pair of lounges with a two-level balcony, and its bowing recreation room forms an ell to the south. Practices had changed since the first buildings of the cluster went up, and McCulloch has an elevator and a set of furniture hewn from wood of the Second College Grant. As the latest in more than a century of experiments at fostering social interaction, the building placed many of its bathroom sinks in the halls on the basis of the lessons of the Choates' famous "bathroom bonding." The building bears the name of trustee Norman E. McCulloch, Jr., ('50).

The "White House" at 13 East Wheelock Street is the residence of the faculty members who are associated with the cluster. It is the last of a small row of nineteenth-century dwellings connected with the Frost family. Medical School Dean Dr. Carlton Pennington Frost ('52), Dartmouth Medical School (DMS) ('56), acquired much of the property lining this side of Wheelock Street and moved his family into a house on the Heorot site around 1875. After Dr. Frost died in 1896, one of his sons, anatomy professor Gilman Dubois Frost ('87), DMS ('92), had this modest two-and-a-half level clapboard house built next door. The building's Tuscan Doric portico faces the athletic park, and according to legend, Gilman Frost's daughter Elisabeth met her future husband on this porch when a tennis match was rained out: he was college architect Jens Larson. Gilman Frost died in 1942 and the college later acquired the house, renting it and the housekeeper's apartment at the rear to college employees. A spare pergola now extends the portico to the full width of the facade, and a side porch expands the house's utility as an academic headquarters.

24. Faculty Housing

Parkside Apartments
Charles Alonzo Rich, 1912–13
Ledyard Apartments
Larson & Wells, 1920
Parker Apartments
Larson & Wells, 1921
Whitaker Apartments
Jens Fredrick Larson, 1928
North Park Graduate Housing
William Rawn & Associates, 2003
Wheelock and Park Faculty Housing
Truex Cullins & Partners, 2000–2001

Dartmouth doubled its faculty to forty-four between 1893 and 1899, raising the number to sixty-nine within a decade and reaching one hundred by 1913. Most new faculty members had difficulty finding a room to rent, and no donors responded to President Tucker's plea for "an apartment house, or a terrace of small houses, or single houses."[4] The school went ahead and built its own faculty neighborhoods beyond Park Street, at the eastern edge of the campus. Faculty have continued to move eastward, and several college projects lie about two miles out, along Wheelock Street: an award-winning group of thirty-two houses off Grasse Road (William Rawn Associates, 1992) and a second twenty-three-house group nearby in the Camp Brook area (Anne Lee Wilson, 2000).

The first faculty apartment house in this neighborhood is a two-family building alongside the College Park. Much of the design work fell to a draftsman who was in Rich's office from 1904 to 1914, Howard Major ("my good Major," in Rich's words). Major would go on to a career as a society architect, spreading Colonial architecture on Long Island and designing prominent stuccoed Spanish houses and towns in Florida and the Caribbean over three decades. While Major suggested that a stuccoed apartment house here would appeal to the artistic tastes of professors and noted that a low ground level was "the keynote of the attractiveness of the old Colonial houses," President Nichols' preference for a standard clapboarded house atop a basement won out.[5] The two-level Parkside Apartments terminates in a hipped roof that originally sheltered four servants'

Faculty apartments at Wheelock and Park streets

rooms.

Arts and Crafts tiles decorate the brick stairhall of the Ledyard Apartments, the clapboarded frame building at the northwest corner of Wheelock and Park Streets. The school turned the building over to students at the turn of the twentieth century. Around the corner on North Park Street are the Parker Apartments, named for trustee Joel Parker ('11), Chief Justice of New Hampshire and the chief benefactor of College Park during the late 1860s. During the time that Parker taught medical jurisprudence at Dartmouth, students sometimes spotted him strolling through his park. (The fund he left to establish a law school at his death in 1873 instead created an endowed professorship of law.) Parker also has begun housing students.

"Young married instructors, whose tenure of office is not very definite and whose means are limited, can be furnished simple, inexpensive quarters in attractive duplex houses or small apartment houses," wrote Jens Larson. His C-shaped Whitaker Apartments were meant for eight faculty families. The trio of joined duplexes are similar but wear different clothes, with the superior central unit of frame construction contrasting with the side wings of brick, as if the house of an eighteenth-century family was expanded by more prosperous descendants. The building's namesake is Nathaniel Whitaker, the Presbyterian minister whom founder Eleazar Wheelock sent with Samson Occom on the crucial fundraising tour of Great Britain during the late 1760s.

A row of eleven shingled houses painted in woodsy green and red lines a

Graduate housing on North Park Street

secluded walk on the forested back slope of College Park, giving the appearance
of a summer resort colony of the 1890s. Broad gables, varied dormers, and integral
porches elaborate these apartments aimed at first-year graduate students, each
adopting one of four basic types. The row represents not only the post-1960s
growth in graduate programs but the post-1980s renewal of traditional architecture,
since it replaced a pair of flat-roofed two-level faculty apartment buildings designed
by E. H. and M. K. Hunter in 1957.

Around a common area at the southeast corner of Park Street, the long-ago
site of the agricultural college barns, Dartmouth added a half-dozen clapboard
houses for faculty to the five Larson-designed dwellings that already occupied
the site. The bold corner building's dominant whiteness and the gentle arch of its

recessed monumental gateway bring to mind Charles Rennie Mackintosh's Scottish houses of the early 1900s, here flanked symmetrically by traditional New England dwellings. By the time the complex opened at the turn of the twenty-first century, fewer than a quarter of the faculty still lived in town, and the school was attempting to reverse that trend.

Among the nearby houses that faculty have built for themselves is that of college architect and art instructor Jens Larson at 1 North Balch Street (1927). He designed and later expanded the L-shaped brick building with a frame garage and studio ell. Larson maintained his practice here until moving it to New York in 1945. Writer Corey Ford later bought the place, restarting the Dartmouth Boxing Club here during the 1950s and leaving it to the Rugby Football Club to help fund the future construction of a clubhouse.

25. Park Street Houses of New Hampshire College

The Pettee House (1884) was the first building on North Park Street. From its location at the northeast corner of Wheelock Street, Charles H. Pettee ('74), who was the dean of New Hampshire College, could keep an eye on the farmland to the south. The house later became a college rental.

Thayer Lodge (1888) was built by the state school in part with subsidies from the federal Hatch Act, which aimed to spread "useful and practical information on subjects connected with agriculture, and to promote scientific investigation and experiment respecting the principles and application of agricultural science." When New Hampshire's Agriculture Experiment Station moved to Durham, where it still operates, the state sold the building to the Thayer School of Engineering. The Thayer School remained its headquarters for a decade. As a college apartment building, Thayer Lodge saw many of its details fall in line with the domestic conventions of the neighborhood.

The Farm Manager's House is the 1780s Cape Cod dwelling standing hard against Park Street. It was the farmhouse of the Chase Farm at the time the agricultural college bought it in 1869. The agricultural school surrounded the house with sometimes-lavish state farm outbuildings during the 1870s, most of which Dartmouth demolished during 1922.

1. George Francis Wilson, will (January 12, 1883), quoted in Halsey C. Edgerton, compiler, *Terms of Gifts and Endowments and an Annotated Copy of the Charter of Trustees of Dartmouth College* (Hanover, N.H.: Dartmouth College, 1940), 301.

2. Robert Frost, interview (1958), quoted in "Under That Arch: A Keepsake Issued by the Dartmouth College Library on the Occasion of the Opening of Its Robert Frost Room," (Hanover, N.H.: Dartmouth College Library, 1962).

3. Personnel memorandum regarding Harry Artemas Wells, DP-10(15): 32, President Nichols' Papers, Dartmouth College Archives.

4. William Jewett Tucker, "The Material Development of the College" (address June 26, 1906), printed in Dartmouth Bi-monthly, 1, no. 6 (August, 1906), 310.

5. Howard Major to Ernest Fox Nichols (April 6, 1912), Buildings folder, President Nichols' Papers, Dartmouth College Archives.

WALK THREE: ATHLETICS

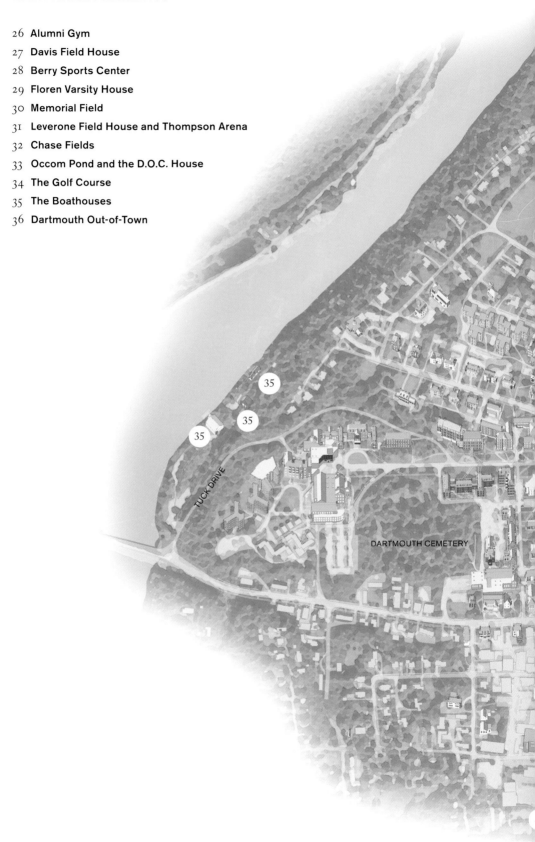

Farm fields turned to sport

Dartmouth's location amid the farms and hills of a river valley has allowed it to keep most of its athletic facilities close. Many of these facilities occupy the old state farm south of Wheelock Street, where they moved in 1893 from the school's original sports field, the Green. The first games played in Hanover took place on the Green, whether cricket or indigenous soccerlike games popularized during the early nineteenth century. Intercollegiate sports at Dartmouth began in 1866, when the school's baseball nine (1862) lost to Amherst's Nicean Baseball Club on the Green. Students fielded a rugby team during the late 1870s that played its first intercollegiate football match in 1881, this time beating Amherst on the Green. The Green was the site of a quarter-mile track for the school's first track meet (1875). These events disrupted each other as well as the peace and quiet of the town, but they provided enough material that students could write a history of athletics at the school in 1893.

The school's first athletic building was the Bissell Gymnasium (Richards & Park, 1866–67; demolished 1958), a red-brick Victorian hall that faced the south side of the Green. The Hanover-born George Henry Bissell, whom a classmate called "the palest, weakest member" of the class of 1845, donated the building. The bowling alleys that were typical of college gymnasia occupied Bissell's ground level, while a double-height gymnasium space occupied the second level. The faculty mandated that a gymnastics instructor provide a "system of physical culture" to promote students' "health and bodily vigor," requiring whole classes to synchronize their jumping jacks or weightlifting. Baseball managed to move out of the gym after students paid for a Baseball Cage on Cemetery Lane (1889; demolished 1912).

The decision of the state to sell its experimental farm provided an extraordinary opportunity. Alumni Gym followed the Alumni Oval there, and during the late twentieth century a second center of facilities opened across Park Street, still on the college farm. Although new athletic facilities represent the one building type for which Dartmouth has retained some of its postwar stylistic freedom, the school also has pushed to rejuvenate its historic athletic buildings rather than replace them.

26. Alumni Gym

Charles Alonzo Rich, 1909–11; Eggers & Higgins, 1962–63;
Fleck & Lewis, 1972, 1973; Gwathmey Siegel & Associates, 1989;
Lavallee/Brensinger, 2005–2006
Spaulding Pool
Rich & Mathesius, 1919–20; Fleck & Lewis, 1980
Manley Multipurpose Rooms
Jens Fredrick Larson, 1931; Lavallee/Brensinger, 2005

Alumni Gym

For some time the greatest and grandest building on campus, Alumni Gymnasium was a project of the students, who started pledging funds during 1906, and especially of the alumni, who borrowed construction funds from the school. The school also helped by donating the services of Buildings Superintendent Edgar H. Hunter, while the college architect gave his initial design services.

Two antagonistic functions were competing for attention in the design of gyms of the day. One was the schoolwide fitness training program, which required a wood-floored drill hall and exercise equipment, while the other was the practicing of intercollegiate sports teams, which tended to require a vast dirt-floored cage with few breakable windows. Making the two volumes work together in a single building was a design challenge that Charles Rich answered with the apparently novel solution of a layered cross: the drill hall would straddle the cage. Although the massing pinched the center of the cage, it still permitted athletes to pass freely below. The cross-shaped form would give Alumni Gym an affinity with the most prominent of the industrial offspring of the Roman bath, the great urban railroad station of the late nineteenth century—if the long cage represents a ticket hall, then the drill hall must be the trainshed extending to the rear. An elegant solution for Dartmouth's problem, this form would not become a standard of gym design, in part because cages grew too large; by the late 1920s, they evolved into the freestanding fieldhouse.

The thermal window of Dartmouth's drill hall dominates the prominent central frontispiece of Alumni Gym, flanked by heavy bastions. A few of the Romanesque forms the architect had employed in Harlem during the 1880s appeared in the building, such as the tripartite arched screen and the granite block capitals of the entrance. The gym's rear facade is strongly Romanesque, displaying a full-

Michael Pool in Alumni Gym

height arcade and crow-stepped gable. The building's modified pediment and its prominent monitor roof give it a kinship with the school's nearby Heating Plant of 1898.

The upstairs drill hall or "gymnasium" was the heart of the gym and would see decades of basketball games, Junior Promenade dances, the occasional rained-out Commencement, and many large-scale class examinations. The school filled the room with a plethora of exercise machines when it reopened the space as a fitness center following a 2006 renovation, allowing sunlight to filter through the original metal truss roof and the new ductwork. A new elevator tower and mezzanine occupy the front of the room, behind the great thermal.

Ancillary spaces are stacked below the drill hall, focusing on the first-level Trophy Room. Alumni lavished considerable attention on this space, separately commissioning the architect to design a broad passage lined with columned alcoves. Professor Keyes deployed his taste in furniture to create a gentlemen's club with some of the atmosphere of a reliquarium (at least one football was noted as still bearing the blood of the victors). More specialized spaces elsewhere have since surpassed the Trophy Room, and only the small Modernist wood Oberlander Lounge carries on part of the original function here, the other alcoves having been infilled with offices.

The cage portion of the building began as a great dirt floor 360 feet long below a metal-truss roof nearly 40 feet above. It was not unlike a New York National Guard cavalry armory the architect had designed in 1884. The Trophy Room formed a solitary bridge across the center of the space, allowing the building's full-length cinder running track to pass beneath it. Above the floor was a cantilevered gallery carrying a board running track that was the fastest in the world for a time after a 1939 resurfacing. Baseball teams played on a regulation-sized diamond in the western half of the cage, while track and field events initially occupied the eastern half below a series of suspended rooms for handball, fencing, and boxing.

The gym's vast sturdiness has made it one of the most-modified buildings on campus. During the early 1960s, the school installed a permanent basketball floor and stands in the western half of the cage and excavated the dirt floor of the eastern part for the school's main swimming pool. Named for longtime coach Karl B. Michael, the pool was designed by R. Jackson Smith ('36) of Eggers & Higgins, a former swim team captain. A long-standing lack of ventilation required a new circulation system and allowed the re-exposure of the high metal truss roof during 2006.

In contrast, Dartmouth's initial pool is an addition to the rear of the gym. Former New Hampshire governor Rolland Harty Spaulding, whose New England mills produced fiberboard and leatherboard, offered in 1917 to give whatever a

Davis Field House

worthwhile pool would cost. Charles Rich produced a design that year, but the World War I shut down construction across the country and halted the Spaulding Pool project. The war affected students directly, having prompted a number to volunteer for ambulance duty beginning in 1915. Others raised money to ship a pair of Ford ambulances to the American Field Service. Among the twenty Dartmouth students of A.F.S. Section No. 28 was ambulance driver Stanley Hill ('18), who was killed during the summer of 1918 in the second battle of the Marne, near Rheims. As he requested, the proceeds of his life insurance policy went toward a Dartmouth pool.

The contributions of Spaulding and Hill form two distinct parts of the pool that the college built after the war concluded. The pool room proper is built of brick on a steel frame and originally featured a multicentered barrel vault thirty feet above the water, lit by five large chandeliers. The basin below is a massive monolith of unreinforced concrete. Professor Keyes specified that the room would be lined with decorative tilework like that of a pool found on a private estate, since a conventional scheme of white tiles might make the room unappealing in snowy weather. Keyes asked Leon Victor Solon, the head of the Art Department of the American Encaustic Tiling Company, to design the tiles. (Solon, who presented the pool in the architectural press, also collaborated with Rich to remodel a Manhattan rowhouse into an extravagant Aetco showroom.) Spaulding's restrained decorative scheme is based on a series of tan wall panels set off by wide blue bands. Alternate panels contain elaborately rendered pairs of yellow dolphins in low relief, while similar dolphins are painted on the room's green wooden benches. Adjacent to the pool room is the Hill Memorial Shower, a solemn space of shallow cross-vaults dedicated to "brave and clean young manhood," according to the wall plaque. A suspended barrel vault and three-sided mezzanine for the general women's locker room now obscure Spaulding's ceiling, but the shower room remains in use and enough of the pool's decoration remains visible to give a hint of Spaulding's original appearance.

The western analogue of Spaulding Pool is a simple three-story Manley Multipurpose Rooms. The Athletic Council originally built the Georgian addition to contain ten American singles squash courts, with a doubles court alongside the gym. When the squash team switched to international rules and newly-widened courts in Berry Gym, this building took on a new use.

27. Davis Field House
Jens Fredrick Larson, 1926

Between helping alumni complete the gym and giving a hockey rink at the gym's
east end (Jens Fredrick Larson, 1929; demolished 1985), Boston businessman
Howard Clark Davis, a member of the class of 1906, gave the college this carefully
domestic varsity house. Standing at the west end of the gymnasium, the building
presents its front facade to the gridiron, although its street facade to the rear is
nearly identical. Klauder and Wise described the building in their campus-design
book as a "pleasant home complete in itself," and the building's original function
was to house visiting teams, fulfilling an early-century Athletic Council plan to
open a rooming house on Main Street. Varsity teams and their lockers, offices, and
equipment rooms moved into this specialized headquarters from the crowded gym,
installing their team trophies in the second-level Hall-Bennett Lounge. From the
building's basement, a tunnel originally let the football team charge directly onto
Memorial Field.

28. Berry Sports Center
Gwathmey Siegel & Associates, 1987

A bridge leads from Alumni Gym to the John W. Berry Sports Center to the east.
Berry's siting is the result of the effort of master planner Lo-Yi Chan to prevent
the complex from turning its back on the town by facing westward to the Green
instead of northward to the street. While the glass barrel-vault lighting Berry Gym's
axial corridor aligns directly with the thermal window at the end of the old gym, the
new building is unmistakably of its own era—a long, low, steamship of a museum
that represents the final note of the school's initial adoption of Modernism. The
building's minimalist brick exterior displays a coolly projecting white-paneled bow
window and cast-stone details, while the interior maintains the nautical feel by
deploying balustrades of curving pipe rails with attached wire mesh panels.

Berry's largest space is Leede Arena, a multipurpose basketball hall that
occupies almost exactly the footprint of the predecessor Davis Rink. Named for
basketball star and independent oilman Ed Leede ('49), the room is considerably
more spacious than the old basketball gym in the west wing of Alumni Gym,
although it is just as bold in asserting its industrial heritage, suggesting the beauty
inherent in the planar geometries of ground-faced concrete block divided into stark
bays by white-painted steel columns. This hall also anchors the ceremonial route
of East Wheelock Street, since it is where the seniors form up before making their
Commencement procession to the Green. The building contains other spaces
including the Herrick Court, an unusual international exhibition squash court with
three glass walls.

Berry Sports Center, Park Street facade

29. Floren Varsity House

Centerbrook Architects, 2006–2007

Floren Varsity House

This is the familiar story of Ivy athletics at the turn of the century: more athletes are playing more intercollegiate sports, shrinking the relative fan base to a point at which so many students compete that there might be no one left to do the cheering. Centerbrook Architects drew up a master plan for the growth of athletic facilities in 1999, and the Floren Varsity House, which reduced the football field's capacity from about 18,000 to 13,000, is the plan's most visible result. The building is shoehorned onto a narrow interstitial site where it can serve as a backdrop for both the right field line of Rolfe Field and the East Stand of Memorial Field. The restrained Modernism of the brick-clad, flat-roofed building includes the closest thing Dartmouth has to a luxury skybox,

Memorial Field, grandstand entrance

a single lounge that looks down at the fifty-yard line. A variety of varsity sports have their headquarters here, sharing larger spaces for meeting or exercising. The building carries the name of Douglas C. Floren ('63) and his family.

30. Memorial Field
> *Thomas Butler, 1892–93; Larson & Wells, 1921–23; 1950s;*
> *Clark Companies, 2006*
> *Red Rolfe Field*
> *Larson & Wells, 1921–23; 2007*

Students of the land-grant college cultivated the front field of the state farm for almost twenty-five years before Dartmouth purchased it during 1892 and let alumni turn it into an athletic park. A cinder oval track ringed a field for football and baseball, flanked by a frame shingle-style grandstand that seated 800 (1893; burned 1911). Just as importantly, a high board fence around the park gave spectators an incentive to pay at the turnstile. The school realigned the field slightly to the northeast after World War I, renamed the expanded park Memorial Field, and built a replacement grandstand of concrete faced in brick. Jens Larson's great Roman aqueduct is both a severe proscenium terminating the Lebanon Street vista and an open gateway to the football spectacle behind it. The grandstand's projecting central bay contains a monumental memorial arch that recalls the 112

Leverone Field House

Dartmouth men who died in World War I, some of whom had played football on this field, and many of whom had dug practice trenches here, on what is now Rolfe Field. (Football coach Frank Cavanaugh ('99), meanwhile, continued coaching elsewhere as the Iron Major.) Although the grandstand's central bay has been attenuated over the years into a blank-walled tower to screen the rear of a green-paneled Modernist press box, the mood of the building has not become any lighter.

Once through the arch, the visitor emerges into a grandstand built to seat 7,100 people. The Cornell team that dedicated the field handed Dartmouth a 32–7 defeat, the only loss in a thirty-game run that included a national championship in 1925. The place has brought good luck since, with its most remarkable moment occurring in 1940: after an officiating error gave Cornell an extra chance to win, both teams developed their films, the official acknowledged his mistake, and Cornell magnanimously and uniquely conceded the Fifth Down Game to Dartmouth. The eight schools signing the 1945 football agreement that underlies the Ivy League began round-robin games in 1956, and although Dartmouth's fortunes would rise and fall in cycles, this team was the one with the most victories and championships by the league's fiftieth anniversary.

Although the wooden seating opposite the grandstand gave way in 1968 to larger metal bleachers, Memorial Field has remained a one-sided park. The games against Harvard and Yale that were popular during the decade prior to 1978 brought the park to its peak attendance of more than 20,416. Since then, the league moved to a smaller division within the N.C.A.A. (1981), and attendance has dropped. Memorial Field's ennobling enclosure is no less focused on fierce competition among students, and it still leaves plenty of room for the occasional Dartmouth dog to wander out during a game. Something about the sight of red and yellow leaves above the alumni wrapped in their Black Watch tartan blankets walking up Crosby Street as the band forms up for a victory parade helps make Memorial Field the quintessence of college football.

Red Rolfe Field, the baseball diamond east of the football field, hosts Dartmouth's oldest intercollegiate sport. The ball games on the Green during the eighteenth century predate the invention of baseball, and informal or inter-class teams were playing some version of baseball by the 1830s. The Green's northwest corner became the college's official baseball ground, with a backstop against the Wentworth Street fence and bleachers along the Main Street first-baseline. Baseball moved to the Alumni Oval when it opened, and the present diamond emerged as part of the Memorial Field project. Reputed to be one of the Ivy League's toughest parks, the modest Red Rolfe Field has bleachers seating about one thousand and a pair of simple brick dugouts, one with a frame second level for the press. During 1969, the school named the field for Robert Abial "Red" Rolfe ('31), the New York Yankees third baseman who was one of the legendary Bronx Bombers of 1936 to 1939 and went on to manage the Detroit Tigers and was the Athletic Director at Dartmouth from 1954 to 1967.

31. Leverone Field House and Thompson Arena

Leverone Field House
Pier Luigi Nervi with Campbell & Aldrich, 1962–63
Thompson Arena
Pier Luigi Nervi with Campbell, Aldrich & Nulty, 1973–76

Dartmouth's Business Manager Richard W. Olmstead ('32) was a fan of the imaginative Italian engineer Pier Luigi Nervi and visited him in Rome, admiring the engineer's repetition of cool, crystalline geometric units to create refined and poetic concrete buildings. Nervi roofed trainsheds, sports arenas, and other vast open rooms, starting with the radically airy concrete hangars built for the Italian Air Force during the 1930s and culminating in the circular Palazetto dello Sport in Rome for the 1960 Olympics. Dartmouth's trustees commissioned a field house design from the engineer that would be the first project he completed in North America. The candy-machine mogul Nathaniel Leverone ('06), the founder of the Automatic

Center ice, Thompson Arena

Canteen Company of America (1929) and the man who helped spread vending machines through the break rooms of the nation, funded the project.

Leverone Field House has no walls, just a great barrel-vaulted roof sixty-three feet high at the center. Workers cast the roof's individual diamonds and triangles on the ground, hoisted them above a movable centering scaffold, and poured reinforced concrete into the gaps to create the span. Massive angled legs lining the sides of the building transmit its force into the ground, all but hidden within a set of incongruously rectilinear ancillary rooms of brick. Curtain walls of glass and steel panels seal up the building's ends. Newer generations of materials have replaced the building's original wooden track and practice surface over the years, allowing Leverone to play regular host to the Ivy League's Indoor Heptagonal Championship track meet and practices for many other sports.

Thompson ice arena is the larger but less obvious of Nervi's two Hanover buildings, since it is recessed into the ground and hides intriguingly behind a row of early-twentieth-century houses. One-ton precast triangles paired at the base replace Leverone's diamonds as the essential building unit, and Thompson's roof leaves its muscular ribs in plain sight along its flanks. As the largest hall in town, the arena represents a radical change from the predecessor ice surface of Davis Rink: Thompson's sixty-four-foot vault allows for more than twice as many spectators and a lavishly larger sheet of ice. It is the home of men's and women's hockey and the school's national-caliber figure skating team. The building is named for trustee and Rhode Island banker and conglomerateur Rupert C. Thompson, Jr. ('28).

Lacrosse at Scully-Fahey Field

32. Chase Fields

Boss Tennis Center
Bread Loaf Corporation, 2000
Fieldhouse
Freeman French Freeman, 2007
Scully-Fahey Field
Saucier & Flynn with Clark Companies, 1999–2000
Burnham Field
Freeman French Freeman, 2007

A growing collection of sports venues occupies the fields of the former Chase Farm east of Park Street. Following the end of state ownership in 1892, the land continued in farm use until the college acquired it in 1921. An old barn served as a field house into the 1950s, and little development occurred here until Thompson arrived in the 1970s. The ice arena's parking lot became the center of a group of specialized venues. The Boss Tennis Center, which rests largely below ground level, features an oversized stepped and parapetted brick gable whose clock serves as a symbolic and practical reference to Alumni Gym. The tennis center, named in memory of All-Ivy player Alexis Boss ('93), provides an unexpectedly interesting approach: after passing between a pair of brick gateposts, the visitor travels along a concrete causeway raised on steel piers to arrive at the

Boss Tennis Center

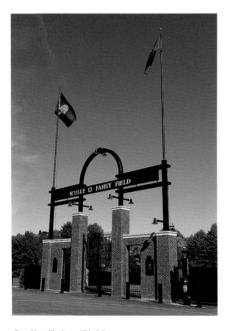

Scully-Fahey Field gate

boxy Gordon Pavilion, which marks the building's entrance. Inside, a spectator mezzanine gives a view of the six doubles courts that occupy the building's single large room.

Across the parking lot is a small Fieldhouse with a gently curving shed roof sheathed in copper. It faces Blackman Fields Nos. 1 and 2 (2000), lighted football practice fields that recall Robert L. Blackman, who coached from 1955 to 1970 and took at least a part of seven of the first fifteen Ivy championships, racking up a record number of victories at the school. Beyond are the several numbered Chase Fields, portions of the farm that have not yet been altered extensively.

Two 1,600-seat grandstands flank the Fieldhouse. To the east is an artificial turf field for the lacrosse and field hockey teams that also sees use by the cricket club, the Frisbee team, and others. It is named for lacrosse All-American Donald Scully ('49) and varsity sportsman Peter Fahey ('68), Th. ('70), an investment banker, trustee, and Thayer Overseer. The field's entrance features Dartmouth's boldest freestanding gateway, a set of tall brick pillars spanned by a sculptural steel arch. To the west is the grandstand of the soccer field named for coach Alden "Whitey" Burnham, who began guiding the team in 1960 (he also coached wrestling and lacrosse and administered athletics for thirty years). Among Burnham's early players were David Smoyer ('63) and Bill Smoyer ('67), whose father Stanley ('34), an attorney and officer with Johnson & Johnson, was the field's major donor.

33. Occom Pond and the D.O.C. House

Occom Pond
Thomas Wilson Dorr Worthen, 1899–1900
The D.O.C. House
Jens Fredrick Larson, 1928, 1940; 1986

The D.O.C. House

An artificial pond of about nine acres occupies a little valley-within-a-valley below the namesake Occom Ridge. Previously a cow pasture known as Clement's Swamp, the pond's site was a potential residential zone in the college's development program until Webster Avenue resident Elizabeth Washburn Worthen suggested in 1897 that it should become an ornamental pond. Charles P. Chase ('69), the college treasurer and the owner of the wetland, agreed "to reserve it perpetually as an open ground" and allowed Worthen's husband to flood the bowl with stormwater runoff.[1] Because the earthen dam that originally impounded the water could not survive the muskrats, and so the Occom Pond Association (1901) replaced it with a fifty-foot-wide concrete dam faced in stone. Dr. Howard N. Kingsford completed the effect by providing a pair of swans and a flock of mallards. The pond has been the site of decades of Carnival events, including speed-skating races, which began here in 1911. Under college ownership, Occom Pond passed its centennial surrounded by new plantings meant to decrease the annual algae bloom.

Overlooking the north end of the pond is the square-pillared portico of the D.O.C. House. The one-level stone building with its shingled frame wings stands atop a full basement that originally featured a short canal to the pond, allowing skaters to lace up on the ice while still indoors. The class of 1900 gave the building as a permanent Winter Carnival headquarters and a country club for skiers and skaters, supporting Carnival's opening ceremonies, ski-jumping competitions, and field events that took place on the adjacent golf course. The establishment initially operated as a restaurant open to the public, and the 1938 W.P.A. guide described it as a popular place for outdoorspeople to gather. Although the original donors expanded the kitchen and added a dining room in 1940 in an effort to improve

its viability, the restaurant was not always profitable and eventually closed to the public. The D.O.C. House still sees occasional use hosting catered events and housing the Dartmouth Cross Country Ski Center, which rents skis and grooms twenty-five kilometers of trails on the golf course and beyond.

34. The Golf Course

Hilton Field
1896; 1899; Orrin Smith, 1918–21; Ralph Martin Barton, 1932–33;
Ron Prichard, 2000–2002
The Hanover Country Club House
Nineteenth century; Homer Eaton Keyes, 1916–17; 1929
Pine Park and the Vale of Tempe

The college's historic but distinctly unstuffy golf course has been a favored haunt of Hanoverians for more than a century. During 1896, the Hanover Country Club laid out a rough nine-hole course on this borrowed site between the river and the Vale of Tempe, at the time a thirty-acre farm field. The club expanded its course to temporary eighteen holes in 1897 and bought the field in 1899, building a permanent nine-hole course. *The Boston Sunday Herald* described the course charitably as having "sufficiently irregular ground to make progress fascinating." The college bought the course in 1914, using mostly funds given by trustee Henry Hoyt Hilton ('90), a Chicago colleague of Lewis Parkhurst's in the schoolbook publishers Ginn & Co. Between 1918 and 1921, Hilton also funded an eastward expansion of Hilton Field across the Vale of Tempe. This expansion added the nine holes that now are numbered six through seventeen. Getting across the vale required a steel pedestrian trestle, again a Hilton gift (1921). The Country Club grew rapidly after the First World War, with the college's golf team winning the national championship during 1921.

Professor Ralph Barton ('04) and golf team coach Tommy Keane designed an additional nine-hole course during the early 1930s. Two-thirds of it lay inconveniently across Lyme Road and during 1970 dwindled to a well-regarded four-hole practice area. The three near holes were swallowed up by a cross-country ski area, indicating the importance of Hanover's golf course to the history of skiing. The first slalom race in the country took place on a course that Professor Charles A. Proctor, 1900, laid out on Golf Course Hill in 1925. During 1929, the Outing Club replaced its 1921 steel ski jump in the Vale of Tempe with the country's first and longest-lived large collegiate jump. The iconic swoop of the tall jump trestle built by the Boston Bridge Company poked above the trees for decades, providing an image that would remain on the Country Club's logo even after the school demolished the jump during 1993. The fourteenth hole of the golf course is known

OPPOSITE: *Skating on Occom Pond*

The Hanover Country Club House

as the Ski Jump Hole and had to shift occasionally over the years to accommodate longer jumps. With Hilton Field often described by the euphemistic term "traditional" by the 1990s, Robert Keeler ('36) funded a doubling of the number of bunkers and the creation of four replacement holes (eleven and twelve, sixteen and seventeen), adding seven hundred yards to the course.

The Country Club's headquarters is a shingle-clad cottage whose original name of "the golf barn" explains its rudimentary origin as an agricultural outbuilding nearby. Moved to the first hole, the barn was convenient to Occom Pond and Golf Course Hill and became the first headquarters for Winter Carnival. Professor Keyes, who lived across the street, used Hilton funds to remove the animal stalls, renovate the hayloft, and turn the barn into a two-and-a-half-level house clad in shingles to the eaves, with small, square-paned windows. The connected Caddy House (1929) became a snack bar in 1981. Although the Club intends a future clubhouse on Lyme Road to make the old building redundant, the college is expected to keep this historic structure around.

Between the golf course and the river lies the nineteenth-century forest of Pine Park, containing Romantic glens where Girl Brook flows through the Vale of Tempe to meet the river. A rope ferry operated here during the eighteenth century, and Robert Frost and many before him walked contemplatively through the Vale where students occasionally presented Shakespeare plays. When the Diamond Match Company planned to cut about forty-five acres of riverside forest at the turn of the century, a group of benefactors bought the land to preserve it. Emily Hitchcock

Hilton Field, The Hanover Country Club

left an adjacent parcel of similar size during 1912. The Park Managers continue to maintain the Goat Path, the Cathedral Aisle, and the other trails that run through the area.

35. The Boathouses

Fuller Boathouse
1940
The Friends of Dartmouth Rowing Boathouse
Banwell Architects, 1987
Tom Dent Cabin
B.L. Krause, 1963
The Ledyard Monument, 1907
The Ledyard Canoe Club
Eugene French Magenau, 1930

Students began building boathouses on the left bank of the Connecticut during the mid-nineteenth century, including one of 1857 that stood for only a few months before a flood erased it. The Dartmouth Boat Club bought a six-oared cedar shell and an existing boathouse just above the bridge in 1873, soon adding another building and proving its seriousness by hiring a coach and bringing up a craftsman to repair its boats. Its boathouse fell to a storm in 1877, however. Boathouses and a

Boat Club reappeared during the 1890s, and students attempted a revival in 1919, but it was not until the advent of a new Boathouse (1934; destroyed 1952) that organized rowing could become a permanent sport at Hanover.

The second building of the rowing renaissance of the 1930s is the Fuller Boathouse, a long one-level building given by former Massachusetts Governor Alvan Tufts Fuller. The nave and side aisles of the utilitarian white-painted clapboard building contain a fleet of recreational shells, as well as a boat repair shop and training rooms. A smaller storage building is located nearby, and a Small Boathouse stands near the water.

The Wilder Dam of 1950 reformed the river at Hanover as a glassy rower's paradise. Local rowing clubs sprang up, the National Rowing Team began using the site for summer training in 1972, and the river began making cinematic appearances as the archetypal setting for an Ivy League crew. The symbol of this post dam growth is the big Friends of Dartmouth Rowing Boathouse. From the bank, it appears as a windowless white clapboard building topped by broad roofs and a lighted monitor. On the river side, however, one sees an imposing front-gabled Postmodern composition. Three green-doored portals topped by flattened arches puncture the building's brick-clad river level, where the Rowing Club keeps about thirty of its boats. Utilitarian stacks of square windows light the white-painted second level, while a bent-timber truss frames the gable above the building's signature Syrian-arched window opening; inside is a high-ceilinged social room focused on a freestanding fireplace.

Just uphill from the boathouses is a college cabin given by alumni who had played sports under Tom Dent, the school's first coach of lacrosse, starting in 1926, and its soccer coach from 1924 to 1960. The Athletic Department intended Tom Dent Cabin to house informal team dinners within walking distance of campus, and Athletics Director Red Rolfe raised funds and asked a friend to design the simple cabin. Sheathed largely in milled logs and painted a uniform forest service brown, the small front-gabled frame building features a small kitchen and a large fireplace that continues to warm gatherings and retreats for all types of groups.

This stretch of riverbank has always been convenient for putting in a boat, which is why freshman John Ledyard, displaying the visionary thirst for experience that would make him a celebrated world traveler, picked this site as the one where he would build a canoe and escape from college in 1773. As Dartmouth's patron saint of adventure, Ledyard has inspired generations of students since. With the help of friends, Ledyard "Felled a giant pine / from which he made a canoe / and in it descended the river to Hartford Connecticut," as the plaque here proclaims. Within a few years, Ledyard sailed on merchant ships to the Barbary Coast; joined or was pressed into the British Army; transferred to the Royal Marines; sailed on the *Resolution* under William Bligh as part of Captain Cook's third voyage of 1776 to 1780; became the first American to see much of the West Coast, including

The Ledyard Canoe Club

Alaska's Cook Inlet; and received several tattoos in Tahiti. He and Thomas Jefferson planned to explore North America from west to east, an expedition that Ledyard began in Hamburg, Germany, and ended in Siberia, when Empress Catherine II ordered him out of Russia. A later expedition for the African Association of London brought Ledyard to Cairo, where he died at thirty-eight. Biographer James Zug notes that Ledyard was not impressed with the Nile and wrote Jefferson to say that it looked rather like the Connecticut River.

Jefferson found Ledyard "a man of genius, of some science, and of fearless courage and enterprise."[2] Melville, on the other hand, commented in *Moby-Dick* that "the mere crossing of Siberia in a sledge drawn by dogs as Ledyard did... I say, may not be the very best mode of attaining a high social polish."[3] Ledyard himself claimed that he was "eccentric, irregular, unafraid, unaccountable, curious & without vanity, majestic as a comet."[4] Ledyard's fame and untimely passing encouraged people to mark the sites of his life's events, starting with the spot where he felled the tree on this riverbank. Those who had helped Ledyard build the canoe or were familiar with the voyage pointed out the site, and although landowner Dr. Dixi Crosby D.M.S ('24) uprooted the stump, he commemorated the locale by proposing that the town name its new free bridge for John Ledyard in 1859. The Dartmouth Scientific Association heard monument proposals during the 1870s, but

The Boathouse

it took until 1907 for the present rough-hewn block of granite with its bronze tablet to appear. The flowers that usually grow at its base are watered by the canoe club's student custodian.

The Ledyard Monument is a touchstone for poets. Robert Frost said in 1955 that "I go every year, once a year, to touch Ledyard's monument down there, as the patron saint of freshmen who run away."[5] Richard Eberhart ('26) also felt the pull of the marker, writing in the poem *John Ledyard* (1972) that "Only death remains / To tell us / How great we were / Speaks the voice of the voyager / From fading bronze letters, / Great with desire."[6]

The American traveler was the natural namesake for a canoe club that formed during 1919. Outing Club benefactor John E. Johnson ('66) helped the club purchase one of the rudimentary vertical-board-sided boathouses that then stood north of the bridge. The club's first expedition was a failed 1920 attempt to recreate Ledyard's journey to the Atlantic, although the voyageurs made it all the way to the destination of Long Island Sound the following year. A crew of students and alumni has recreated the Trip to the Sea nearly every spring since.

Johnson also funded the club's territorial expansion by giving it the Third Island, about six miles upriver. The club built the Johnny Johnson Cabin there (ca. 1923; destroyed 1953), and college treasurer Charles Parker Chase ('69) soon gave Occom Island, three miles upriver (Occom Cabin, 1921, destroyed 1936) and lent the two-level Chase Cabin on Chase Island, a mile to the south (destroyed 1953).

When the club built its headquarters by the monument, Johnson again provided the funds, while senior Eugene Magenau ('30) designed the building with approval from Jens Larson. The long two-part clubhouse is clad in white-painted shingles. Its dormered north end contains storage bays for much of the club's fleet, including the 15-paddler war canoe, Wakonda Auga (1977). The lower south end of the building presents a broad shed-roofed portico over the club's main entrance. Few spots on campus encapsulate the self-imposed spur to adventure better than the club's meeting room inside, its walls and ceiling festooned with mementos from hundreds of water-borne expeditions and a few on land, including an annual canoe portage to the summit of Mount Moosilauke.

The Corey Ford Rugby Clubhouse

36. Dartmouth Out-of-Town

The borders of campus have never limited students seeking physical exertion. John Ledyard led a 1772 winter camping trip to Velvet Rocks east of town, on today's Appalachian Trail, and long country rambles became a practice during the nineteenth century. An 1866 expedition by fifteen "Dartmouth Mountaineers" climbed Mount Lafayette while transforming into a glee club at their campsites in towns along the route. Swimming and skating on the river were popular from the eighteenth century onward, and snowshoe races sprang up during the 1880s. Among the permanent athletic facilities more than three-quarters of a mile from the Green, the first was the Hanover Country Club. Opposite the golf course and about a mile and a quarter north of the Green stands the Corey Ford Rugby Clubhouse (Randall T. Mudge & Associates, 2004–2005). The Rugby Football Club (1951) was the first American college team to play in Britain (1958) and began planning a clubhouse during the mid-1960s. Comparative literature professor Herbert Faulkner West, a fan of the club's amateur spirit, suggested facetiously that the club should take over Memorial Field and let the (American) football team have the fields on Lyme Road—where, coincidentally, the rugby clubhouse now stands. It was the arrival in Hanover of novelist and humorist Corey Ford that would plant the seed of the present building, as Ford wrote:

Well, the fact is that rugby took up me. My home here in Hanover adjoins the college playing-fields; and so in the course of time it has been adopted as headquarters of the Dartmouth Rugby Club, an independent organization which has no home of its own. I am hailed as "Coach" for want of a better title.[7]

On his death in 1969, Ford left his house to fund a home for rugby. The project got little further than schematic drawings for a Chase Field house until the club commissioned a design during the late 1990s. Split down the middle between the D.R.F.C. and the Dartmouth Women's Rugby Club (1979), the hulking great building resembles a Victorian boathouse, sheathed in unpainted cedar shakes and trimmed in green. A high bow window and an overhanging cross-gable dominate the front facade, where a broad deck looks out over the Brophy Match Pitch. The field entrance is set below grade, in the brick-clad basement; behind the building, on the road side, lies the Battle Training Ground. Although not the first college rugby clubhouse in the country, it is arguably the finest, and one of the first in the world to contain equal facilities for men and women.

Northeast of the Rugby Clubhouse and about two miles from the Green is the small Oak Hill ski area. This was the site of the country's first overhead-cable ski lift, a J-bar system that the Outing Club created during 1935 before the chairlift was invented. The present importance of the hill lies in its ski jump and in the trails that began to appear here during the 1960s and were revamped during 2003. The centerpiece of the Ski Team's home range is the 13.5k Silver Fox Trail, site of Carnival races and N.C.A.A. championships. No smaller Dartmouth building has a longer name than the Oak Hill Ticket Booth & Warming Hut.

The Dartmouth Skiway lies in the narrow valley beyond Lyme Center, about fourteen miles from the Green by shuttle bus and much closer than the school's original skiing destination of Mount Moosilauke. A single Poma lift served the Skiway's first six trails on Holt's Ledge during 1956, while skiers originally warmed up in the Peter Brundage Lodge (W. Brooke Fleck, 1956–57, 1959–60; demolished 2000) and sped past the twenty-bed Nunnemacher Cabin (1957). The college later upgraded Holt's Ledge to a J-bar (1960) and double-chair lift (1977). The Skiway has expanded to thirty trails encompassing more than one hundred skiable acres, many of its trails located behind the lodge on Winslow Mountain (1967) and served by its quad lift (1993) and Jeremiah Thompson ('96) Memorial Start House (2007). In 1985, the college funded the crucial snowmaking system that allows the Skiway to remain the place where students take gym classes and where the region skis. Dartmouth has had representatives in every Winter Olympics, and many of them trained here.

The McLane Family Lodge from Holt's Ledge at the Dartmouth Skiway

A quadrupling in visitorship during the Skiway's first half-century required the school to replace the original lodge. The two angled wings of the green-clapboarded McLane Family Lodge (Banwell Architects, 2000) are hinged about a flat-roofed central entrance tower, with a stone-pillared loggia providing a reference to the portico of the D.O.C. House. A lofty post-and-beam structural system of ash organizes the building's interior into a 400-seat dining room, a ski store, and other spaces. Skier and investor P. Andrews McLane '69, Tuck School (Tu) ('73) was the building's principal donor.

South of the Green by a mile, the Sachem Field complex comprises a varsity softball field (1995) and seven grass fields for practice, intramural sports, and club matches, as well as local youth soccer. The school has used the former farm fields for sports since the 1960s.

The red barns of the Dartmouth Riding Center are prominent on the 180-acre Morton Farm, about six miles east of campus in the village of Etna. The Laramie family supplemented the farmhouse (ca. 1792) with a set of dairy barns before selling the complex to American Express president Bill Morton ('32) in 1969. Morton bred Charolais cattle there until he gave the farm to the college in 1978. The farm's metal-sided riding rink (Huntington Farm Buildings, 1979) also is a Morton gift, a counterpart to the farm's outdoor rink as well as the surrounding pastures and forest trails. Morton Farm serves as the headquarters of the Equestrian Team and the Outing Club's Boots & Saddles Club (1928) and offers a variety of programs to the community.

The narrow Mascoma Lake stretches for five miles through the township of Enfield, a dozen miles southeast of Hanover. Dartmouth students were rowing on the lake by 1833, but it was not until 1950 that they would erect a permanent venue, when the Dartmouth Corinthian Yacht Club (1931) built its functional Allen Boathouse on the lake's eastern shore. Designed by John Lansing Bennett ('46), Th ('50), the flat-roofed cinderblock building named for coach Arthur E. Allen, Jr. ('32) watches over about four dozen sailboats.

The Minary Conference Center (1928) is located in Holderness, N.H., about fifty-five road miles east of campus. The former Bertha Schrafft estate features a meeting space in the upper level of its boathouse, which project out into the tranquil Squam Lake. CBS head William S. Paley, a later owner, gave the property to Dartmouth in 1970 in the name of friend and advisor John Minary ('29). The Minary Center hosts retreats for the Board of Trustees and makes itself available to outside groups.

Dartmouth holds its Moosilauke Ravine Lodge (Richard D. Butterfield, 1938–1939) as dearly as any college could hold a mountain retreat that lies 53.6 miles northward along the Appalachian Trail. Mount Moosilauke is the southwesternmost of the big White Mountains, the closest four thousand-foot peak to Hanover, and has long occupied the imagination of the college. Students were climbing

The Moosilauke Ravine Lodge

the mountain by the early nineteenth century, and it became a Northeastern vacation site, with entrepreneurs cutting a carriage road to the top and erecting the Prospect House there (1860; 1881; burned 1942). Professor Charles H. Hitchcock explored Moosilauke as part of a state geological survey and mounted an expedition to "camp out" on the summit during the winter of 1869. D.O.C. founder Fred Harris's original club proposal of 1909 suggested the group mount an annual expedition, "say to Moosilak," and one of the Outing Club's first cabins was the Great Bear Cabin on the mountain (1914; burned 1926). The club became the owner of Moosilauke's entire summit in 1920 and established its Summit Camp there. (The school later gave the summit to the state.)

With an alumnus managing the commercial logging that was taking place on Mount Moosilauke during the 1920s, the D.O.C. was able to acquire Parker Young

Logging Company Camp No. 2 and part of the ravine in which it stood. Students went to work turning the logging camp into a ski resort, renovating its horse stable into a chalet and cutting the pioneering Hell's Highway ski trail down to the camp. During an era when ski lifts were almost nonexistent, the Moosilauke Ravine Camp was a popular destination. The Down-Mountain Race of 1927, on Moosilauke's winding Carriage Road, was the first modern downhill race in the country, its 1933 running served as the first National Downhill Championship.

After a fire destroyed the rudimentary Ravine Camp during 1935, Richard D. Butterfield ('30), an associate in Jens Larson's office, worked with Professor Richard Goddard ('20) to draft a set of plans for a giant new base lodge for the ski area. Under the guidance of Dartmouth forest guru Ross McKinney, loggers from the nearby town of Warren labored with horse teams to fell two-ton spruce trees to build the new building. The two-level cross-gabled Ravine Lodge that resulted embodies a simple way of building on a grand scale, according to historian David Hooke. Its heart is a large multilevel dining room lined with old trail signs and focused on a large rock fireplace. Bunkhouses of various vintages and levels of luxury stand near the building. This complex was sometimes too large to be commercially viable, especially after skiing moved to large, mechanized ski resorts, and the Ravine Lodge closed during 1963.

It took the 1970s and the expansion of the Outing Club's Freshman Trips program (1935) to bring the lodge finally and firmly into the heart of the college. By the early twenty-first century, ninety percent of incoming students were sharing the preorientation experience, receiving a powerful impression of the Ravine Lodge as the embodiment of the college's relation to the woods. During those parts of the season when the students of the "Lodge Croo" are not hosting trippees, they open up the Lodge to the public.

Finally and farthest-flung is a piece of Dartmouth that lies hard along the Maine border, unvisited by most students. The state of New Hampshire donated the wild 26,800-acre township of the Second College Grant, 140 miles from campus, during 1807. It was the second grant after a 1789 donation of the township of Clarksville, which itself followed a failed attempt by the Royal Province to grant the township of Landaff in 1770. The school rented mostly to farmers, loggers, and trappers, although by the 1920s alumni and college administrators were enjoying the hunting there. The D.O.C. and the college built a total of eleven cabins in the Grant between 1947 and 1996, including the Gate Camp (1962) for the Caretaker of the Grant and the Management Center (1951) for the College Forester. The Forester manages what logging still occurs in the Grant under a long-term sustainable-harvesting plan to produce the lumber that goes into the furniture of almost every new building on campus. Outdoorspeople in search of a wild place often begin their adventures in the Grant by crossing the suspension bridge over Hellgate Gorge, near the confluence of the Swift Diamond and Dead Diamond Rivers.

The Minary Conference Center

1. John Charles Olmsted to William Jewett Tucker (December 18,1899),
   Olmsted Associates Papers, Job File 1385, Library of Congress.
2. Thomas Jefferson, *The Autobiography of Thomas Jefferson*
   (New York: G.P. Putnam's Sons, 1914), 103.
3. Herman Melville, *Moby-Dick, or the Whale* (New York: Hendricks
   House, 1952), 30.
4. John Ledyard to Deborah Ledyard, quoted in James Zug, *American
   Traveler: The Life and Adventures of John Ledyard, the Man Who
   Dreamed of Walking the World* (New York: Basic Books, 2005), 214.
5. Robert Frost, "The Commencement Address," *Dartmouth Alumni
   Magazine* 47, 10 (July 1955), 14.
6. Richard Eberhart, "John Ledyard," *Fields of Grace* (New York:
   Oxford University Press, 1972), 11–12.
7. Corey Ford, "Football for Fun" (1959), Folder 76, ML-30,
   Ford Papers, Dartmouth College Archives.

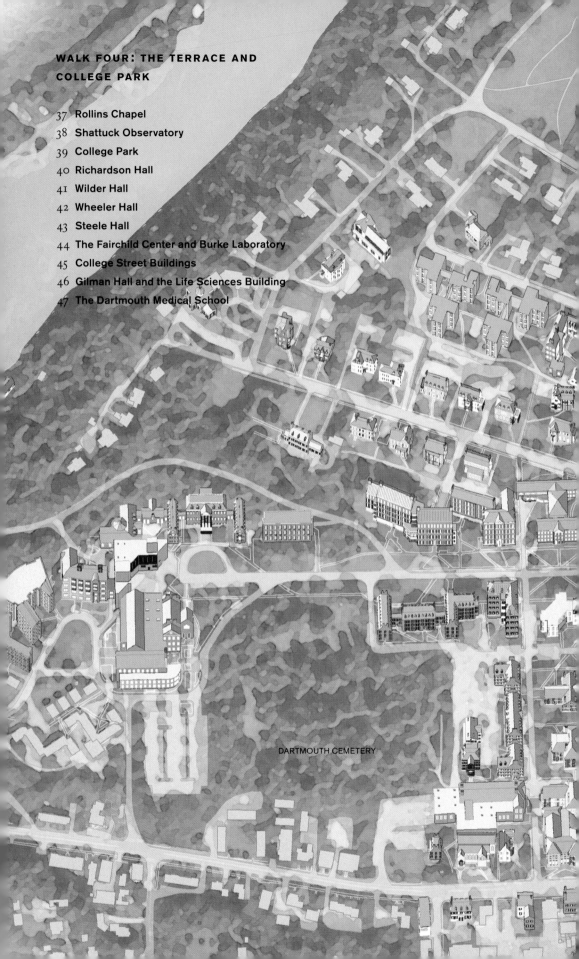

WALK FOUR: THE TERRACE AND
COLLEGE PARK

DARTMOUTH CEMETERY

College Street's science area

The modest rise on which Dartmouth Hall stands is called Observatory Hill. The school tends to erect buildings on the hill only reluctantly, hampered by the exposed bedrock and restrained by a past decision to reserve the area as a park or greensward. Students adopted the hill's natural monuments as places of ceremony during the early nineteenth century, later reshaping its landscape into a more romantic form as a way of enhancing this sacred precinct. The school placed a trio of open quadrangles along the hill's College Street flank, sometimes using dynamite to level the slope into an urban figure that late-nineteenth-century planners called "the Terrace." Although construction bit dramatically at the park's edges and diminished its sense of otherness again during the 1930s, the park still presents a picturesque nineteenth-century counterpoint to the rectilinear Green nearby, and it remains the place where seniors hold Class Day and where many can find a bit of forested solitude.

Today, the terrace along College Street represents an organized process of erecting medicoscientific buildings that has been ongoing for about two hundred years. The Medical school was here first, as founder Dr. Nathan Smith used state and college funds to erect a miniature version of Dartmouth Hall in brick as his school's main building in 1811, behind the present Steele Hall. Expanding the top level with an iron-and-glass clerestory for the Stoughton Museum (1871–73) and adding a dissecting room (1894) allowed the building to house Dartmouth's medical education for generations. Shattuck Observatory followed as a blend of science and Romantic folly, providing part of the reason for establishing the park itself. Buildings for physics and chemistry followed.

The expansion of the sciences along the terrace shows not only continuity but disjunction, and marks the site of the college's only real historic preservation mistake. The 1963 demolition of the Medical School was excused at the time on the basis that renovating the hall—Dartmouth's oldest building—would have been too expensive. The other remnants of the medical campus here fell later: the Nathan Smith Laboratory (Edgar Hayes Hunter, 1907; demolished 1990) and the North Lab, a house built by Professor Hardy and used as the presidential mansion and later as a sorority (1876; demolished 2000). Room would seem to remain for another century's expansion to the north, although the college's siting of a senior society in the path of future development suggests that the linear growth of the terrace has come to an end.

Rollins Chapel

37. Rollins Chapel

John Lyman Faxon, 1884–85; Homer Eaton Keyes and
Edgar Hayes Hunter, 1908, 1912

The importance of Rollins Chapel to the life of Dartmouth has changed dramatically over time. The building occupies a site reserved in 1838 for a companion to Reed Hall, although it is the furthest thing from Reed in stylistic terms; the chapel is the only campus building in full Richardsonian Romanesque mode. It is also the only stone building in the center of campus, with the pink granite of its cyclopean masonry having come from quarries in nearby Lebanon township. Quarries of Longmeadow, Massachusetts, supplied the building's brown sandstone trim, including the carved heads of a lion and a man that comprise the entire gargoyle population of the campus.

Chancel window by James Ballantine and Son, depicting John the Baptist

The predecessor Old Chapel in Dartmouth Hall was a small, chilly, smoky chamber with uncomfortable pews that lent themselves to inter-class pranks. The school's 1867 decision to move the altar to the west end, putting the seniors first in line for the exit, failed to prevent fighting among the classes fleeing the room after a sermon. Robert Frost enjoyed one 1892 battle in which his class "fought it out with the sophomores across pews and everything (it was in the Old Chapel) with old cushions and even footstools for weapons."[1] Relief from the barbaric conditions would come with a gift from former New Hampshire state legislator Edward Ashton Rollins ('51), then a banker in Philadelphia.

John Lyman Faxon designed Rollins Chapel as his only project at Dartmouth. Most of his work was in and around Boston, Massachusetts, and his First Baptist Church in Newton (1888) would be a virtual twin to the Dartmouth chapel, albeit slightly more elaborate in its decoration. Even Rollins Chapel, with its varied medievalesque details, including carved sandstone piers and inventive strap-ironwork, as well as a large stone carving of the college's 1773 seal, turned out "a little more adorned, elaborate, and expensive than was contemplated" by the donor, Rollins wrote.[2] (This was the case even after the school declined to use white marble that Redfield Proctor ('51) offered to donate from his Vermont quarries.) After the chapel opened, donors honored the school's deceased presidents with memorial windows, making it through six of the first eight presidents before apparently halting in 1905.

The building's original footprint was essentially a Greek cross with an octagonal tower alongside the entrance porch. Its nave and transepts could seat six hundred worshipers facing the curved apse in the east end, all sheltered beneath a timber roof resting on a set of great brick crossing arches and ranks of jointed wooden crucks. The result was an airy if not very bright space for students to gather in and hear the president each morning.

As much as anything, Rollins Chapel is a memorial to the regimen of mandatory chapel exercises that Dartmouth enforced from 1770 until 1925. The system imposed an administrative burden on the school that came to involve taking tickets and docking class credit for unpermitted absences, and it tied Rollins's size directly

Rollins Chapel crossing and north transept

to enrollment.

As the college grew, workers had to expand the building's capacity by half through a west-end gallery and seats in the apse during the early twentieth century. The installation of a peal of three bells in the tower during 1903 allowed students sprinting across the Green for chapel to refine their estimates of how much time they had left. The chapel's major expansion of 1908 required workers to roll the apse back about thirty feet to the east, leaving a gap in which Professor Keyes designed a new skylit blue-green choir with small side chapels. The building seated about nine hundred, but critic Montgomery Schuyler noted that the addition harmed its original proportions. Just four years later, the school dismantled the ends of the transepts and lengthened each one by twenty feet, also extending the west-end gallery and bringing the lectern from the apse to the crossing to give everyone a view. This brought the building's capacity to about 1,200.

The school would have had to expand the chapel again if it had not eased attendance requirements in 1917. When the whole affair became optional in 1925, daily attendance dropped by about ninety-seven percent. The chapel instantly became far too large, and its functional redundancy coincided with a national reaction against Victorian architecture. John Russell Pope proposed to place a spare white chapel of brick on Rollins' site during 1922, and President Hopkins later suggested moving the white clapboard College Church to the site. Hopkins, in fact, seemed especially interested in demolishing the building, and he asked Ralph Adams Cram to sketch an admittedly unnecessary replacement chapel for Observatory Hill. The school brightened the interior of the unpopular building in 1955 and walled up some of Keyes's side chapels to create a sacristy and robbing room in 1965. Those moves made Rollins into an official interfaith worship center and performance hall, a functional change that also prompted the school to return the lectern to the apse and cover the memorial windows behind it. While rebuilding the west facade (1985–86), the school made the interior colors closer to the originals and reopened some of the infilled arches; a later, historically minded whole-building renovation (2006–2007) finally restored Dartmouth's oldest significant interior space and revealed the memorial windows in the apse once

Shattuck Observatory, with 1913 telescope building at left

more. In an era when colleges commonly install libraries in their underused chapels, this prime space at the center of campus patiently continues to play host to a variety of small daily services and the occasional wedding, awaiting a second use.

38. Shattuck Observatory
Ammi Burnham Young, 1853–54; 1958

The oldest building dedicated to science at the college is a monument to the capable Young brothers of Lebanon, New Hampshire: Ammi Burnham Young (architect), Dyer B. Young (contractor), and Professor Ira Young ('28) (astronomer). Professor Young's son Charles Augustus Young ('53) sketched the building's initial plans while still a teenager and would go on to direct the observatory.

Two years after Ira Young built the town's first frame observatory in his backyard, about where North Massachusetts Hall stands (1850), the Boston physician George Cheyne Shattuck ('03) donated a permanent observatory at Dartmouth. A shallow-pitched roof and basic cornice give the simple Classical building an air of repose. Sited on solid bedrock amid today's tall Larches near the top of Observatory Hill, Ammi Young's last project in Hanover has the appearance of a folly. Its Latin cross plan centers on a twenty-five foot cylindrical tower that terminates in a steel dome built in 1958, a replacement for the original wooden dome. Inside, the building's three wings originally housed a library, computing room, and transit room. A granite cylinder six feet in diameter supports the telescope.

After Charles Young became the third generation in his family to assume the Appleton Professorship of Natural Philosophy in 1866, and he made several changes to the observatory. He convinced a donor to fund a connection to Western Union's telegraph network in 1869 in order to find the building's longitude; he traded in the original telescope in 1871 for the larger instrument that is still in use; and around 1874 he had the school paint the building white to keep it cool. Young left in 1877 for a long career at Princeton, and the observatory has changed relatively little since. Although Jens Larson's southern addition went unbuilt, two handsome auxiliary temples appeared nearby. The first, which opens by sliding its roof longitudinally (Harry Artemas Wells, 1913), was a gift of Dr. Shattuck's grandson, Frederick C. Shattuck. The second temple splits its roof along the ridge and was the gift of its designer, John W. Lovely (1938). Since Shattuck's last official director retired in 1964 and the college began maintaining shares of powerful telescopes elsewhere, Shattuck has become a curiosity, although it still hosts astronomy classes and is sometimes open to the public.

39. College Park

*1854; Lee & Follen, 1868; Robert Fletcher and
Arthur Sherburne Hardy, 1879; 1882; 1895*

The sacred grove of College Park is a symbol of Dartmouth's origins and remains the site of an annual student pilgrimage. Encompassing a hill that rises above the Hanover Plain, the park's topography and protruding bedrock preserved it from significant development and led Eleazar Wheelock to quarry foundation stone here during the 1770s. Along with the rest of the township, the hill was largely denuded by the mid-nineteenth century, aside from a few clusters of trees. The college took its first official aesthetic step there in 1854, when President Lord suggested that an observatory would not only be useful but "will doubtless prove in a high degree ornamental."[3] The trustees then resolved that the field "in which the observatory is situated be appropriated as college grounds and never more for pasturage."[4] Coinciding with the creation of Central Park and its sometimes intentionally wild topography, treasurer Daniel Blaisdell ('27) suggested in 1863 that the school should plant trees in the park and mark out roads and paths according to a landscape plan. Blaisdell sought out former trustee and state Chief Justice Joel Parker ('11) to fund the project, and Parker became an enthusiastic backer. During 1867, he ordered 7,500 seedlings from André Leroy, a horticulturist in Angers, France.

The problem was that without a landscape plan, no one knew where to plant Joel Parker's trees. "Mr. Blaisdell has ordered some Freshmen to go and dig

Bartlett Tower

Detail of Robert Frost

holes for these trees, wherever they think a tree should stand," wrote one observer.[5] The school commissioned a plan in 1867 from Boston landscape architects Francis L. Lee and Charles Follen, and the architects did not finish their design until the following year. Follen helped suggest many of the 7,500 plants in Parker's second order of 1868, this time including decorative shrubs, some of them exotic. Parker also bought up land to expand the park to the south and east. The resulting "College Grounds" or "Dartmouth Park" was considered an attractive place, and the town laid out the prosperous residential row of Park Street behind it around 1870.

Two West Point artillerymen whose houses stood near the flanks of the park redesigned the landscape a dozen years after the work of Lee & Follen. Professor Robert Fletcher, who would direct the Thayer School of Engineering and the Town Water Works, was the main designer of the new landscape, while construction supervision fell to the cosmopolitan mathematics professor and future diplomat Arthur Sherburne Hardy. He had studied engineering at the École des Beaux Arts and elsewhere in Paris and possessed a deeply Romantic sensibility that filled his novels and poems with nature imagery. Starting with student-drawn topographical maps of the 32-acre site, the two engineers planned curving walks lined with hedges for pedestrians, separate roads for carriages, hidden seats and arbors, terraces, rustic bridges, and gazebos or "summer houses." The main cast-iron gazebo would stand on the western hilltop near Bartlett Tower, while a wooden counterpart erected by the college carpenter would occupy the eastern summit. President Bartlett contributed the labor force by convincing students to volunteer for the work starting in 1879. Faculty helped out,

Plaque at base of Bartlett Tower

and townspeople lent horse teams. A prospect tower and mysterious grotto arrived by 1895, and the following year New York Judge Horace Russell ('65) funded some finishing touches, including a wooden footbridge to span a ravine on the park's western side.

Landscape architect Charles Eliot's 1893 proposal for an academic quadrangle in the park, which the college built as Fayerweather Row, was merely the first encroachment. Richardson, Wilder, Ripley, Woodward, and Smith Halls backed up close to Shattuck Observatory and the Bema by the early 1930s, and a pair of Faculty Apartments occupied wooded sites along Park Street a quarter-century later. Yet the school sited these buildings here with some reluctance. Since 1900, the trustees had declared that the park would be held "as a reservation" free from buildings. Projects that the school declined to build in the park include a "Hillside" dormitory behind Richardson Hall (1911), a President's House (1920s), a Gothic chapel (1920s), and a Modernist dormitory behind Ripley (1965). Although the park's gazebos and bridges are long gone, the park's European Larches have become some of the tallest in New England, and the landscape retains its naturalistic appearance.

Among the trees spared the deforestation of the eighteenth and nineteenth centuries was a lone White Pine from about 1783 that stood at the top of the hill. It was not beautiful, but its outstanding site and the fact that it had two picturesque trunks made it notable. By the 1830s, seniors had begun to gather around the Old Pine on the eve of Commencement to have a "farewell smoke" from what they regarded as peace pipes and sing a parting hymn. The Old Pine became a locus for students' sentimental connection to the park and their college.

The Pine was ephemeral, of course. The tree was dying even before lightning struck it in 1887 and a windstorm caused severe damage during 1892. The college finally put the tree out of its misery following Class Day of 1895, when Bartlett Tower opened nearby as a permanent replacement. Richard Hovey and others wrote a flurry of memorial poems, and in 1900 the nascent student government, Palaeopitus, based its name on a Latinization of the phrase "Old Pine." Students attached as much importance to the stump of the old tree as they had to the tree itself. During 1912, a committee of alumni treated the stump with fungicide and encircled it with a concrete coping bearing a plaque, and since then, the stump's authenticity has become much less important than its persistence as a sort of holy relic, a carefully tended monument to a symbol. Although students dropped the pipes from the ceremony in 1993, along with the late-nineteenth century practice of shattering the pipes on the stump, the annual Class Day continues to conclude at the Old Pine in College Park.

A substitute for the Old Pine, Bartlett Tower, is the folly at the center of President Bartlett's reworking of College Park. The slim seventy-one-foot cylindrical tower of stone was built in stages over more than a decade after Bartlett suggested it in 1884. Members of the class of 1885 laid the foundation themselves, and the ten succeeding classes gathered hornblende schist from the park, carted it to the construction site, and funded the work of stonemason Timothy Sullivan and several others who laid the courses in increments of three to eight feet each year. The college donated the eighty-six spiraling interior steps and the conical roof to complete the structure. The only representational sculpture on Dartmouth's campus, a bronze cast of a seated Robert Frost given by the Class of 1961 (George W. Lundeen, 1996), rests nearby.

Students moved the oratorical portion of Class Day to the natural amphitheater located just down the hill from the Old Pine. The space, now called the Bema, became a focal point of Bartlett's later improvement campaign, as the president called on the class of 1882 to build a pair of stone structures there. The less important one was the Grotto, a recess in one of the amphitheater's steep and rocky walls that students framed opportunistically with a flat-roofed three-pillared portico of rough quarried stone. Initially impressive, it seems to have had little purpose and was dismantled.

The more important structure in the amphitheater is a permanent stone platform that students assembled on the long northern slope in 1882. Students compared this terrace to a bema, a speaking platform of ancient Greece, and the name soon came to refer to the amphitheater as a whole. Eventually students would create the back-form of the acronym of "Big Empty Meeting Area." Because the Bema also was the site of Commencements from 1932 to 1952, the school installed the now-crumbling tiered concrete platform at the narrow east end of the space in 1932.

40. Richardson Hall
Lamb & Rich, 1897–98

The brick building with Manhattan pretensions is the first dormitory Charles Rich designed for Dartmouth, and the first new dormitory the school built in more than fifty years. Alumni criticized the building for what they perceived as its softness (it required no outhouse and included bathtubs in some of its rooms), and Richardson remained a relatively expensive place to live for many years.

By the end of the nineteenth century, students living in dormitories had a choice between the four old-fashioned and decrepit instructional/residential

Richardson Hall

buildings of Dartmouth Row. The school added some beds by converting houses into dormitories during the mid-1890s, an insufficient effort. The school then decided to erect Richardson on the edge of College Park, demolishing an old student boarding house on College Street to open up the view to the dormitory. Richardson's rusticated Portland granite basement and its semidomed distyle Ionic entrance portico receive considerable prominence, working with the proliferation of dormers and intersecting roofs to give Richardson the appearance of a metropolitan mansion of the period. The building originally contained an intentional variety of room types and prices, the better to foster a "democratic" mix of inhabitants of all social classes. The trustees named the hall for Massachusetts Supreme Judicial Court Justice James Bailey Richardson ('57), the first alumnus selected under the school's unique 1891 system of term-limited trusteeships for alumni.

Student traditions seem to cling to Richardson, for some reason, with particular strength. Students established the Ledyard Canoe Club on the ground floor in 1920; made the top room an unofficial Cabin & Trail Club headquarters for more

Wilder Hall, rear addition

than a decade prior to 1982; lived in the building during World War II, when most dormitories housed students of the Naval Training School; and resisted the coeducation of the building until 1988. As many dormitories did at the turn of the millennium, Richardson lost a stack of rooms to make space for an internal fire exit. At the same time, the school enclosed the building's central stair in glass, hoping to preserve the boldness of its configuration within the dormitory's entry hall.

41. Wilder Hall

Lamb & Rich, 1897–99; 1948–49; 1951; Centerbrook Architects, 1999–2001

The original floorplan of the Wilder Physical Laboratory represents a momentary high-water mark for Dartmouth's interest in specialized, university-style scientific research. The school altered the building later, refocusing it on teaching and thereby mapping out a shift that appeared throughout the institution.

Along with giving a dormitory to Wellesley College in his Massachusetts hometown, paper magnate Charles T. Wilder split his philanthropy between Dartmouth and his mill town of Olcott Falls, Vermont, located just downriver from Hanover. Living in a shingled mansion across the river from his pulp mill, Charles Wilder exhibited the generous paternalism expected of the area's largest employer: his Wilder Brothers' Paper Co. provided boarding houses in Olcott Falls laid out gridded streets on which it built company houses. Wilder personally gave the village a frame Congregational church (1890), where Dartmouth students and

LEFT: D_2D *and Wilder Hall entrance*
RIGHT: *Wilder Hall entrance*

faculty conducted the services, and he donated the Wilder Club and Library
(Louis Sheldon Newton, 1899). Most important, Wilder funded a proper carriage
bridge to replace the Olcott Falls's old suspended footbridge, requiring only that
the village rename itself in his honor, which it did.

Charles Wilder's largest gift went to Dartmouth. Friend and physician Carlton
P. Frost, the dean of the Medical School and the father of physics department
astronomer Edwin Brant Frost, suggested that Wilder give a physics building. The
front facade of the three-level T-shaped brick physics laboratory follows the slightly
Jacobean design the architect had given the main building at Barnard College
(Milbank Hall) in 1896, itself probably descended from an unbuilt design for a
Milbank Memorial Pavilion at Roosevelt Hospital. Wilder's end pavilions project
only slightly, but the building gives the same impression of a flat-roofed mansion
in an exuberant freely Classical style. Exaggerated granite voussoirs and a large
swagged keystone surround Wilder's double-height arched opening, while oval
windows lined by florid terra-cotta elements flank the entrance. Emphatic quoining
establishes the building's corners, and a stone balustrade originally delineated its
roof.

Dartmouth's physicists, particularly Professor Charles Franklin Emerson ('68),
conceived the building's research-oriented floorplan. Another key contributor was
Ernest Fox Nichols, who was hired as a physics professor during 1898 and became
the lab's first director, establishing Dartmouth's modern tradition of physical
research. A visitor who passed the black iron columns in the lobby and reached

Wilder's skylit upper levels originally would have seen a variety of specialized faculty research laboratories, as historians Sanborn Brown and Leonard Rieser note. These spaces fulfilled Wilder's promise by hosting several groundbreaking experiments, including Professor Nichols's and Assistant Professor Gordon F. Hull's pioneering of a method for measuring the pressure exerted by light.

The bloom lasted only a short time, however, hastened by Nichols's departure after just five years. Wilder soon resembled all of the other academic buildings on campus after workers converted it into a teaching laboratory for required physics classes. The school added a pair of unornamented wings during the late 1940s, and during the 1970s, Wilder effectively became a subsidiary element within the larger Fairchild complex. A more sympathetic addition of the late 1990s enhanced the laboratories and created a new rear facade, its polychrome brick entrance providing a pixilated reference to the building's front voussoirs and even referencing the old building's missing balustrade. A new elevator tower topped with a dominant white cornice and pyramidal roof add to the whimsy of this new entrance facing the park. Wilder enters its second century of teaching physics, still negotiating the balance between teaching and research.

42. Wheeler Hall
Charles Alonzo Rich, 1904–1905

In contrast to its idiosyncratic neighbors, Wheeler Hall established the basic form and palette that Dartmouth would apply to most of its future dormitories—a "Colonial" building three or four levels high that adopts a simple rectilinear plan atop a granite foundation and terminates in a hipped or side-gabled roof clad in copper and punctuated by dormers. The prototypical wall material would be red brick laid in Flemish bond, often interspersed randomly with black headers, while Classical details and windows would be rendered in white-painted wood or occasionally granite. Shutters of Dartmouth Green complete the picture. Wheeler had most of these elements, and a few unique ones. Its H-shaped footprint creates shallow arms that terminate in parapetted gables, for example. In addition, the building's front and rear facades are almost indistinguishable. The Roman Doric of the two-columned entrance portico on the south, which subtly trumps the Tuscan Doric of the north, is one of the few signs of the building's true front.

The building's namesake is John Brooks Wheeler of Orford, New Hampshire, who wrote the trustees in 1816 to observe that Dartmouth's initial legal defeat in the New Hampshire Supreme Court created "one of those instances in which good is educed from evil."[6] He donated one thousand dollars to cover legal fees, a gift that historian Leon Burr Richardson of the class of 1900 described as the most timely and consequential gift in the history of the college. The school then

Wheeler Hall, south entrance

was able to appeal the Dartmouth College Case to the United States Supreme Court. Coincidentally, the frame building that the college had to move to make room for Wheeler Hall had been the sole building that the college managed to occupy during the university controversy. Originally known as the Dartmouth Assembly Rooms, it was built in 1807 behind Rollins Chapel, where it stood when the college rented it after being evicted from Dartmouth Hall. The building moved several times and was demolished in 1928.

Steele Hall with penthouse addition

43. Steele Hall
Larson & Wells, 1920–1921; 1958; Centerbrook Architects, 1999–2000

Steele Hall entrance

Largely the gift of trustee Sanford H. Steele ('70) in memory of his brother, Benjamin Hinman Steele ('57), the building forms one side of Wilder Hall's three-sided quadrangle. Steele's businesslike massing focuses attention on its flat-roofed, rectangular main block, which reads as three stories below an attic. The building's shallow flanking wings originally stood three levels high but were topped off in 1958. A cool and relatively low-relief limestone Classicism clothes the building, focusing on a quartet of giant-scale Corinthian entrance pilasters supporting a conventional segmented arched pediment—quite different from the round-arched forms Larson would standardize in the near future.

A millennial renovation achieved the opposite effect of Wilder Hall's early generalizing alterations by turning Steele's general teaching laboratories into research laboratories for chemistry faculty. The project set a steel-framed penthouse of dark glass atop the building, sheltered by a broad, Classicallypitched copper-clad gambrel roof. The addition's stout brick chimneys and rooftop ventilators required new internal foundations below ground. The architects of the project signed it on the back, where two curled brackets rendered in silhouette support a small entrance roof.

44. The Fairchild Center and Burke Laboratory

The Sherman Fairchild Physical Sciences Center
Shepley Bulfinch Richardson & Abbott, 1974
Burke Laboratory
Ellenzweig Associates with R.M. Kliment & Frances Halsband
Associates, 1990–1992

A boxy concrete tower sheathed in glass serves as the hub within a pinwheel of buildings. Two of those buildings are Wilder and Steele Halls, the third is a mundane four-level classroom and laboratory wing extending behind the tower, and the fourth, an east wing heading into College Park, was contemplated but never built.

The tower is a thing of contrasts: taller than the adjacent buildings, yet not slim enough to read as a traditional campus spire; Modernist in style where its neighbors are Classical; based on a massive central spine of Brutalist concrete, yet sheathed in glass; diaphanous for most of its height, but topped by a heavy, flat brow. The tower's styling and its chilly interior are descended directly from the architects' award-winning design for the iconic cable car terminal at the California ski resort of Squaw Valley (1960). Here, the architects organized the building around a diagonal axis that slices through the tower in the form of an atrium, punching through the tower's flat roof as a triangular skylight. One of the tower's more sensitive moves is its celebration of the former exterior walls of its neighbors by reframing them as interior surfaces, a practice that has been imitated throughout the campus.

The generic four-level academic building behind the entrance tower fails to live up to expectations. The wing is clad in mildly purplish exposed-aggregate concrete panels, apparently part of a modular construction system of prefabricated elements developed by the Ford Foundation and the Toronto school system. The Kresge Library and the departments of geography and the physical sciences occupy this wing.

The science center came with a university-style program of landscaping and outdoor sculpture, the most extensive attempted at Dartmouth. The tower's poured concrete interior walls continue outdoors, channeling visitors away from Wilder

Burke Laboratory

and Steele and toward Fairchild's broad and interesting concrete stair. At the foot of the stair is an endless whorl of bronze titled D_2D (Charles O. Perry, 1974) that declares the center's purpose to be the study of everything from atoms to galaxies. The school also inserted the monumental 135-foot-long *Thel* (Beverly Pepper, 1976–77) in the quadrangle below the science center, arranging its pointy forms to slice toward Fairchild's entrance. The archipelago of irregular hollow pyramids made from white-enameled Cor-Ten steel panels and webbing drew comparisons to an outcropping of New Hampshire granite, a New England church, Caspar David Friedrich's 1924 painting *The Polar Sea*, and an airplane crash.

Fairchild's mute academic wing was a back side of the campus for twenty years before the school transformed it with the addition of the Burke Chemistry Laboratory. New meets old in a projecting entrance pavilion, cleverly creating the impression that the two adjoining structures are merely wings of a single building. Trademark touches of the architects appear throughout the entrance, such as in the granite-clad colonnade with its corners sliced off in plan. The paneled stair hall that organizes the laboratory's interior separates the offices from the teaching and research laboratories, which require heavy ventilation.

45. College Street Buildings

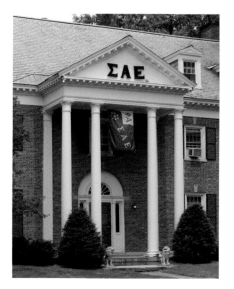

Sigma Alpha Epsilon house

The removal of most of Elm Street for Berry Library has not diminished the unique prominence of the Sigma Alpha Epsilon house (Wells & Hudson, 1927–28). The fraternity, founded in 1904, demolished its 1809 frame house and built this brick building on the site, fronting it with a giant-scale quadristylar portico with oddly slim Tower of the Winds columns. The portico stares effectively down several blocks toward the center of campus. Although other fraternities originally operated nearby, the building now stands alone, and some of Denise Scott Brown's early-1990s conjectural plans for Berry Row indicated the value of this site for an academic building. For the moment, however, the development of the northern part of the campus accommodates the house and gives new prominence to the building's balanced and fully detailed rear facade.

Two neighboring white-painted clapboard houses are crucial props in the preservation of a somewhat villagelike atmosphere along College Street. The house at 42 College Street (ca. 1820) served as the hospital of Dr. Dixi Crosby, the multitalented dynamo who taught from 1838 to 1870 at the medical school, which stood across the street. Crosby introduced ether anesthesia to Hanover during the late 1840s, and his retirement helped spur the plans for a new hospital that Hiram Hitchcock later would adopt. Crosby's estate sold the house in 1873 to Thayer School Dean Robert Fletcher, who would remain for sixty-three years. The building still serves as a residence under college ownership, housing faculty, town residents, medical students, fraternity or sorority members, or its current occupants, ten students in an immersive linguistic experience known as La Casa that is sponsored by the Department of Spanish and Portuguese.

The pre-1855 house at 44 College Street remained a private residence until the college and hospital acquired it jointly during the 1950s. The variety of succeeding functions has included a Russian-language immersion program and the college's office for international students.

Although Hanover lacks the dreaming spires of a medieval college town, the 125-foot steeple of the Church of Christ at Dartmouth College (Hobart Upjohn with

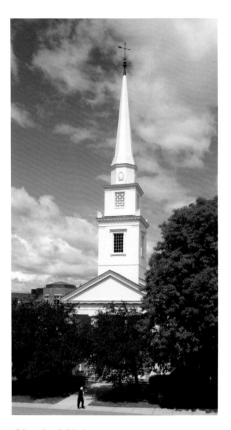

Church of Christ

Wells, Hudson & Granger, 1934–35; 1962) plays nicely against Baker Tower in the view of pedestrians passing on College Street. It is called "the White Church" in reference to *the* White Church, the white clapboard building finished in 1795 that was the original home of the congregation on the Green. The Congregational society was a foundation of Eleazar Wheelock that remained intimately intertwined with the college for generations, with the school holding its Sunday services and more than 110 commencements in the White Church. It was an 1804 controversy over the church's practice of giving the pastorate to whoever was the professor of theology that eventually caused the college trustees to expel John Wheelock from the presidency, precipitating the Dartmouth College Case. Stanford White remodeled the interior of the original church on the Green in 1889, and a spectacular blaze destroyed it in 1931, leading to the construction of the present building here.

The brick church, with its quadristylar Greek Doric temple front, is more sober than its Palladian-windowed forbear. Various additions including those that house the Eleazar Wheelock Student Center spill into the ravine behind the church, their flat-roofed Modernism prompting designers to suggest that the college and the church should cooperate to add a friendlier face to the building's rear. Whatever result emerges, both the town and the campus would seem to be enriched by the presence of the congregation on College Street.

One of the college's two all-male senior societies, Dragon (Randall T. Mudge & Associates, 1995–96) began in 1898 as a weekly dinner club. The group has managed to go through an unusual succession of buildings. Before World War I, it turned Kappa Kappa Kappa's original Italianate hall into a white-painted, blank-walled hexastylar Roman Doric temple. A 1920s Larson design for a proper house on the northwest corner of Webster Avenue did not come about, so the group put a brick meeting hall next to the Sigma Alpha Epsilon house on Elm Street (1931; demolished 1995). Preparing for Berry Library, the college proposed to build a new hall behind the Roth Center, but neighbors objected. This site on the wooded

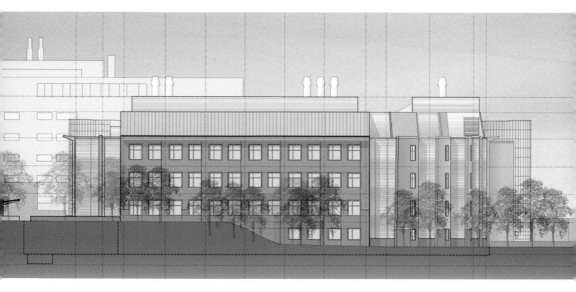

Rendering of Life Sciences Center, Lyme Road facade

slope beyond Burke Laboratory, also owned by the college, was the second choice. The group sought grandiosity rather than mystery in its Georgian hall, especially through the use of an elaborate brick entrance stair. The goal of reusing elements of the predecessor building dictated much of the form: interior paneling, the front door and its surround, and the slim portico columns all were part of Larson's earlier hall.

46. Gilman Hall and the Class of 1978 Life Sciences Center

Gilman Hall
Shepley Bulfinch Richardson & Abbott, 1963–64
The Life Sciences Building
Bohlin Cywinski Jackson, 2007–10

The distance separating the Charles Gilman Life Sciences Laboratory from the Green belies the building's function as the home of the college's biology department. The department originated as the departments of botany and zoology of the Chandler School of Science & the Arts, which joined Dartmouth in 1892, and united as a single department during the late 1950s. The department provided Dartmouth with its first proper Ph.D. programs, in biochemistry, pharmacology, and physiology, and the college erected this building to house those programs and the rest of the department in proximity to the medical school. The six-level building is part of the medical campus but resists the horizontality of its neighbors, using white spandrels and entablatures to tie its windows into vertical bands. A white-painted metal rail at the cornice serves as a Classical baluster while protecting visitors to the Mabel and Charles Murdough Experimental Greenhouse, which occupies most of the building's roof.

The Life Sciences Center represents the creeping colonization of the medical campus by undergraduate uses. The Medical School keeps basic science education in Hanover but concentrates its clinical and research buildings in Lebanon, and it offered the combined sites of three of its own buildings for large college laboratories: the long, two-level Butler Hall down the hill (1964), the 1980s Modular Lab on the courtyard, and Strasenburgh Hall. The resulting rampart of a building, although the farthest academic building from the Green at 685 yards, fully lives up to its vital campus responsibility of serving as a containing wall, indicating with the greatest clarity what is inside the campus and what is outside. By playing its bulk against Observatory Hill, the building also forms a gateway to the college and the town, at the only place where the perceived boundaries of both communities coincide, marking the transition from a woody rural landscape directly to the built fabric of the campus. The building's unbalanced and essentially medieval footprint also works with the forms of its neighbors to enclose a spacious Medical School quadrangle, supplying a broad exterior stair specifically to host the medical graduation ceremony following Dartmouth's commencement on the Green.

47. The Dartmouth Medical School

Remsen
Shepley Bulfinch Richardson & Abbott, 1959–60, 1963, 1968
Vail
Shepley Bulfinch Richardon & Abbott, 1971–73
Kellogg Auditorium
Shepley Bulfinch Richardson & Abbott, 1962; FPO, 1998
Dana Biomedical Library
Shepley Bulfinch Richardson & Abbott, 1962–63, 1972–73

The outpost of medical education at the north end of Dartmouth's campus has seemed a small world unto itself, easily walkable from the center of town but not on the way to very much. The Medical School was built here in spurts between 1960 and 1973. Its buildings display a vast scale and anonymous Modernism that contrast with the rest of the campus and belie Dartmouth's otherwise unitary undergraduate focus.

Dr. Nathan Smith founded the Medical School in 1797 and built an important brick building for it on College Street, allowing the school to turn out M.D. degrees

Remsen and Vail, with Dana Library at left

for more than a century. A curricular decline related to the limits of the clinical training available at the hospital caused the school to lose its accreditation in 1914, however, the school continued as a two-year preparatory institution. The medical school remained a basic science school for nearly fifty years, preparing students to complete their medical degrees at other institutions, often Harvard Medical School. During the mid-1950s, Dartmouth president John Sloan Dickey issued an ultimatum to do something about the school once and for all, either remaking it as a top medical school or dropping it altogether.

First, the school essentially refounded itself as a two-year institution, obtaining grants to construct a new campus about 250 yards north of the old one. James R. Clapp, Jr., of Shepley Bulfinch Richardson & Abbott designed the first wave of buildings that went up from 1959 to 1963 along College Street, adopting the rectilinear alignment of the existing hospital's nineteenth-century grid. The new medical buildings were Remsen, Kellogg, and Dana, while Dartmouth's consulting architects Campbell, Aldrich & Nulty added the Strasenburgh Hall dormitory (1962–63; demolished 2007) to complete the ensemble. All four buildings adopted a traditional red brick and limestone palette, but little else about them comported with the scale, massing, fenestration, or detailing of their prewar neighbors.

The five-level Remsen Medical Sciences Building was the first and most important building of the rejuvenated two-year medical school. The limestone elements that surround the building's paired square window openings distinguish Remsen from later additions. The building's long flat-roofed entrance pavilion extends toward the courtyard that forms the school's formal entrance, marking

Remsen as the school's initial headquarters on this site. Inside, the school installed its administration and initially assigned one level to each of the school's six departments. The school added a penthouse level in 1968 and named the building for Martin D. Remsen of White River Junction during 1974.

A boxy auditorium given by the W. K. Kellogg Foundation connects to the rear of Remsen by a long skybridge. Taking advantage of the tunnel network surviving from the demolished hospital, the college terminated its cross-campus steam line here during the late 1990s, adding a schoolwide water-chilling plant to the south end of the auditorium.

Because the Dana Library has a partially undergraduate function, planners considered a variety of southerly sites for it. It ended up as a five-story pavilion within the medical complex that joins Gilman Hall through a glassed-in passage. With a street facade somewhat more interesting than those of its neighbors, the square-plan main block of the library features tall multilevel window openings in its lower three levels and a top level, added in 1972, whose darkened openings follow a different rhythm. A largely blank-walled rear ell contains the stacks. Inside the library, the Quinn Memorial Room guards the medical school's relics, including the desk of founder Nathan Smith. The library bears the name of the Charles A. Dana Foundation.

Not content to train future physicians in the basic sciences, the leadership of the Medical School worked with the college's science departments to bring full-fledged graduate education to Dartmouth for the first time in 1964. First was a Ph.D. program in molecular biology, and other programs followed. The change seemed to pit the new stars of research against the existing educators, and the exciting and apparently money-draining nature of the new programs threatened to overshadow the medical school's goal of providing students with a vigorous medical education. A bitter faculty row and a flurry of resignations ensued, as school historian Constance Putnam writes, all based on Dartmouth's basic college/ university conflict. Then the medical school gritted its teeth, acknowledged that its primary purpose still was teaching, and it retained the molecular biology program on the grounds that teaching is done best when it is informed by research—and that both are necessary and possible.

The refounding that saved the medical school also led to the loss of its tangible past. In 1963, Dartmouth demolished the Medical Building that had defined the school's original campus on the slopes of College Park. Parts of the building's Stoughton Cabinet went to Dana and elsewhere, part of its gallery and stair went into Remsen, but the most visible act of preservation was the retention of an image of the building on the Medical School's coat of arms.

The return of the Medical School's M.D. program in 1970 occasioned a second round of construction on College Street. The eight-level James D. Vail Medical Sciences Building (1971–73) is a northern extension of Remsen, still in red brick

Dana Library entrance

but now with recessed windows peering out warily from segmented horizontal bands. In contrast to its neighbor's stepped-back penthouse, Vail's largely blind-walled brow projects top-heavily. An underground extension contains the frequently used Chilcott Auditorium (1974).

The move of the Dartmouth-Hitchcock Medical Center to the woods southeast of town in 1991 encouraged the medical school to create a campus there largely for research and clinical education. The continually growing group of S.B.R.A.-designed buildings alongside the hospital in Lebanon includes the Matthews-Fuller Health Sciences Library (1992); the basic-science labs of the Borwell Research Building (1993); the Barbara E. Rubin Building (1995; 2003); and the C. Everett Koop Medical Science Complex, comprising LeBaron Commons (2008), the Translational Research Building (2007–2009), and the Center for Evaluative Clinical Sciences (2007–2009).

Down the steep hillside from the medical campus, in the parking lots of Dewey Field, stands the Dewey One Maintenance Building (FPO, 1997), a brown shed-roofed metal industrial building that relieves the facilities headquarters on Lebanon Street of the responsibility for storing vehicles and equipment.

1. Robert Frost to Harold Goddard Rugg (April 20, 1915), in Lawrance Thompson, ed., *Selected Letters of Robert Frost* (New York: Holt, Rinehart and Winston, 1964), 167.

2. Edward Ashton Rollins to Samuel Colcord Bartlett (June 20, 1885), DP-8, President Bartlett's Papers, Dartmouth College Archives.

3. Nathan Lord, "Annual Report to the Trustees of Dartmouth College," 3, Ms. 85440, Dartmouth College Archives.

4. Trustees of Dartmouth College, Minutes (1854), quoted in Frederic S. Page, "College Park," *Dartmouth Alumni Magazine* 24, no. 2 (November 1931), 112.

5. William Thayer Smith to Asa Dodge Smith (February 26, 1861), in College Park Vertical File, Dartmouth College Archives.

6. John Brooks Wheeler to the Trustees of Dartmouth College ([n.d.], 1816), Ms. 816900.3, Dartmouth College Archives, quoted in Leon Burr Richardson, *History of Dartmouth College* (Hanover, N.H.: Dartmouth College Publications, 1932), I:361.

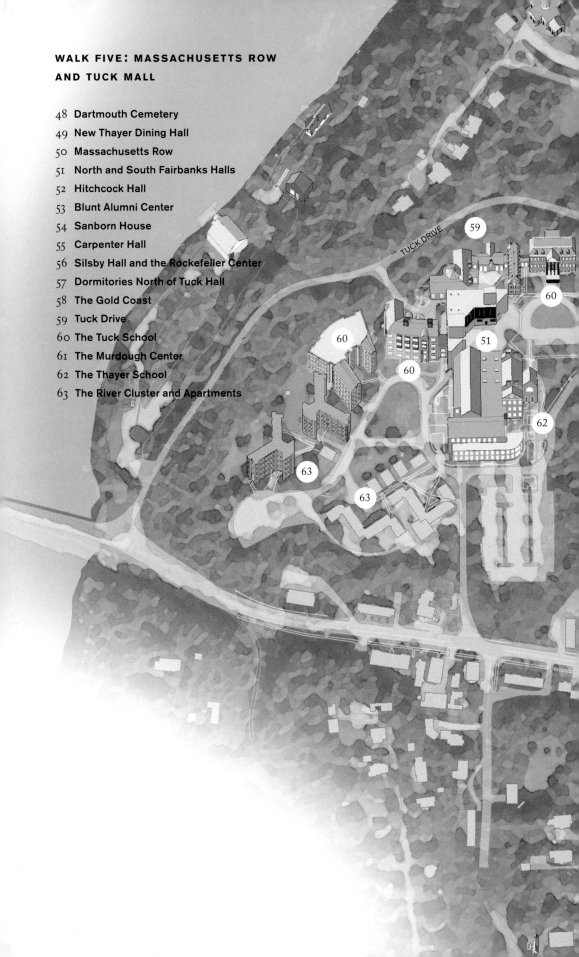

WALK FIVE: MASSACHUSETTS ROW AND TUCK MALL

WEBSTER AVENUE

60

TUCK MALL

57

56

55

58

52

MASS ROW

53

NORTH MAIN STREET

54

WENTWORTH STREET

COLLEGE STREET

50

DARTMOUTH CEMETERY

51

48

49

THE GREEN

Westward to the Hitchcock Estate

On a campus that tends to expand slowly over property acquired in large chunks, the district that lines the Beaux-Arts ensemble of Tuck Mall represents a very large chunk. Emily Hitchcock, the widow of Hiram Hitchcock, left her country estate to the college in 1912, giving a forty-five-acre parcel that encompassed everything from Main Street down to the river, bordered on the north by Webster Avenue and on the south by the houses of West Wheelock Street. The acquisition gave Dartmouth an opportunity to make long-term plans, and the estate became the place where many plans were abandoned. The terrain of the estate makes it difficult to build on. It offers only a narrow causeway of level ground where it meets Main Street. Charles Rich worked with landscape architect Bremer Whidden Pond to lay out an axis along this causeway as a guide for Hitchcock Hall, an axis that John Russell Pope would refine in his 1922 master plan for the campus. Pope's proposal still envisioned the mall as only a shallow court flanked by Hitchcock Hall and Russell Sage Hall, which Pope's office designed with Larson & Wells. A tangential dormitory group was intended to sail away alongside Webster's Vale, and although that tangent recurred in Larson's plans of the 1920s, Butterfield Hall was the only building to follow it at first.

The long rectilinear Tuck Mall visible today developed after Baker Library anchored the east end. As late as 1926, a broad meadow still was all that there was to see. Landscape architect Charles A. Platt assisted Jens Larson in extending the mall during 1928 and 1929, still nominally intending to follow Pope's idea of sinking an open-air Greek theater at the mall's terminus above the river. The area around the theater site became the center of Dartmouth's professional schools of business and engineering, an intense complex made for small-group learning and that is dependent on passages and courtyards in a way that no other part of Dartmouth's campus is.

Dartmouth rediscovered its mall after World War II, using the professional schools' backyard as a place for temporary housing and for dormitories that seemed not to fit on the older parts of campus. The college's architects proposed a dining hall for one side of the mall (1967, unbuilt), erected a dormitory for the business school in 1968, and made the major decision to place a library on the site proposed for the theater at the west end of the mall. It was the right move symbolically and functionally, but the building's awkward execution continues to imply the substitution of a memorable and confident end to the mall, or at least a screen of pine trees. The professional schools that share the library continue to expand and grow closer, and the college continues to build dormitories, leaving the mall a work in progress.

Intersecting with the mall is a walking street called Massachusetts Row, an organizational armature for a little neighborhood of student-oriented buildings that

The Dartmouth Cemetery

emerged around 1900. The street matured in 1937 with the construction of Thayer Dining Hall and the demolition of Chandler Hall, removing Young's building and the 1898 Lamb & Rich addition that partially blocked Mass Row. The resulting channel of space stretched all the way to Webster Avenue, where it petered out until the mid-1980s, when Lo-Yi Chan terminated it by framing the allee with the porte-cochere of the Rockefeller Center. (The south end of the Row still lacks an effective end.) The school has recognized the importance of the small platz before the dining hall, an accidental crossroads that is the most "urban" place on the campus and the object of considerable planning as the hub of a "campus center."

48. The Dartmouth Cemetery
1771; 1876

Eleazar Wheelock created a counterpart to the Green about four hundred feet away when he set aside the Dartmouth Cemetery. The plot's first occupant was Wheelock's stepson John Maltby, and his slab lies near the entrance to the cemetery's original acre on Cemetery Lane. Citizens raised money to fence the burial ground in 1833, during the same period when the college and town were fencing the Green. The Dartmouth Cemetery Association (1845) soon took up the tasks of planting trees and expanding the funerary infrastructure, adding more land to the north in 1876. A footbridge (ca. 1882, later demolished) carried visitors across the ravine that divides the two sections of the cemetery. As a close relative of College Park, the cemetery followed similar evolutions, and during the 1890s, donations funded improvements of the two landscapes as a pair.

The most notable monument in the cemetery is Eleazar Wheelock's horizontal slab, a 1905 reproduction of a tablet that was placed in 1814 as a substitute for the original 1779 gravestone. The heavily textual slab offers a blunt challenge to the reader who leans over to decipher its letters:

> By the gospel he subdued the ferocity of the savage
> and to the civilized he opened new paths of science.
> Traveler,
> Go, if you can, and deserve
> The sublime reward of such merit.

More than forty of the school's earliest professors are buried here, along with most of the college presidents who died before the early 1960s. President John Kemeny, who died in 1992, also is buried in the cemetery. Students' Row contains the remains of seven students who died of consumption or drowning during the days before there was a railroad to take their bodies home. Each student's literary society typically paid for his grave marker, and a service for one of Daniel Webster's United Fraternity classmates saw one of his earliest public speeches: "By the grass that nods over the mounds of Sumner, Merrill, and Cook, now rests a fourth son of Dartmouth, constituting another monument of man's mortality." Although the cemetery's nearly four acres are closed to most burials in favor of Hanover's postwar cemetery across Mink Brook, south of town, a few spots remain.

49. New Thayer Dining Hall
Kieran Timberlake Associates, 2008–10

A 1929 proposal for a massive student union and dining hall south of the Green would have allowed the school to demolish College Hall, but the Depression put an end to the idea. An influential 1936 social life survey suggested that such a building was still needed, but by then the Hopkins Center had reserved the site south of the Green. So the school built the Thayer Dining Hall (Jens Frederick Larson, 1937; demolished 2008) behind its precursor, College Hall. The building took the name of Harry Bates Thayer ('79), long a motivating force on the trustees' building committee and the executive who had given future college president Ernest Martin Hopkins a summer job at Western Electric during 1910 (Thayer himself had become president of AT&T in 1919). Thayer Hall's long double-height dining room retained its all-you-can-eat atmosphere until the mid-1990s, although numerous additions to the building left the dining hall cramped and relatively inaccessible. The '53 Commons and a temporary dining hall of the early twenty-first century removed enough pressure from Thayer to let the school demolish it and replace it with a new dining hall.

50. Massachusetts Row

Middle Massachusetts Hall
Charles Alonzo Rich, 1907–1908
North and South Massachusetts Halls
Charles Alonzo Rich, 1911–12

President Tucker proposed that groups of alumni living in Massachusetts, New Hampshire, New York, and Illinois might each build a dormitory and give it to the college, or at least cover the interest on a construction loan. When no one took up the idea, the school had to fund Massachusetts Hall itself, keeping the name in recognition of the fact that more than a third of all students by the turn of the century were from Massachusetts. Boston was known as "the second home of the College."

Built with speed on a previously vacant plot, Massachusetts Hall shows the simple but effective planning of the period: its grassy forecourt is framed behind two of the buildings that face the Green, and it peeks between them to establish an axis to the north door of Dartmouth Hall. The building's entrance portico features two pairs of giant-scale columns of the Tower of the Winds order supporting a flat-roof, making the "Colonial" Massachusetts the last dormitory for many decades with so prominent a central feature.

The bookend buildings of North and South Massachusetts Halls are shaped by the same housing crunch that pressed the campus throughout the early twentieth century. Planners decided at the last minute that the site of a "Hillside" dormitory proposed for the backyard of Richardson Hall was unsatisfactory, and they looked for another site. Splitting the program in two created twin L-shaped buildings flanking Massachusetts Hall and connected to it by short colonnades.

North and South Massachusetts marked the first appearance on the campus of something called a "resort room" or "living room," effectively forming the architectural origin of the "cluster" system of the 1980s and the Student Life Initiative that followed. A resort room terminated the first-level corridor of each dormitory and was expressed on the exterior by a large bay window. First envisioned for Hillside, the rooms were meant to provide "small but truly democratic units" within the dormitories, places where students of all backgrounds could mingle by a fireplace, surrounded by oak paneling. They were successful enough that the school soon placed similar rooms in the existing Sanborn Hall

Middle Massachusetts Hall

(since demolished) and in the new Hitchcock Hall. What was good for men's education seems to have been totally inadequate for women at the time, however, as Rich's contemporary plans for Northrop and Gillet Houses at Smith College in Northampton, Massachusetts, demonstrate: although that linked pair of buildings adopted the footprint and palette of North and South Massachusetts, their planning within Smith's house system made them effectively family residences blown up to dormitory size, complete with parlors, dining rooms, and apartments for housemothers.

South Fairbanks Hall

51. North and South Fairbanks Halls
South Fairbanks Hall
Charles Alonzo Rich, 1903
North Fairbanks Hall
Larson & Wells, 1925; 1963

To compete with the Chandler Scientific School's first fraternity (Phi Zeta Mu, 1857), a group of Chandler students formed a society called Sigma Delta Pi in 1858. Occasionally operating under the name of Vitruvian, the group thrived, and it obtained a charter from the state legislature in 1871. It soon established two short-lived chapters at other schools and in 1882 bought a plot of land on Cemetery Lane for a house. After becoming a chapter of Beta Theta Pi in 1889, the group had Vitruvian alumnus Charles Alonzo Rich ('75) design its building in 1893.

The simple wood-framed and clapboard-sided Beta Theta Pi house, now South Fairbanks Hall, emerged after a decade of slow fundraising. Its awkwardly monumental front facade is a Classical confection that dates the building's origin to the era of the World's Columbian Exposition. As an example of the hall-and-lodge form of clubhouse that was conventional at the time, South Fairbanks originally contained in its rear ell a high-ceilinged goat room known as Vitruvian Hall. This model fell out of fashion by the First World War, and new houses took the form of single volumes that subsumed the meeting room above or below the living quarters, subordinating secrecy to domesticity.

Rendering of Hitchcock Hall's west facade with social-room addition

The fraternity's decision to obtain a new building led it to a site on Webster Avenue, and the college bought the old house in 1932. A succession of occupants included the pool-shooting graduates' club, the admissions office, and the William Jewett Tucker Foundation (1951), which made the building its headquarters during 1992. The foundation promotes community service in the name of Dartmouth's socially minded ninth president, a progressive backer of one of Boston's first settlement houses.

North Fairbanks Hall is the largest building the college ever moved. The wood-framed Georgian hall began as a preparatory school gymnasium on Elm Street, near the entrance to Berry Library. In the two-story gymnasium space that occupied the building's basement, the Clark School played basketball against Hanover High and other opponents over a period of nearly thirty years. After Dartmouth bought the Clark campus in 1953, it installed a ninety-eight-seat theater in the building and made it the headquarters of the Dartmouth Film Society (1949). The purchase also provided the occasion to name the building for Professor Arthur Fairbanks ('86), the long-time director of the Boston Museum of Fine Arts. As the college prepared a space for the Kiewit Computation Center during the early 1960s, it rolled Fairbanks to its present site behind Mass Row. A new raised basement underpins the building, and a clapboard lean-to connects it to its neighbor, South Fairbanks. Although the Film Society later moved out, the building continued to house part of the film and television studies department for decades.

52. Hitchcock Hall

Charles Alonzo Rich, 1912–13; Atkin Olshin Lawson-Bell Architects, 2006–2007

Hitchcock Hall turns the corner between two eras. By pioneering development on the frontier of the largest campus expansion since the school's founding, the dormitory ended a period of relatively limited urbanistic achievements and formed a gateway to the growth of the Roaring Twenties. One arm of the L-shaped building aligns with Massachusetts Row, thereby deferring to the Green, while the other arm faces optimistically to the north alongside what would become Tuck Mall. Later buildings reiterated Hitchcock's L-shaped footprint as they made their way down the Mall.

Hitchcock Hall originated in the trustees' desire to have a spare foundation on hand just in case enrollments grew the following year. President Nichols wrote the architect at his summer home in Sugar Hill, New Hampshire during 1912: "I do not see how it will be possible for us to escape building another dormitory to be ready for use a year from now." The school built the foundation and covered it for the winter. During the spring of 1913, freshman enrollment made the new building unavoidable.

Hitchcock lives up to the scale of the later Tuck Mall. Its four levels stand above a basement and terminate in a shallow-pitched hipped roof, making Hitchcock the largest and tallest dormitory Rich designed at Dartmouth. Only an arch inset above each entrance relieves the monotony of the window openings in the building's two main facades; a pedimented Ionic portico of limestone flanked by a pair of cartouches indicates the precedence of the Tuck Mall side. Inside, a firewall originally separated the two halves of the "double dormitory," causing the building's original one-level social room to take the form of an addition open to the two halves from within the crook of the ell. As part of the systemwide social expansion of the 1980s, the college raised the roof of the social room to install a mezzanine (Charles G. Hilgenhurst & Associates, 1985). The original social room finally made way for a full-height elevator tower addition during a 2006 renovation of Hitchcock, a project that scoured the building's interior and added the western entrance and portico.

53. Blunt Alumni Center

1810; Lamb & Rich, 1896; Benjamin Thompson Associates, 1980

The oldest building in Hanover to remain on its original site is Crosby House, the brick dwelling that forms the nucleus of the Blunt Alumni Center. The house began as an unelaborated side-gabled building for Professor Zephaniah Swift Moore ('93), who taught Latin and Greek for about five years before assuming the

The Blunt Alumni Center

presidency of Williams College and then helping to establish Amherst College. Medical School professor Dr. Dixi Crosby DMS ('24), who acquired the house in 1838, instigated the most important event to take place there, the world's first scientific examination of crude oil.

Dr. Francis Beattie Brewer ('43) visited Crosby in 1853 with a bottle of the supposedly medicinal oil that was seeping from land that his lumber company leased near Titusville, Pennsylvania. Crosby and his neighbor, chemistry professor Oliver Payson Hubbard, found that the oil had potential for lighting lamps. Son Albert Harrison Crosby ('48) convinced another visitor, George Henry Bissell ('45), to fund an expedition to Pennsylvania. Bissell was a Hanover native practicing law in New York, and he joined with a former law partner to establish the Pennsylvania Rock Oil Company. The company struck oil in 1859, and within six years of Dr. Crosby's effective establishment of the petroleum industry, Bissell was able to donate a gymnasium to Dartmouth.

Crosby's family sold the house to Dartmouth during 1884 for use as a faculty rental. When uncontrolled Tucker-era enrollment surges led the college to turn its Main Street houses into dormitories, the 1896 remodeling of Crosby House was the most radical Colonial Revival project of the group. The architect added a giant-scale quadristylar temple front of fluted Ionic columns and planted a hipped-roofed attic level atop the house. A large T-shaped frame dormitory annex at the rear allowed the combined building to house about forty-four students. The last residents moved out in 1949, when the Alumni Records Office, charged with coordinating the college's famously loyal (and notoriously fierce) graduates, moved from Parkhurst Hall next door.

Sanborn House

A 1980 reworking of Crosby House created the Blunt Alumni Center, named for Chicago attorney Carleton Blunt ('26). The design was by the firm of Benjamin Thompson, who had worked with Walter Gropius and retained his Bauhaus simplicity, replacing the house's frame addition with a minimalist brick of similar scale. The columns stayed on the house, flanked by downward-pointing canister spotlights. Thompson's firm had pioneered the "festival marketplace" during the mid-1970s by adapting Boston's Fanieul Hall and other historic urban buildings into lively bazaars, and here the firm turned the open first level of the house into the Zimmerman Lounge, blowing up an 1890s photograph of North Main Street to cover an entire wall.

54. Sanborn House
Jens Fredrick Larson, 1928–29

Planners selected the site for an English house as part of a larger scheme for creating a topographic representation of the primary elements of a liberal arts college: an art building was to stand to the northwest of Baker Library, an English building to the southwest, a music building to the southeast, and a general museum to the northeast. The latter two were not built, but the first two emerged as Carpenter Hall and Sanborn House.

As early as 1917, New York attorney Edwin Webster Sanborn ('78) was hoping to be the one to leave the school a new main library in his will. Sanborn was still

Carpenter Hall

alive to be irritated, however, when the college accepted George Baker's library gift in 1925. Sanborn offered a book endowment instead, yet he still wanted a building to bear the name of his father, professor Edwin David Sanborn ('32). In part because the younger Sanborn inherited book royalties earned and invested by his sister, the writer Katherine Abbott Sanborn, he was able to fulfill his wish and add a bequest for a new building for the English Department—complete with its own library.

The L-shaped Sanborn House joins Baker through an arcade and a basement-level passage. One of Larson's finest and most detailed productions, the red-brick

Georgian building is unusually exuberant, especially for Dartmouth. Its varied and carefully crafted interiors impart a sense of thoughtful, tweedy collegiality and attempt to inspire brilliance in the teaching of the literature of the English language. Indeed, planners originally imbued the rooms with particular pedagogical roles. Several rooms display leaded windows containing the coats of arms of great writers; the Rupert Brooke Room presents a medievalesque theme; the Shakespeare Room features a high-relief carving of Shakespeare's arms in wood above the mantle; and the Wren Room is an interpretation of the salon in Belton House (William Winde, 1685), a Lincolnshire house long attributed to Christopher Wren. The Sanborn English Library fills the building's east wing, a quiet double-height space of alcoves and balconies clearly built for drinking tea in (and students continue to serve tea there weekdays at four o'clock during term time).

Sanborn House's Poetry Room is special because it is lined with early-nineteenth-century wallpaper depicting scenes of the Bay of Naples salvaged from the study of Professor Sanborn. A long-time professor of Oratory and Belles Lettres who served as well as the college librarian and was the first Winkley Professor of Anglo-Saxon, Professor Sanborn worked for decades in a study that occupied an ell projecting from the family house on the west side of the Green (1810; Lamb & Rich, 1894; demolished 1929). His son initially wanted to maintain a connection to the past by attaching his father's frame study itself to the new English building but practicality determined that it would be enough to install the wallpaper, along with the mantle, window surrounds, furniture, and other elements from Professor Sanborn's study.

55. Carpenter Hall
Jens Fredrick Larson, 1928–29; Fleck & Lewis, 1968

The art department faculty requested a headquarters building that was dynamic, imaginative, and architecturally significant, preferably designed by Eliel Saarinen. Donor Frank Pierce Carpenter, however, asked to reserve the donor's right to select the architect. The Manchester banker was the long-time president of the Amoskeag Paper Mills and his city's largest benefactor, the donor of classical buildings for the city library, the historical society, the Y.M.C.A., and the Y.W.C.A.; his architect was Edward L. Tilton of New York. Carpenter Hall thus became the most significant test of Dartmouth's policy of requiring that all new construction be planned and designed by the college architect, Jens Larson. In this case, President Hopkins denied both the faculty and the donor by sending the project to Larson, reaffirming the idea that the campus was a total work of art whose harmony would be disturbed by even a skilful attempt at distinction, as Hopkins put it.

The resulting design serves as an essential act of campus-making and shows considerable imagination in its handling of an awkward program. Attenuating the building's first-level arcade disguised part of the blank-walled gallery that occupied the building's top level, and setting a row of limestone plaques in an implied attic story covered the other half of the problem. Standing atop a high, half-exposed basement and supporting a gabled pediment on a quartet of giant-scale Doric pilasters of brick, Carpenter Hall expresses more grandeur and refinement than any Dartmouth building of its size. With Sanborn House and Baker Library, it frames the east end of Tuck Mall in a Beaux-Arts courtyard.

Carpenter's skylit gallery became a set of classrooms after the Hood Museum opened, but the building continues to house its original occupants, the departments of art history and anthropology, along with the department of women's studies (1978). A variety of lectures takes place in the basement's Herbert Faulkner West Lecture Room, while the Sherman Art Library's sixteenth-century mantelpiece from Chenonceau, France, still manages to glower over its small reading room. A passage cut through the library's modest stack addition gives access to the Berry Library circulation desk, a proximity planned from the beginning as the college sought to allow an independent departmental library to exist while retaining the focus on the main library.

56. Silsby Hall and the Rockefeller Center

Silsby Hall
Jens Fredrick Larson, 1927–28
The Rockefeller Center
Prentice & Chan, Olhausen Architects, 1983–84

Silsby Hall takes the form of the letter T, its cross-bar presenting the building's front facade to Tuck Mall. An elaborated reference to Dartmouth Hall, the tripartite facade features an entrance pavilion bearing four giant-scale Doric pilasters of brick atop a ground-level arcade. Behind this dominant range lies the stem of the T, facing Main Street. The school named the Natural Science Building for Ozias Silsby of the class of 1785 after the death of his grandson, T. Julien Silsby, who had funded the project between 1916 and 1934. Silsby Hall continues to house most of the school's social science departments.

Architect Lo-Yi Chan observed Silsby's unbalanced appearance while growing up in Hanover and attending college and described the hall as "an armchair with one missing arm." His design for the major addition of the Nelson A. Rockefeller Center for the Social Sciences finally added the chair's second arm. This was a time of aesthetic transition: Classical architecture was back in the mainstream and once more acceptable to the school's administration. Although the college had just completed its geometrically pure Maxwell Hall, Charles Moore had begun designing the postmodern Hood Museum. The Rockefeller Center is Dartmouth's

Silsby Hall, Tuck Mall entrance

first building to express this shift, and the transition can be mapped precisely to the building's northeast corner, where the abstract geometries of Rockefeller's long north facade encounter the Georgian formality of its archeological east facade. The stylistic loyalties of the building's other facades lie somewhere between the two poles and include a referential arcade to the west and an elaborated copper pediment that makes no pretence of being old. If Rockefeller had been built even five years earlier, its act of precisely replicating Silsby's historic facade would have been out of the question, its designer said, while the whole addition might have been indistinguishable from Silsby if it had gone up only a few years later, others have noted.

At the rear of the building, Chan placed a high porte cochere to terminate Massachusetts Row. Brick paving made its first appearance on campus as a floor for the pedestrian route that passes along the rear of Silsby and Rockefeller. Dartmouth named the building for Nelson Rockefeller ('30) and turned much of it over to the school's public affairs foundation, which sponsors presidential primary debates and a variety of other events.

57. The Russell Sage Cluster

Russell Sage Hall
Larson & Wells with the Office of John Russell Pope, 1922–23
Butterfield Hall
Jens Fredrick Larson, 1939–40, Charles G. Hilgenhurst & Associates, 1988
Fahey and McLane Halls
Atkin Olshin Lawson-Bell Architects, 2005–2006

If the site of Baker Library on Tuck Mall is analogous to that of the Capitol on the National Mall in Washington, D.C., then Russell Sage Hall predicts the position of John Russell Pope's National Gallery of Art of 1941. The comparisons end there, however—although the only building erected in strict accordance with Pope's

Butterfield Hall

1922 plan for Dartmouth is balanced and refined, it displays no particular Pope touches. The pitch of its gable is broader than that of many Larson buildings, its domestic shutters leave relatively little wall surface visible, and the building's white-painted wooden window trim articulates its facades with a sprightliness absent from its opposite number, Hitchcock Hall; each of Sage's two main entrances also received some ornament in the form of a columned wooden portico. The charitable foundation that funded the building was established by Margaret Olivia Sage during 1907 for "the improvement of social and living conditions in the United States" in memory of her financier husband, and it often donated educational buildings before focusing on social science research after World War II.

Butterfield Hall is Larson's last design on the campus but not his best. A reduced construction budget and a Deco-era shift to a stripped and planar Classicism impoverished the dormitory's appearance; yet it is still a part of the forty-year red-brick-and-shutters era of housing, a prosperous forty-year period in which two architects designed all of the old dormitories that are still in use.

Russell Sage Hall, Tuck Mall entrance

Butterfield is uniquely eccentric in its massing. Its side-gabled main block is a simplified version of Streeter Hall, with a small copper-sheathed entrance gable, yet at its east end it incorporates a lower mansarded wing. The school eventually filled the gap between the wing and the nearby Russell Sage Hall with a social room still known as the Hyphen. Butterfield was not without attractions on the interior, and it originally featured a ping-pong room and basement ski lockers meant to help it compete with fraternity facilities. The building takes the name of Ralph Butterfield ('39), an eccentric Kansas City merchant and amateur geologist who had once participated in an unsuccessful night mission to steal quartz crystals from a local farmer's field. He gave the natural history museum that stood at the north end of the Green (Lamb & Rich, 1895; demolished 1929) before Baker Library.

The paired dormitories, Fahey and McLane Halls, are a rebuttal to the planning mentality of the 1950s, which had seen the campus as already being "full" and lacking any space for new buildings except at its extreme peripheries. Fahey Hall faces Tuck Mall and links through a two-level social hinge to the larger McLane Hall, which angles off in the same way that Butterfield does. Both buildings modify Butterfield's basic form, expanding its seven bays to eleven and stacking an attic story atop the third level. A traditional side-gabled roof sheathed in copper terminates each building, featuring a vestigial central pediment like that of their older neighbor. Taking advantage of the slope of the mall, McLane Hall also features a granite-clad basement level. The architects originally proposed a trio of buildings for this site, but the dot-com downturn of 2000 put the project on hold, and its revival sensibly adopted this reduced scale. The buildings bear the names of Helen and trustee Peter Fahey ('68), Th ('70) and Peter McLane ('37).

McLane and Fahey Halls

58. The Gold Coast

Gile Hall
Jens Fredrick Larson, 1928; F.P.O., 1999
Streeter Hall
Jens Fredrick Larson, 1929
Lord Hall
Jens Fredrick Larson, 1929

Ghana's colonial name of "The Gold Coast" is a reference to its mineral wealth, and by the late nineteenth century the phrase described the apartments that private developers built to house many of the wealthiest students at Harvard. To refer to "a Gold Coast" at Dartmouth during the early 1900s was to raise that cautionary example, expressing the fear of what would happen if Dartmouth failed to build its own dormitories and open them to all. The group of dormitories on the south side

Gile, Streeter, and Lord Halls

of Tuck Mall was nicknamed the Gold Coast in joking hyperbole: although the group of three buildings might have commanded rents above the average, it did not become an enclave of wealth.

The architectural harmony of the group belies the differences between its three members. The subsidiaries Gile and Lord flank Streeter Hall, each adopting a different footprint. High arcaded breezeways recalling Baker Library connect the buildings and signal a high point of Dartmouth's Georgian Revival. The calm of the lawn and the trees in front of the halls, the intimacy of the buildings' flat-topped gabled roofs, and the visual interest supplied by their overscaled chimneys and gable-end wheel windows together communicate an unpretentious traditionalism, making a statement about the importance of student life outside the classroom and creating some of the most successful dormitories at Dartmouth.

The buildings bear the names of influential trustees. Named for Medical School Dean Dr. John M. Gile ('87), DMS ('91), the first building completed in the Gold Coast also is the largest, and has been expanded eastward by a sympathetic bay that houses a fire stair. The long centerpiece building is named for Frank S. Streeter ('74), Concord counsel to New England commercial powers and a fixture on the trustees' building committee. Latin professor John King Lord ('68), who served as acting president, is remembered in the westernmost building, where the slope of the ground allows for a set of basement rooms.

59. Tuck Drive

Bremer Whidden Pond with Arthur W. Dean, 1914; Saucier & Flynn, 2005–2006

The artistic and manual labor that went into the quiet road leading up to the campus is difficult to overstate. Tuck drive is an aesthetic bypass, a 3,800-foot private "highway" built to avoid the depressingly eroded stripmine of a welcome that was West Wheelock Street at the time. Edward Tuck's landscape benefaction begins just uphill from the bridge, where the first formal gateposts on the campus were built to mark the entrance to the drive. From there, Tuck Drive traverses the face of the bluff before turning to climb into the winding and tree-shaded ravine known as Webster's Vale, following a route that students had long used in their regular rambles down to the bridge. As the drive emerges from the top of the vale, it locates its formal end in front of McLane Hall, where a second set of gateposts originally stood. A pair of short branching streets connected the drive to existing roadways, one to Webster Avenue (it is now covered by McLane) and one to the driveway of the Hitchcock Mansion and thence to Main Street, a route later incorporated into Tuck Mall.

Reverend Frank Wakely Gunsaulus

The overriding theme of Tuck's landscape project was the incorporation of aesthetic concerns into an already challenging engineering task. Bremer Whidden Pond ('07), a Boston landscape architect in the Olmsted Brothers' office, began surveying the grounds after the Hitchcock Estate came into the hands of the college during 1912. (Following this project, Pond would form a landscape firm with Francis Asbury Robinson ('08) and then teach at Harvard for more than three decades.) Business Manager Homer Eaton Keyes calculated that the "demands of art," which included the costs of preserving trees and shrubs along the route of the drive, would add as much as fifty percent to

Rendering of The Living–Learning Complex

the cost of the project.[1] Massachusetts highway engineer Arthur W. Dean handled the technical aspects of the hillside cut, while the labor fell to a group of forty Italian immigrants, apparently organized through a traditional padrone labor-broker system. They lived in temporary shanties on the bluff at the end of Webster Avenue.

Workers initially surfaced Tuck Drive with bituminous macadam and flanked parts of it with granite-block gutters laid in concrete. The drive's safety barriers are paired timber rails suspended from simple granite posts, similar to the Senior Fence on the Green. A great deal of the character of the drive comes from the retaining walls of split-faced granite that line much of its length. Although the expansion of the boathouse parking lot threatens the lower drive, Pond's design remains largely intact, its mossy stones and tall trees still communicating its original innocent sense of the automobile's place in nature.

60. The Tuck School

Tuck Hall
Jens Fredrick Larson, 1929–30; Centerbrook Architects, 1992
Woodbury and Chase Houses
Jens Fredrick Larson, 1929–30
Stell Hall
Jens Fredrick Larson, 1930; Centerbrook Architects, 1993
Buchanan Hall
Campbell and Aldrich, 1967–68
Byrne Hall
Centerbrook Architects, 1990–92
Whittemore Hall
Goody Clancy Architects, 1999–2000

The Living-Learning Complex
Goody Clancy Architects, 2007–
2008

Whittemore Hall

The Tuck School of Business arose on the Green from the gifts of Dartmouth's greatest benefactor, international financier Edward Tuck ('62). After the school had operated for a quarter-century, the fact that its students had to live in different parts of the campus bothered President Hopkins. He suggested building a new home for the business school, and Edward Tuck responded with enthusiasm, stating that he would rather not let anyone else fund the project. The Tuck School sold its original building to the college and erected its permanent home alongside Tuck Mall, a group of four confident Georgian buildings that make a statement about business education during the Depression. The institution continues to focus on a small, full-time, two-year program leading to the Master of Business Administration, and from its perch at the edge of Webster's Vale it has achieved a world stature.

The administration building is named for the donor and symbolizes the institution. What might be a late-seventeenth-century English country house

Chase House and Tuck Hall

displays a white-painted wooden Ionic portico, the only such portico Larson employed at Dartmouth, to create something like a Long Island stockbroker's mansion. The building and its flanking wings achieve an intimacy appropriate for a campus where students live, and Tuck Hall continues to contain offices and classrooms of the institution. It connects to the flanking Chase and Woodbury Houses through double-height arcades that were infilled and topped with attic stories in 1993. The paved cul-de-sac known as Tuck Circle is the site of the school's investiture ceremony the day before Commencement each year.

Dartmouth's trustees named Tuck Hall's original dormitory wings for treasury secretaries (and Supreme Court justices, and senators) Levi Woodbury of the class of 1809 and Salmon P. Chase of the class of 1826. These gambrel-roofed ranges face the courtyard and represent a hybrid of the housing forms that were in use on other parts of Dartmouth's campus. The school remodeled the buildings' living spaces and basement courts for handball and racquetball into classrooms and offices during the late 1980s (Chase) and 2001 (Woodbury).

Being relatively monastic in nature, a business school deserves a "refectory" instead of a standard college dining hall. Dartmouth's trustees named the fourth member of the original Tuck group for the family of Julia Stell, Edward Tuck's wife, and joined it to Chase House. Stell Hall is a small T-shaped building whose front facade is lined with high arched window openings disposed about a central sundial. The formal dining room inside is one of Dartmouth's finer interiors, intending to inspire students through its evocative use of paneling, portraiture, and high trusses with corbels and pendants. Attaching a newer dining hall to Stell's west end has rephrased the old refectory as a formal corridor, restored for cocktails and small group meetings.

Buchanan Hall was the Tuck School's first foray outside its home in thirty-eight years, and the only element of the professional schools' complex to reach toward the Green rather than away from it. The Tuck School declined a proposal from Buckminster Fuller and instead had Dartmouth's consulting architect design a low-slung flat-roofed building, innocuously Modernist in its use of a concrete frame with brick infill across three levels. An underground connection to the neighboring Woodbury House enabled the seventy-two Tuckies who originally occupied the dormitory to set new records of troglodism, remaining indoors for months at a time. The Tuck School started its early Minority Business Executive Program here in 1980, and its experience with that and other executive programs suggested a need for something more than a simple dormitory, something like a hotel. The opening of the Living-Learning Center allowed the school to make Buchanan into an office building. The school renamed the building known initially as the Tuck Mall Dorm for William Buchanan ('24) in 1987.

Byrne Hall, the main dining hall of the Tuck School, handles its role as an urban intervention somewhat better than its role as a purely architectural statement. Low and cottagelike, with triangular eyelid dormers and a roof that dominates its diminutive one-level facade, the building contrasts sharply with the high formality of the adjoining Stell Hall. Yet Byrne succeeds in framing the Southwell Courtyard, a space more intimate and fully realized than any comparable court on Dartmouth's campus. (The courtyard covers an underground auditorium.) At the rear, the ell-shaped dining hall steps five levels down the steep hillside. A white-painted lantern with a balustrade of chinoiserie marks the building's octagonal PepsiCo Dining Room, Dartmouth's only significant domed space and the center of the variety of auditoriums and classrooms located inside Byrne Hall. The building is named for Dorothy and John J. Byrne, Jr., an insurance executive and Tuck Overseer.

Whittemore Hall is an adventurous dormitory that is required to provide the amenities of a hotel in order to house summer executive programs. Off the rear of the business complex, the crisply-detailed red-brick dormitory has license to adopt a different style. It might be an example of the optimistic Dutch workers' housing of World War I, with the addition of a battery of projecting metal-clad bays. A high sundial occupies a broad, lancet-shaped parapet atop the building's full-height entrance pavilion, drawing attention to what amounts to a second public entrance to the Tuck School. Inside is the Great Hall, a lobby that focuses on a two-story fireplace. Behind Whittemore is a stone-faced concrete viaduct that Jens Larson designed to access Stell's kitchen, now cut off from vehicle traffic. The bridge supports the McCormack Courtyard at the springing line of its round Roman arches, a part of the Whittemore project that hides the school's garage and loading dock beneath the suspended plaza. Whittemore Hall is named for Tuck Overseer

The Murdough Center

and Morgan Stanley partner Frederick B. Whittemore ('53), Tu ('54).

Finally, the H-shaped Living-Learning Complex at the west end of the Tuck School provides further evidence of the professional schools' affinity for an urbanism of intimate scale and accretive form (as usual, passages connect the building to the rest of the school underground). Designed in a vocabulary similar to that of Whittemore Hall, the brick building comprises a pair of bent ranges of unequal lengths containing living spaces for Tuck's expanding population. A glass-walled crossbar for classrooms and social spaces connects the ranges, with ground-level colonnades framing the Class of 1980 Courtyard on the school side. The comparable space on the river side of the crossbar is roofed as the McLaughlin Atrium.

61. The Murdough Center
Campbell, Aldrich & Nulty, 1971–73

The planners of the 1920s did not expect it to end this way, but the professional schools flanking Tuck Mall's wastefully vacant west end needed library space desperately. Dartmouth decided to link the business and engineering schools through a shared red-brick building that emerges from deep in the hillside, a half-sunk five-level building topped by a flat roof. Named for Grace and Thomas Gorden Murdough ('26), the Modernist building's abstract geometric footprint avoids angles other than forty-five and ninety degrees in plan and suggests the square-doughnut form of the architects' Amherst College Science Center (1974), here sliced on the diagonal. The undifferentiated brick walls of the building's front facade create a backdrop for a cool curtain-walled jetty of dark-gray glass gridded with black anodized aluminum, marking the entrance to the building's heart, the joint business and engineering library named for Theodora and Stanley Feldberg ('46). A stepped concrete plaza of lively topography brings to mind both the Greek theater that Pope proposed for this site and the plaza of the Boston City Hall, a project that the architects helped design.

Under the plaza is the largest of the Murdough Center's joint teaching spaces, the 350-seat Cook Auditorium. Murdough's interiors have been reworked several times since the designers originally specified a characteristically 1970s palette of yellow, orange, and red interior surfaces, intended to brighten up the Hanover winter.

62. The Thayer School
Cummings Hall
Jens Fredrick Larson, 1938–39; 1946–47; Venturi, Rauch, &
Scott Brown with Payette Associates, 1989–90
MacLean Engineering Sciences Center
Koetter, Kim & Associates with Lim Consultants, 2004–2006

Dartmouth graduates pursued engineering well before the discipline was professionalized, among them Rufus Graves of the class of 1791, who in 1796 designed an astounding single-arched timber bridge that spanned the river at Hanover for the first time but collapsed after eight years. The school's most important engineer was Sylvanus Thayer ('07), who attended the United States Military Academy after graduating from Dartmouth and directed the construction of fortifications at Norfolk, Virginia, during the War of 1812. He studied engineering in Paris at the Ecole Polytechnique and accepted President Monroe's appointment to the superintendence of West Point in 1817. Until departing in 1833, he worked to utterly reorganize West Point into the nation's first college of engineering, justifying the description that appears on the Academy's 1883 statue of him as "Father of the United States Military Academy."

The study of engineering remained an undergraduate pursuit in the United States for decades after Thayer's innovations at West Point. Dartmouth's Chandler Scientific School, which opened during 1852, followed the typical undergraduate model to produce engineers and architects who designed canals and reservoirs and skyscrapers. It was after the Civil War that Sylvanus Thayer reformed American engineering education for a second time, in 1867 giving his engineering library and

The MacLean ESC and Cummings Hall

a fund of $70,000 to endow "a School or Department of Architecture and Civil Engineering" at Dartmouth. This gift created the nation's first graduate school of civil engineering, since one condition of the gift was that the school was "to be essentially, though not formally, post-graduate" (all but about fifteen percent of students were college graduates from its 1871 opening, and the school became formally limited to post-graduate students around 1888).[2] When General Thayer died in 1872, the bulk of his estate went to establishing the Thayer Academy and a free library in Braintree, Massachusetts.

General Thayer recommended that Dartmouth hire Lieutenant Robert Fletcher, a West Point graduate, to direct the new engineering school. Fletcher established the institution almost single-handedly largely in Thornton Hall. The school acquired its first distinct headquarters (Thayer Lodge) in 1892, and following Edgar H. Hunter's extensive 1911–12 renovation of the old Bissell Gymnasium, it spent the next twenty-seven years facing the Green.

Horace S. Cummings, a state senator and Washington telephone executive, was a boyhood friend and 1862 classmate of Edward Tuck. The building given in his memory by his widow, Jeannette I. Cummings, would be a permanent home for the engineering school adjacent to Tuck's own benefaction at the end of Tuck Mall. As the last major project that Larson completed at Dartmouth (his pre- and postwar designs for a Classical Hopkins Center were not built), Cummings Hall is essentially an enlarged version of Larson's earlier Hitchcock Clinic. The engineering school's stolid brick box with subordinate longitudinal wings stands but two levels above a high basement, topped by simple side-gabled roofs. Placing the first-level entrance atop a sweeping stair did little to overcome the diminutive scale

MacLean's GlycoFi Atrium

of the building's enclosed entrance porch; nevertheless, a dominant brick parapet traversing the entire central block of the building proclaimed it the HORACE CUMMINGS MEMORIAL. The original bequest soon funded a pair of wings for electrical and mechanical engineering, plain ells that framed an outdoor courtyard behind Cummings. That courtyard, although occupied by a temporary building in 1967, set up the most inventive and successful addition ever on the campus in the late 1980s.

Robert Venturi's addition to Cummings did three things. It introduced a bold entrance pavilion at the center of the building's facade; it closed off the school's rear courtyard with a businesslike crossbar range; and it roofed over that courtyard with a flat-roofed clerestory. Each of these interventions defies expectations slightly by shifting or rescaling familiar elements. The dainty two-level red brick entrance pavilion, for example, is highly orthodox in form. The lantern-topped building with its paneled chamber has been described as a lay chapel or a Palladianized medieval town hall. Even the presentation drawings, crowded with labels in curling script, focused on a traditional sectional view of the building's great Palladian window, invoking the history of architecture. But the building is still playful: the flat-arched openings that screen each of its two side entrances somehow fail to align with the entrance doors behind them, and the building's prow features a set of slate panels as a sort of advertisement overrun with text announcing the name and purpose of the school. The addition turned Cummings's courtyard into a clerestoried Great Hall surrounded by former exterior walls. The spilling glacier of a stair at the head of the hall derives from Michelangelo's stair at the Laurentian Library in Florence of the 1550s and other Renaissance favorites of Venturi, and it leads to the simple range placed at the rear of the building for offices and workspaces. The plain, flush-windowed range offers the firm's trademark stepped-back gable as it serves as an academic laboratory loft.

The MacLean Engineering Sciences Center further encases Cummings, adding a voluminous brick laboratory range to the south and sending a bright and delicate glass bridge northward to the Murdough Center. The designers' urbanist outlook informed their decision to use a brick drum with an engaged ground-level colonnade to lead the visitor around the building's southeast corner. A small

The MacLean ESC

front gateway opens onto the building's recessed entrance courtyard, where a hodgepodge of bays and pillboxes of glass or copper looks like a miniature representation of a city. Beyond the entrance, the full-depth glazed GlycoFi Atrium joins the building to Cummings Hall. Yet another harmonious distinction in the professional schools' complex, MacLean represents an ongoing process of incremental development. The lab addition creates extra space for master's-degree programs and the B.S.E., which is the only undergraduate degree Dartmouth offers other than the A.B. The hall is named for Mary Ann and Barry MacLean ('60), Th ('61), a Thayer Overseer and C.E.O. of the MacLean-Fogg Company.

63. The River Cluster and Apartments

French and Judge Halls
Campbell & Aldrich, 1960–61
Channing Cox Hall
Shepley Bulfinch Richardson & Abbott, 1975–76
Maxwell Hall
Shepley Bulfinch Richardson & Abbott, 1981–82

At the extreme margin of the Hanover Plain is an amoebalike expanse of grass that has the potential to become a full-fledged campus space. No building seems to have occupied this green until after World War II, when the peripheral nature of the site made it a repository for housing of expedience. A great wheel of prefabricated wartime residential units that Dartmouth trucked from the shipyards of South Portland, Maine, during 1945 and 1946 had its center about where Maxwell Hall stands today. Along with flanking buildings and another rank of units in the Thayer School parking lot, "Wigwam Circle" was a project funded by the Federal Housing Development Agency to house married students, largely veterans, during the first years of the G.I. Bill. (A temporary village of prefabricated two-level dorms called the Tree Houses—Birch, Elm, Maple, Oak, and Spruce—would occupy the same area during 2001, remaining for half a dozen years.)

With loans from the United States Housing and Home Finance Administration, the school removed Wigwam Circle in 1958 and replaced it with the only dormitories Dartmouth built during the 1960s, a trio of somewhat experimental Modernist buildings initially called North, Middle, and South Wigwam. These buildings appeared in presentation drawings accompanied by a winged late-model car, perhaps acknowledging the buildings' remoteness and their essential suburbanity, since they stood closer to Vermont than to Dartmouth's Green. The buildings emerged directly from the lessons of the Choates' experiment, and the school even delayed building them to study the Choates further, testing students' reaction to a mockup of a Wigwam room that it created within one of the Choates. Everyone had praised the Choates' large common rooms, but even supporters agreed that other dormitories did not need their faculty apartments, especially if having to subsidize faculty apartments would raise student rents (since the school required the dormitory system to pay for itself). The new Wigwam dorms, which became known as the River Cluster, therefore omitted faculty residences.

Resembling contemporary public housing projects, the four-level buildings of the River Cluster occupied randomly-scattered Y-shaped footprints. Each building received the same mildly International-style facade, a Choate-like checkerboard of brick infill panels alternating with metal window-and-spandrel combinations, their brown color helping the buildings fade into leafy obscurity. At the base of each Y was a lounge and entrance; yet each building deployed its stairs at the extreme ends of the wings, forcing students to tromp through the two bathrooms at the heart of the building to reach the other end of any given floor. The school solved that problem by inserting a triangular-plan stair at the center of each building during 1986. The school named the buildings for trustees: International Paper head John Holmes Hinman ('08), attorney and arbitrator John Roy "Judge" McLane ('07), and Boston & Maine president Edward Sanborn French ('06). When Hinman Hall made way for the Tuck School's Living-Learning Complex during 2006, McLane Hall became Judge Hall, the only building at Dartmouth to carry a person's nickname.

The school's first experiments with student apartments during the 1970s and 1980s were two small zigzags of brick designed to harmonize with the River Cluster. A bridge at each of the buildings' three-levels spans the gap between zig and zag. The four-bedroom suites house independent upperclass students as well as groups based on affinities for particular languages, cultures, or fraternities. Channing Cox Hall is named for early-1920s Massachusetts Governor Channing Harris Cox ('01), who established a library fund to memorialize the other three brothers in his Manchester, New Hampshire family. Maxwell Hall uses the same kit of parts as its predecessor but contains the Max Kade German Center along with the apartments. The brick box alongside Maxwell, which originally housed racquetball courts, became the Daniels Climbing Gym in 1994.

1. Homer Eaton Keyes to Ernest Fox Nichols (March 28, 1914), Treasurer's Papers, Tuck Drive, DA-2(19):19, Dartmouth College Archives, quoted in Alan Saucier and William Flynn, "Dartmouth College Historical Evolution and Preservation: Strategies for the Landscape" (Lebanon, N.H.: Saucier & Flynn, Landscape Architects, 1996), I:35.

2. Dartmouth College, [Catalog of Dartmouth College and the Associated Schools for the Academic Year 1867–1868] (Hanover, N.H.: Dartmouth College, 1867), quoted in William Phelps Kimball, *The First Hundred Years of Thayer School of Engineering at Dartmouth College* (Hanover, N.H.: University Press of New England, 1971), 14.

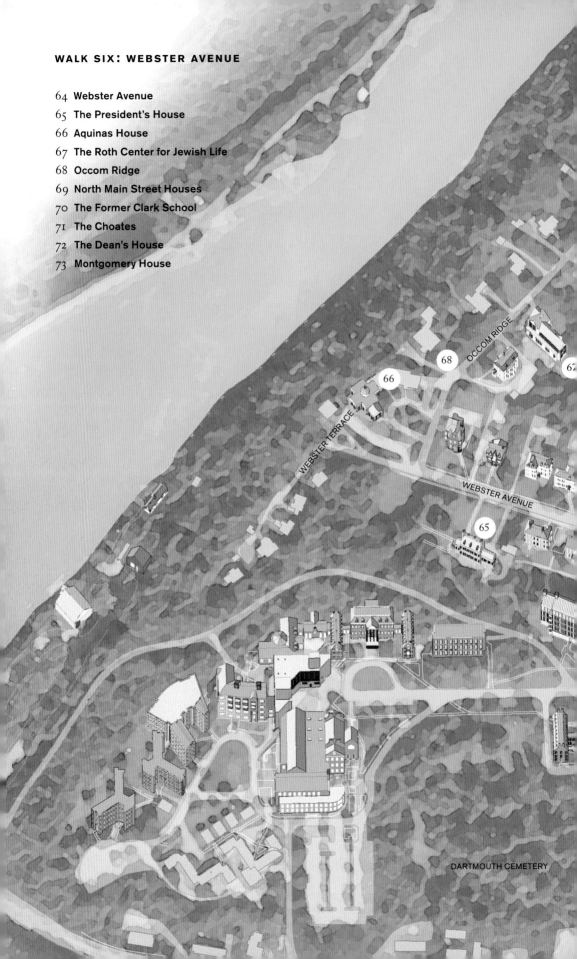

WALK SIX: WEBSTER AVENUE

OCCOM POND

73

CLEMENT ROAD

ROPE FERRY ROAD

72

CHOATE ROAD

MAYNARD STREET

70

69

71

70

64

THE GREEN

Hanover's residential northwest

Institutional and recreational uses continually nip at the edges of the residential quarter north of Webster Avenue, a neighborhood that now lies landlocked behind the college. This territory was largely farmland until the 1890s, when the college platted part of it as a residential development, and private organizations used other parts for an ornamental pond, a forest preserve, and a golf course. Rope Ferry Road (1795), which ran to meet the river at the mouth of the Vale of Tempe until the golf course occupied its end, became the site of the town's largest and most prosperous-looking houses. Fraternities gradually migrated to Webster Avenue along the south side of the neighborhood, but the dominant institution during much of the twentieth century was the Clark School, a preparatory school that straddled Main Street. The school's seven buildings were a boon to the college when Dartmouth bought them in 1953. Dartmouth built its first International Style buildings on the prep school's sports field along Choate Road.

64. Webster Avenue

Webster Avenue gradually became a "fraternity row," a street lined with half of the houses of Dartmouth's independent social organizations. Although the street's first private fraternity house went up in 1902, the majority of its buildings did not come into fraternity ownership until after World War II. In a town with few bars and no college dives, the basements of Webster Avenue still turn into some of the chief foci of students' social attention on weekends, but the perception that the street is a place for wild parties might have peaked during the 1960s. Now a third of the houses admit women as members, and two-thirds have jettisoned any affiliations they had with a national group. The presence of the Catholic student center and the President's House make this street less monolithic than its reputation might suggest.

Webster Avenue began as a college real estate development meant to foster good community relations. Dartmouth's academic expansion in the Quadrangle scheme north of the Green was displacing residents, mostly faculty, and President Tucker announced during 1895 that the school would make a "suitable provision for residential removals" on a plot of farmland that it had purchased. The new street would be lined on one side by faculty houses and would join North Main Street near the cottage where Daniel Webster was reputed to have roomed, taking the name of "Webster Park" or "Webster Avenue." The first lots went on sale during 1896, and the Boston firm of Henry Hyde Dwight and Howland Shaw Chandler designed a row of five frame houses to sell to faculty. The houses, which became more Romantic in turn from west to east, all strove nevertheless to present a

Alpha Chi Alpha house

bilaterally symmetrical front facade to the street. The college also sold lots on the street to three fraternities, institutionalizing its concern over social segregation by inserting covenants into the deeds prohibiting the fraternities from housing for more than fourteen residents. The ban extended to all new fraternity houses in 1902, when the school also banned fraternity dining facilities in the interest of maintaining collegiality. The three initial fraternities took until 1915 to complete their buildings.

Although the school acquired Webster Avenue's south side during 1912, it waited until the early 1920s to sell the first four lots there to fraternities. Those groups built their houses of brick for a change, as did the fraternity that got the last empty lot on the north side, and two of the original trio, which replaced their buildings. With the President's House, the street had become a mostly masonry enclave. By the 1960s, one of the original professors' houses had fallen to create the Catholic student center, and fraternities occupied the other four. The faculty avenue had become a fraternity row.

Regular waves of alterations meant to keep the houses in service have eroded the street's character as an early-twentieth-century residential development. Alumni corporations and the college have expanded the buildings' kitchens and living quarters. Students have uniformly repurposed the buildings' basements into grim arenas for "pong," a beer-based table tennis that was a distinctive Dartmouth folkway by the 1960s and has since became a touchstone of American college life. Among exterior elements, downmarket vinyl windows have largely replaced

Phi Delta Alpha house

the houses' original double-hung wood sashes; parking lots have eaten up lawns; students have added unpainted wooden decks; and the school's enforcement of local safety codes has fostered several sympathetic fire-stair additions. Thus the street is a bit more ragged than it was in 1925, but it still manages to broadcast its origin as a planned neighborhood.

The first brick house on the street was the latest in a series of innovative accommodations for Kappa Kappa Kappa, a group that students founded during 1842. The society's original mysterious Italianate frame hall (1860; demolished ca. 1962) stood below Wilson Hall as one of the first freestanding buildings erected by any college fraternity in the country. An unbuilt early-1890s proposal for a combination residence and meeting hall preceded the group's 1894 move to a mansarded house on Main Street (1870; demolished 1926), where the group added a clerestoried but otherwise windowless ell for its meetings. After the building came to the attention of the college as a site for Silsby Hall, the fraternity erected its current two-level red brick house on the corner (Larson & Wells, 1922–23). The modest dwelling concentrates its detail on a projecting bay with a semicircular entrance portico whose Corinthian order the *Architectural*

Forum found "too delicate and refined in character for use at the entrance to an undergraduate fraternity house." (The order might have been mandated by the society's earlier adoption of a Corinthian column as its mystical emblem.) The building's hipped slate-clad roof obscures an attic-level meeting room that is the functional if not the formal descendant of the group's ostentatiously secretive hall on College Street.

Next door is the brick house of the Tabard. The local Chandler School fraternity called Phi Zeta Mu (1857) became a chapter of the national Sigma Chi the year after Dartmouth absorbed Chandler in 1892. After buying one of the original Avenue parcels, the group took the typical period of more than a dozen years to build its frame-constructed Colonial dwelling (John Ashton, 1912). That house burned in 1931, and the group used the foundation to support a brick building (1931–32) by the local firm of engineer Harry Artemas Wells and architect Archer E. Hudson. Both buildings turned their long six-bay front facades to the street and terminated in a hipped roof pierced by a trio of dormers, but they shared few other formal features. This building originally placed a special focus on winter sports, with *The Dartmouth* noting its basement ski racks and its trophy room of the "outing club type," meaning that it had a flagstone floor, a stone fireplace, and rough-hewn ceiling beams. When the student government required fraternities to leave discriminatory national organizations, the group became a local organization in 1960 under the name of Geoffrey Chaucer's Southwark inn. Women joined the society starting in 1980.

At 5 Webster Avenue stands Phi Delta Alpha (Charles Alonzo Rich, 1901–1902; Design-Build Studio, 2004–2005), the grandest fraternity house at Dartmouth. An 1884 chapter of the national Phi Delta Theta built this building, the first fraternity house on the Avenue, by adopting a form then popular among Eastern fraternities—that of the imposing five-bay mansion with a bilaterally symmetrical front facade of attenuated proportions. In this case, the frame building is sheathed in clapboard siding and terminates in a massive gambrel roof that the college architect populated with prominent gabled dormers. The giant-scale Corinthian columns of the pedimented entrance gable frame the requisite portico, this one resting on paired Ionic columns. The house has continued through the usual institutional struggles, including a 1960 secession from the national organization, and the building incorporated a rear kitchen and stair after passing its centennial.

Students who formed a chapter of Kappa Sigma in 1905 saw their group ascend to prominence quickly. It managed to purchase an empty lot at 7 Webster Avenue from Delta Kappa Epsilon, the original buyer, which had hired Charles Rich to design a frame fraternity house that it failed to build. Kappa Sigma built a unique frame Arts & Crafts house (1915; demolished 1937), followed by a conventional side-gabled Georgian design (Wells, Hudson & Granger, 1937). The firm's earlier proposal showed a sprawling brick cottage with angled wings for handball courts and other amenities, but it was too extravagant. The group seceded from the national organization around 1980 and took the name Chi Gamma Epsilon several years later.

History professor Herbert Darling Foster ('85) bought the house at 9 Webster Avenue, one of the original faculty houses (Dwight & Chandler, 1898–99; 1956; 2003). The rectangular clapboard building's Colonial details and essentially pyramidal roof ally it with the architects' Atlantis Hotel in Kennebunk Beach, Maine (1903; since demolished). The house remained a private dwelling following Foster's death in 1927 until Delta Upsilon moved in during the war. After failing to build a replacement brick Georgian house during 1941, the group settled for a shallow two-bay addition for a meeting room in 1956. Under the name of Foley House (1966), the group sold its building to the college in the mid-1980s, making way for a succession of sorority rentals that culminated in the local Kappa Delta Epsilon (1993). The college added a full-height rear addition in 2003.

Cheney Professor of Mathematics Thomas Wilson Dorr Worthen ('72) occupied the boxy clapboarded house at 11 Webster Avenue, the one with Ionic pilasters at the corners (Dwight & Chandler, 1896; Alfred T. Granger Associates, 1958–59). Families and then renters occupied the house into the 1920s, when the Clark School acquired it to use as a dormitory called "Webster House." The college bought the place in 1953 and later sold it to Sigma Phi Epsilon (1908), which built a large but sympathetic addition on the east, complete with a new Doric entry portico. The group seceded from its national organization during the years from 1967 to 1981.

Willard Professor of Rhetoric and Oratory, Fred Parker Emery ('87), built the swooping shingle-style house at 13 Webster Avenue (Dwight & Chandler, 1896; Fleck & Lewis, 1963, 2004). The mass of the building's two-level side-gabled roof overwhelms its ground level, while the whimsical mixture of concave and convex forms, including a pair of pointy-roofed dormers, somehow justify the current nickname of the "Cheese Lodge." Emery's widow occupied the house into the late 1940s, with the college acquiring the building during 1957 and leasing it to the new Alpha Chi Rho (1956). The group soon became the local Alpha Chi Alpha (1963) and added two levels of bedrooms on the rear of the building, in part to house women who visited during Fall Houseparties Weekend. The college demolished the building's original carriage house (it had been connected to the house, furnished rustically, and christened "the Barn") in order to erect another two-level addition during 2004, enclosing a new social space with bedrooms above.

Professor of Zoology William Patten built the house at 15 Webster Avenue and occupied it for several decades (Dwight & Chandler, 1896; W. Brooke Fleck, 1965; 2000). A shingle-style concoction like its neighbor, the house features a corner tower with a conical cap. The Mary Hitchcock Memorial Hospital School of

Nursing leased the building in 1942 as wartime housing, and the house remained a private dwelling until the Tau Epsilon Phi Fraternity acquired it within a few years of forming in 1950. After adding a split-level party room, the group seceded from its national organization under the name of the Harold Parmington Foundation (1969), welcoming women in 1973 and changing its name to Delta Psi Delta not long before folding in 1992. The college bought the house and began renting it to the Epsilon Kappa Theta sorority (1982), a group that had left the national Kappa Alpha Theta for largely religious reasons during 1992.

The last vacant lot on the avenue to go to a fraternity lies on the south side near Main Street. Beta Theta Pi sold its original house (South Fairbanks Hall) to the college and soon completed this building at 6 Webster Avenue (Wells & Hudson, 1932–33). Adopting the C-shaped form of the earlier Sigma Nu house, the hip-roofed building encloses between its wings a broad and shallow giant-scale portico with capitals derived from the Tower of the Winds in Athens. Disciplinary violations cost the group college recognition in 1996, and during 1998 it began renting the house to the Alpha Xi Delta sorority (1997).

Students established a permanent chapter of Zeta Psi in 1920, and soon the group was inhabiting its purpose-built house at 8 Webster Avenue (Larson & Wells, 1925). The long brick mansion displays a Mount Vernon-style portico of square columns on its street front, while its paired internal gable-end chimneys affiliate it with the architects' nearby Gold Coast dormitories.

The prolific Boston firm of Clarence H. Blackall, James Ford Clapp, Sr., and Charles Whittemore designed the 1925 house at number 10 for the Delta Tau Delta fraternity of 1901. The L-shaped building features applied brick arcading at the ground level and terminates in a dormered gambrel roof. Tuscan Doric columns mark both the front and rear entrances of the house, acknowledging the fact that the back door faces in the direction of the Green. During a time when builders made much of "slow-burning" or (alternately) "fireproof" construction, Blackall, who was Jens Larson's mentor, was regarded as a safety expert. He drafted Boston's building codes beginning in 1907 and promoted fireproof construction as the editor of *The Brickbuilder*. Nevertheless, Delta Tau Delta chose the "nonfireproof" option that contemporaries had avoided, and a fire gutted the building in 1929. Local firm Wells & Hudson rebuilt the house that year within the surviving brick shell. The fraternity became a local society called Bones Gate in 1960, adapting its name and motto from those of a pub in Chessington, England. A bay added to the west end of the house encloses a fire stair (Design-Build Studio, 2005).

Moving from an old frame house opposite Webster Avenue's east end, Sigma Nu (1903) built the two-and-a-half level house at number 12 (Larson & Wells, 1925; Haynes & Garthwaite Architects, 2007). Its C-shaped form and paired chimneys derive from Virginia's 1720s Stratford Hall, as filtered through Gilded Age mansions

The President's House

such as the one that Robert W. Cumming built in Newark, New Jersey (McKim, Mead & White, 1896). The house appeared in *Architectural Forum* (1925) and Klauder and Wise's *College Architecture in America* (1929). The group was a local fraternity from 1961 to 1985.

65. The President's House
Peabody, Wilson & Brown, 1926; 1982; 1994

Dartmouth's executive mansion, another Edward Tuck benefaction, is a conventional two-and-a-half level building whose rear facade is nearly identical to its front. This indecisiveness reflects the fact that the building's official address is 1 Tuck Drive while its formal entrance drive faces Webster Avenue. The building does not differ too much from the fraternities nearby, and indeed the most remarkable aspect of the house is its location on Webster Avenue. The trustees considered several alternative sites, including Observatory Hill (it was thought to be a distant backyard) and Lyme Road by the Medical School (it was too disrupted by White Mountain vacation traffic). Before work even finished on the Webster Avenue house, three new fraternities had sprung up to the east, one of them located just over the garden wall. Hopkins soon acknowledged that the siting probably was a mistake and wrote that he expected the eastern rooms of the President's House to be unusable "when fraternity phonographs and musical instruments are in operation."

Aquinas House

66. Aquinas House
Stanley Orcutt, 1961–62

The independent Catholic student center (1953) is a descendant of the local
parish's Newman Club (1924). Zoning did not permit Aquinas House to build the
chapel that Stanley Orcutt designed for its initial site at 13 Choate Road, and
in 1961 the group swapped with the college for this site at the end of Webster
Avenue. The group demolished Professor Louis Dow's house (Dwight & Chandler,
1898–99) and erected a connected trio of buildings that followed loosely
traditional forms. The brick Classicism of St. Clement's Chapel is distinctly of the
1960s in its expression, with a flat roof, spare detailing, and abstract multicolored
window glazing. The building's modified Greek cross plan angles in the direction of
the Green and presents the arriving student with a gabled Doric entrance portico,
its tracery-filled arched transom a cheery nod to Baker Library and the other
buildings on which the architect worked while in Jens Larson's office. The higher
square-plan sanctuary block at the center of the chapel supports an octagonal
cupola that terminates in a green pyramidal roof. The chapel and its basement-
level function hall are connected through the classroom and recreational spaces of
McDonald Hall to the two-story brick Chaplain's House next door.

The Roth Center, Occom Ridge entrance

67. The Roth Center for Jewish Life

R.M. Kliment & Frances Halsband with Randall T. Mudge & Associates, 1996–97

Presenting an ostensibly domestic gable to Occom Ridge, the white-clapboarded Roth Center is made up of two end-gabled boxes joined by a shed-roofed gallery. The larger front volume contains a faceted worship hall roofed by an interlaced set of bolted wooden trusses that critic Donlyn Lyndon called "an ingenious act of architectural prestidigitation."[1] The smaller volume contains the Koreman Library with its suspended steel-framed mezzanine. This part of the building is closest

The Roth Center's Alperin/Hirsch Sanctuary

to the Green and thus contains the building's student entrance. The broad gallery connecting the two volumes is lit by its own truss-framed clerestory. The building carries the name of Manhattan real estate developer Steven Roth ('62).

The building is a community center for both Dartmouth Hillel and the local Jewish congregation, including its Hebrew School. The center was phrased as a comment on Dartmouth's past when it opened during the term of President James O. Freedman. Following the lead of its peers, Dartmouth had limited Jewish enrollment during the late 1920s, and it had asked Jewish and other alumni to screen out some Jewish applicants. The postwar period saw a shift, however, as the school established its Jewish Religious Life Council and students voted to bar chapters of discriminatory national fraternities. The college appointed its first rabbi in 1975, for a Jewish community that was comprised of about five hundred students and residents of the Upper Connecticut River Valley. The community has only grown since then, and the Roth Center is a sign that it is flourishing.

68. Occom Ridge

The college continued the second phase of its 1890s real estate development by laying out a street to intersect with Webster Avenue and run to the northeast, following the base of the high glacial moraine called Occom Ridge. Landscape architect John Charles Olmsted pointed out the flaws in the road during 1899: its "stiff and commonplace" straight-line design defied the picturesque setting, and its location was too low to reach the houses that Olmsted thought should stand atop the ridge. He proposed adding curves, which the college did not do, and erecting a private access road to reach the ridge, which the college soon did. The college commissioned architect Louis Sheldon Newton to design the varied row of six houses (numbered 14 through 24 Occom Ridge, 1899–1900) to sell to faculty and officers. A lone neighbor to the north followed (26 Occom Ridge, 1907) and another row of six later appeared farther north (30 through 40 Occom Ridge, 1915–18).

Occom Ridge is named for the Mohegan minister Samson Occom, who probably would have wanted less than anyone to have his name attached to the landscapes of Hanover. He never visited the college, and he regretted helping raise the funds that Wheelock diverted to creating an English college, writing bitterly in 1771 that the too-grand Dartmouth would "be Naturally ashamed to Suckle the Tawnees."[2] Occom later helped establish the experimental Christian Indian settlement of Brothertown, New York, and he left the largest body of writings in English created by any colonial Native American.

A short distance along Occom Ridge stands the half-shingled frame Delta Delta Delta house (Lamb & Rich, 1898–99), which began as a faculty duplex known as Ridge House. Its Colonial design makes it a discounted version of the fashionable mansions that the architect was designing on Long Island and in the New Jersey highlands at the time. The trios of Tuscan columns in the corner entrance porticos, the bay windows, and the dormered gambrel roof all suggest picturesque country ease, in a modest way. "It is a long, plain, boxy affair and painted yellow," according to John Olmsted.[3] As the college's first faculty housing, Ridge House was the school's most strident nineteenth-century answer to the local housing crunch, a perennial problem exacerbated by the "renaissance" that Tucker began in 1893. The first tenant in the northern half of the house was the new physics professor Ernest Fox Nichols, who would go on to be president of the college. Faculty and later graduate students and employees succeeded him, with one of the last families to live in the southern half being that of Professor James Wright (during 1976), also a future president. Students and societies then began to occupy the house, and the Delta Delta Delta sorority moved in during the early 1990s. Workers punched through the interior partitions to finally unite the building's two equal halves in 1994.

Across the street from Ridge House is the William Jewett Tucker House (Charles Alonzo Rich, 1907–1908), a modest frame saltbox where the college president retired to write. The building's steeply pitched shingled roof and painted white chimney give it an appropriately cottagelike aspect. The design of the house was a gift of the college architect based on Tucker's initial sketches.

69. North Main Street Houses

The largely residential district north of Webster Avenue arose amid farm fields during the mid-nineteenth century. Fraternities and group homes for nurses dominated North Main Street by the end of the century, and later the college began planting academic buildings, sometimes large and obtrusive. After the 1960s, the school's growth become subtler, as Dartmouth focused on leaving the edges of the block south of Maynard relatively intact. The school tended to preserve and expand the nineteenth-century frame houses it encountered and gave the new academic buildings porches and side-gabled roofs so that they might fit in.

The only brick fraternity on the campus to wear white paint, Gamma Delta Chi, is one of the last of the prewar society buildings (Wells, Hudson & Granger, 1937). Students founded the group in 1921 and soon acquired a frame house on this site, merging with another fraternity in 1935 in preparation for construction (the group absorbed a third fraternity and the alumni of a defunct fourth group the following year). The house is unusual not only in its color but its scale and massing, with a huge gable-end chimney facing the street. A monumental square-columned side portico shelters the main entrance in the building's large rear ell, and the whole ensemble terminates in a slate-covered deck-on-gable roof studded with gabled dormers. The floor of the portico covers a cavernous subterranean squash court now used for basketball.

Webster Cottage (1780) is a small Cape Cod house that college tutor Sylvanus Ripley ('71) built on its original site at the southwest corner of Webster Avenue. Henry Fowle Durant (a.k.a. Henry Welles Smith), who would establish Wellesley College in Massachusetts, was born in the house, and Mary Tolford McMurphy and her niece Lucy Jane McMurphy ran Dartmouth's most popular eating club here from 1836 to 1900. A doubtful oral tradition had Daniel Webster rooming here in 1800, hence the name, but the real value of the place lies in its twentieth-century Colonial revivalism. After the college bought the house in 1900, it rented the place to antiques connoisseur Alice Van Leer Carrick and her husband Prescott Orde Skinner, a professor of French and Italian. Carrick spent the next half-century decorating and furnishing the house, using her extensive writings and lectures as a national authority on antiques to pitch Colonial design in general and this historic dwelling in particular as repositories of aesthetic virtue.

Carrick penned the opening salvo in the first issue of the magazine *Antiques* (1922), founded by former art professor and administrator Homer Eaton Keyes, and she specialized in giving friendly opinions on how to make any house more homelike. She wrote in 1922 of Webster Cottage:

> That's the real beauty of Colonial decoration properly valued. Superfluous furnishings seem a waste of ideas, and a desolation of bad taste. You observe that the whole scheme of my mantel decoration is restrained—a bust of Dante, four candle-sticks, and as many silhouettes. The central candlesticks are French, and at a Paris rag-fair cost two francs.

As the subject of two of Carrick's books, *Collector's Luck* (1919) and *The*

LALACS House

Next-to-Nothing House (1922), the cottage became a national beacon of the Colonial Revival movement. Carrick had to designate visiting hours for the tourists who wanted to see the house. The college moved Webster Cottage twice ahead of waves of development—once around 1927 to create a lawn for Silsby's northeast corner, and once in 1967 to make room for Bradley Hall, now the site of Kemeny Hall. The college lent the building to the town's historical society in 1968 for use as its headquarters.

Three houses for Phi Tau have occupied the same shrinking parcel of land in succession. Before today's organization was a coeducational society (1972) or a local fraternity (1956), it was a national fraternity known as Phi Sigma Kappa (1905) that occupied a nineteenth-century frame house on a generously proportioned lot. During the mid-1920s, however, the group substituted a brick fraternity house designed by Dudley Wells Redfield of the class of 1912 and sold one side of the lot for college expansion. Later still, the college supplied the present gambrel-roofed brick building (Wiemann Lamphere Architects, 2002–2003) in return for receiving the rear part of the property. The first new society house in sixty years displays eccentric fenestration that includes a pair of arched openings infilled with square windows on the front facade; the building's enclosed entrance porch is similarly self-effacing, indicating the priority of what goes on inside the building.

Alpha Theta (1940–1941) stands opposite Choate Road. Some of the house's foundation is left from a nineteenth-century frame house acquired by the organization when it was known as Theta Chi (1920). That predecessor building's unfortunate defining moment was a carbon monoxide leak that killed the nine students sleeping there in 1934 and prompted the group to demolish the house. The replacement building, also a side-gabled five-bay house, substitutes a Palladian window and a Tuscan entrance portico for the dominant Victorian gable that had characterized fraternities of the early twentieth century. The building's gable-ends, unusually, are of brick. In 1952, the group was the first on campus to renounce a racially exclusionary clause in the constitution of its national organization, a move that got it kicked out of the organization. The fraternity opened its rolls early to female members (1972–76, 1980) and remains a coeducational organization.

The Native American House (1852; F.P.O., 1994) is an "affinity house" that

The Native American House

reserves its living space for students interested in Native American culture. Dartmouth and its associated schools enrolled between 90 and 120 Native Americans during the first two centuries in Hanover, weakly upholding the obligation to furnish the education of Native American youth "in all liberal Arts and Sciences; and also of English Youth and any others." President John G. Kemeny recommitted the college to its charter in 1970, and Native enrollment would total more than 500 over the next twenty-five years. The college purchased this Gothic-influenced clapboard house in 1993 and expanded it as a Native American social center. The house originated as the commercial bakery of the early-nineteenth-century Smith Cracker & Candy Co., next door to the firm's candy factory to the south. The Smith family lived in a pair of houses farther down the street. After the company shifted production of its Dartmouth Chocolates and Hanover Crackers to a new factory in White River Junction, Vermont, in 1871, this house became a private residence and a fraternity house. The house was a bed-and-breakfast by the early 1950s under the name of Occom Lodge or the Occom Inn, which remained the last private business north of Wheelock Street when the school bought it.

A professor of mathematics and graphics in the Chandler School, Frank Asbury Sherman ('70), had Sherman House built on the corner in 1883. He might have designed it, since he was the architect of Chandler's extensive 1871 remodeling of Moor Hall and the construction of the Hanover Grade School (1877; 1896; demolished 1936). Sigma Phi Epsilon (1908) moved in a few years after Professor Sherman died in 1915. A 1922 update by Larson & Wells turned the slightly gingerbread frame cottage with jerkin-headed roofs into an upright half-timbered

Webster Cottage

Tudor house, a change large enough to illustrate a 1924 article on "Modernizing Old Buildings by Use of Stucco." Although the fraternity had Larson design a gambrel-roofed frame Colonial replacement during 1940, the war halted that plan and required the group to sell its house to the hospital in 1943. Under the name Sherman House, the building housed students in the growing Mary Hitchcock Memorial Hospital School of Nursing. The college acquired the place with the rest of the hospital and during 1997 renovated it as the academic headquarters of the Native American Studies Program.

The house at 38 North Main Street (1874; Haynes & Garthwaite, 2000–2001) has made the same polar shifts as its neighbors, from nurses' home to fraternity and back. Mrs. Abbie A. Pike built the two-and-a-half level side-gabled clapboard house and rented its rooms to professors, and, starting in 1906, to the School of Nursing. The school bought the house outright in 1911 and continued to call it Pike House. Delta Upsilon moved in soon after it formed in 1920 and sold the house back to the nurses' school around 1939 in order to move to Webster Avenue. The college eventually acquired Pike House and in 1999 made it an affinity house for students interested in the Latin-American, Latino, and Caribbean Studies program, calling it LALACS House. Adding a rear ell and large southern extension a few years later expanded the building's housing capacity.

The main block of the two-level clapboard Choate House (1786) was built for Sylvanus Ripley ('71) and originally stood two doors west of today's Webster Hall. As a tavern and residence it saw a number of owners of local prominence, although its namesake, the great orator Senator Rufus Choate of the class of 1819, was merely married there and never was one of the owners. The college did not acquire

the house and its early-nineteenth-century wings until 1910, a late step toward clearing out the Quadrangle north of the Green. Another seventeen years passed before the school moved the house to the present site of the Haldeman Center. Its residential use over, the building housed offices, including some of the Dartmouth Eye Institute. Around 1966, the school demolished another eighteenth-century house to create the building's present site on the corner of Choate Road (1917). The faculty club, a fraction of the mathematics department, and other organizations have occupied the building in succession since then.

LALACS House entrance

70. The Former Clark School

North Hall
Larson & Wells, 1922
Cutter/Shabazz Hall
Jens Fredrick Larson, 1938; F.P.O., 1996
The Asian Studies Center
Hudson & Ingram, 1951, 1957

Greek instructor Clifford P. Clark started a preparatory school in 1918 on a parcel of farmland south of the new Choate Road, not far from his house on Occom Ridge. Hanover had lacked a private preparatory academy since Moor's Charity School folded during the 1850s. Clark's two-year course began sending twelve to fifteen students each year to Dartmouth and a half-dozen elsewhere. During 1920, the school acquired Phineas Clement's old house at 32 North Main Street (1791), coincidentally Hanover's first schoolhouse when it was built facing the Green for Moor's Charity School. The Clark School used the building as a dormitory called Occom House, operating an eating club called Occom Club on the ground level that was open to Dartmouth students. (Dartmouth later renamed the house East Hall and demolished it in 1966). The Clark School also bought a house on the north corner of Main and Elm (1833; demolished 1966) and turned it into a dormitory called Elm House. The school put its athletic field on a large plot of farmland along Choate Road during 1921.

The Clark School's first new building was a gambrel-roofed clapboard dormitory for about fourteen boys and a faculty resident on Choate Road. The Clark School

Cutter/Shabazz Hall

called it Choate House after its site and intended to build three more houses like
it along the athletic field. Although both sides get an entrance portico, the more
elaborate enclosed portico is the one facing the grassy school side rather than
the street. The building's present name of North Hall reflects its position within
the Clark campus when Dartmouth acquired the group in 1953; as Dartmouth's
smallest regular dormitory, the building is obscure.

The Clark School built a gymnasium (now North Fairbanks) east of the Elm
Street corner, acquired a house on Webster Avenue, and reached its architectural
peak when it erected the three-level brick Alumni Hall (now Cutter/Shabazz) at
the head of its sports field. The side-gabled building was meant to blend with
Dartmouth's campus, and the Clark School hired the college architect to design it.
The building's copper-roofed cupola, which originally terminated in a weathervane,
typifies the architect's work and gives the building much in common with the
Lebanon Town Hall (Larson & Wells, 1923–24) or the White River Junction

railroad station (Jens Fredrick Larson, 1937). Shutters indicate that the upper levels contain dormitory rooms, but the round-arched openings of the ground level suggest a public function, in this case a large library and living room. The building's original program also included apartments for two teachers who would oversee the dormitory, and Dartmouth would put those spaces to use in an experimental program soon after it acquired the Clark campus. Even though Dartmouth had never attempted to house faculty with students for the benefit of the latter, the college installed a faculty member in the building in 1954 and employed varying degrees of selectivity to choose the students who would live in the building. Although the experiment with the former prep-school dormitory was fluid and impermanent, its lessons would influence the provision of faculty housing in the adjacent Choate Road Dormitories.

Dartmouth renamed Alumni Hall for the late trustee Victor Macomber Cutter ('03), who had led the New England Region of the New Deal–era National Resources Planning Board. Cutter was known best for his presidency of the United Fruit Company (1924–33), when the quasi-governmental corporation relied on local dictators to violently put down a number of massive labor strikes at its banana plantations throughout Central America. Cutter's name would prove controversial after 1970, when the college turned the building into the headquarters of the Afro-American Society (1966). The society commissioned a series of murals depicting the life of Malcolm X in the ground-level common rooms (Florian Jenkins, 1972), and students sought to rename the building the El Hajj Malik El Shabazz Temple. The college responded with a compromise: as Cutter Hall, the building would contain an affinity housing program called the El Hajj Malik El Shabazz Center for Intellectual Inquiry, dedicated by Dr. Betty Shabazz during 1993. An annual Thurgood Marshall Fellow directs the center, which is open to all students, in connection with the African and African-American Studies Program. The school added a diminutive frame ell in the style of Webster Cottage to the south end of Cutter/Shabazz in 1996 as the Marshall Fellow's official residence.

With the college squeezing from the south, the Clark School commissioned a design for a campus in West Lebanon, New Hampshire (Hudson & Ingram, 1948). It did not come to pass. The Clark School's last act of building turned out to be its construction of a Headmaster's House just prior to the retirements of the founder and the headmaster. A basic two-level side-gabled clapboard pile like its neighbors, the building housed college faculty, the Tucker Foundation, and other groups until the Asian Studies Center moved in during 1985. The Center provides rooms for eight students and a faculty member interested in Asian languages and cultures. During 1952, the Clark school merged with the Cardigan Mountain School, an institution founded by a Dartmouth-connected group in 1945 and then in possession of its own unbuilt master plan for its site in Canaan, New Hampshire, about nineteen miles' drive east of Hanover (Jens Fredrick Larson, 1945). Cardigan immediately sold the seven Clark buildings to Dartmouth.

71. The Choates

Little and Brown Halls
Campbell & Aldrich, 1956–58
Cohen and Bissell Halls
Campbell & Aldrich, 1956–58

The rectilinear cluster of dormitories atop the Clark School's Choate Road athletic field flowed directly from the typewriters of an energetic 1955 faculty committee. The committee attacked Dartmouth's existing dormitories for their long and noisy corridors and their perceived similarity to military barracks, proposing a switch to more intimate small-group accommodations. Each group of students would have the use of a specialized living room, leaving the adjacent bedrooms free for sleeping and studying. Faculty would live in apartments built into the complex and provide some moral education, an attempt to keep up with current educational trends and a reflection of the success of faculty apartments in the experimental Cutter Hall nearby. Other lessons left over from the prep school included the rule that having a main social room is important. Cutter Hall's social room, with its record player and fireplace, was said to have become a good place to entertain women.

The faculty committee met regularly with Dartmouth's chief designer to create the Choate Road dormitories. The college dropped Jens Larson as college architect after the war, and he moved his office to New York (1954) and then to Winston-Salem, North Carolina (1956), to design Wake Forest University. A different sort of designer replaced him as Dartmouth's architect, consulting out of a Boston office: Nelson Wilmarth Aldrich, who had joined with Walter E. Campbell around 1947 to form the successor to the firm of Hogg & Campbell. Campbell & Aldrich would become known for Modernist work at New England colleges, and their first buildings at Dartmouth were the ones to introduce the International Style to campus. The school paper wrote that with these first buildings of President John Sloan Dickey's tenure, Dartmouth was the last major school to adopt Modern architecture. The Federal Housing and Home Finance Agency loaned the school much of the cost of the Choate Road Dormitories.

Aldrich organized the quartet of three-level T-shaped flat-roofed dormitories into two identical pairs. Frames of white-painted steel beams infilled with brick formed the buildings' walls, organized by evenly-spaced window openings with white-painted metal spandrels. The buildings' main entrances, which were nearly hidden from view, gave access to the interior and its cinderblock-walled suites for eight or nine students. Little Hall opened first at the southeast corner of the complex

View alongside Little Hall toward freestanding social room and Brown Hall

and bore the name of the North Dakota banker and trustee Clarence Little ('81). In the northeast corner was the building named for Albert Oscar Brown ('78), a Manchester attorney and banker who, as governor, promoted New Hampshire as a vacationland and suggested that the 1920s highway along the west side of the state be named the Dartmouth College Highway. Cohen Hall, in the northwest corner, carries the name of New York judge William Cohen ('79) and is the place where the school housed the first seventy women to attend Dartmouth, all transfer students who arrived during 1969 before full coeducation in 1972. The school shifted George Bissell's name from the demolished Bissell Gymnasium to the dormitory in the southwest corner of the Choates.

Glass and steel bridges connected the dorms to a pair of raised pods containing student lounges. Half-hidden beneath each social pod was a building that the architects of the Space Age might have called a Faculty Living Unit—not a house but a flat-roofed three-bedroom faculty apartment, freestanding but indistinguishable from the rest of the complex. Each apartment featured a professorial study with its own student entrance.

The Choates failed to radically reorient student social relations. Students liked the pair of raised lounges for their size, but an early survey showed that only one sixth of the small living rooms in the suites contained signs of student life such as radios and furniture. Another sixth of the rooms stood nearly barren after students liberated most of their furniture. The school abandoned the suite idea and turned the living rooms into bedrooms. Up to two professors at a time continued to live in the Choates for about twenty-five years, but the trustees generally declined to burden the dormitory system with the costs of more faculty apartments. Although the school considered expanding the Choates during the late 1990s, it committed instead to investing in buildings that were meant for the long term and began planning to replace the Choates. The buildings' only legacy might be the phenomenon of "Choate bonding," a conviviality that results from sharing a friendly neighborhood bathroom within one of the buildings' isolated wings. The school has sought to emulate the effect in later dormitories.

72. The Dean's House
1917

James Parmelee Richardson ('99), the Parker Professor of Law and Political Science, commissioned the house on the corner at 13 Choate Road. Aquinas House acquired the place about six years after Richardson died in 1947. A swap put the house into the hands of Dartmouth during 1961, and the school made the house the official residence of the Dean of the College.

The office of the dean emerged during 1893 and took its archetypal form until Craven Laycock ('96), who took office during 1913 after two years of assistantship. The stern Yorkshireman dispensed enough kindly advice and painful truth about students' academic performances over the next twenty years to merit a bronze bust outside the Tower Room in Baker Library (Nancy Cox-McCormack, 1931). Dean Laycock also had the honor, unknown at the time, of suspending Theodor Seuss Geisel ('25) from extracurricular activities after an alleged gin party in Geisel's room: Geisel's subsequent cartoons for the *Jack-O-Lantern* used the name "Seuss" for the first time, and he would add the title "Dr." later. The dean's job has expanded to include supervising the educational integrity of almost all of the experiences that students organize outside the classroom, including athletics, clubs, and dormitories.

73. Montgomery House
Larson & Wells, 1924; O.P.D.C. 2007

The house now reserved for visiting Montgomery Fellows was built for the quirky and innovative Adelbert Ames, Jr., a lawyer, artist, and scientist who helped design the pioneering ski tramway at Oak Hill and proposed the arts center south of the Green. Ames is known best for developing the optically illusory Ames Window, the Ames Chair, and especially the Ames Room, in which visual cues make people appear taller or shorter depending on which corner they occupy (1946). The focus of his energies from 1921 onward was a professorship in the Department of Research in Physiological Optics, an organization that he turned into the Dartmouth Eye Institute in 1936. Ames found early success by discovering the eye condition of aniseikonia; while patenting haploscopes and horopters, the institute welcomed researchers and patients from around the world. It moved into a group of buildings at the corner of Main Street and Webster Avenue, and Jens Larson designed a headquarters for it during the early 1930s. Although the Institute received Rockefeller help and a popularity boost from a 1939 *Cosmopolitan* article, it did not manage to erect its building. President Hopkins was wary of keeping specialized research institutes within the college, and Ames's Eye Institute eventually collapsed in 1947.

The two-level brick house at 12 Rope Ferry Road hosted a variety of theorists and philosophers under Ames's ownership. When Harle and Kenneth Montgomery '25 decided during the mid-1970s to establish a fund that would bring eminent scholars and practitioners to interact with the college, Ames's house had the refinement required. Since then, the Montgomery Endowment has made the house into a steady focal point of the school's intellectual life, a presence that trustee David Shipler ('64) called "Dartmouth's quiet institution."

1. Donlyn Lyndon, "Balance and Skew: The Architectural Artistry of R.M. Kliment & Frances Halsband Architects," in Stephen Dobney, ed., *R.M. Kliment & Frances Halsband Architects: Selected and Current Works* (Australia: The Images Publishing Group Pty. Ltd., 1998), 9.

2. Samson Occom to Eleazar Wheelock (July 24, 1771), quoted in Bernd Peyer, "The Betrayal of Samson Occom," *Dartmouth Alumni Magazine* 91, no. 3 (November 1998), 36.

3. John Charles Olmsted (notes of visit September 7, 1899), Olmsted Associates Papers, Job File 1385, Library of Congress.

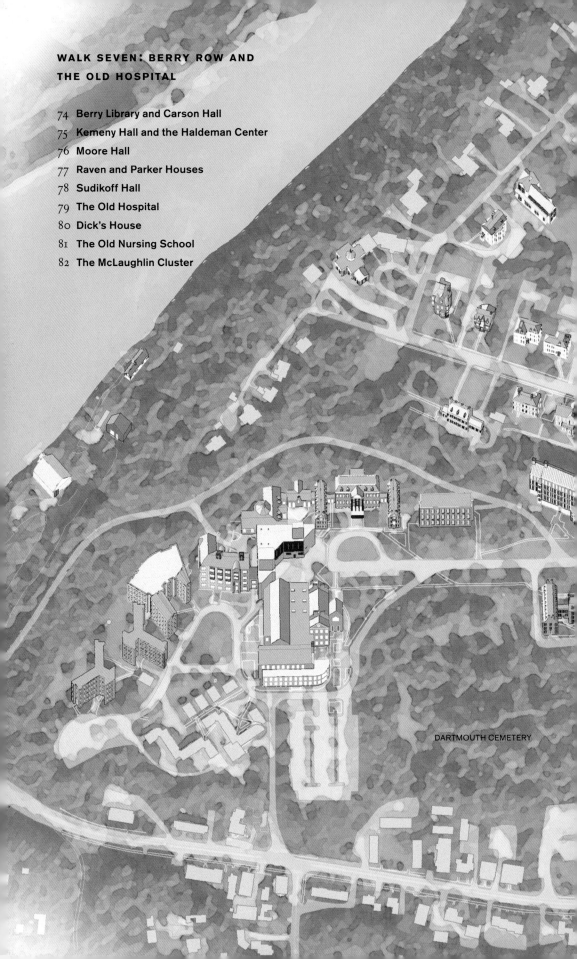

WALK SEVEN: BERRY ROW AND THE OLD HOSPITAL

DARTMOUTH CEMETERY

CLEMENT ROAD

ROPE FERRY ROAD

81

80

79

CHOATE ROAD

82

MAYNARD STREET

82

76

77

77

78

WEBSTER AVENUE

75

74

TUCK MALL

THE GREEN

On the Grounds of the Old Hospital

Through most of the twentieth century, the building at the academic heart of Dartmouth marked the physical periphery of the campus. A few buildings rose in Baker Library's backyard during the 1960s, but they were the only academic structures in this near hinterland. Beyond Baker and Elm Street lay a wide urban block lined mostly with houses and filled mostly with parking lots, its center forming a shallow ravine that ran northward to Maynard Street. Most of the block belonged to the Dartmouth-Hitchcock Medical Center, which lined both sides of Maynard Street, at the top of the ravine.

The hospital made the momentous decision in 1984 that it would leave town, and in 1989 it sold its Hanover property to Dartmouth. The school now had the potential to recenter its academic core at the true physical center of its campus, and it finally was able to follow the imperative to create a contiguous campus ligature running all the way up to its Medical School, originally marooned behind the hospital. The purchase completely reframed the potential utility and beauty of the varied hospital complex itself, a group that Dartmouth finally took over during 1992. The complex included the former campus of a small nursing school, a collection of frame houses, a heavily altered 1890s pavilion hospital, and a huge eight-level Modernist tower built on the original hospital lawn during the 1960s. The purchase also recast the college's 1960s buildings behind Baker as impediments to any campus space that might emerge within the block north of Elm Street, and much of the school's planning would be driven by the need to find new homes for the occupants of the doomed Bradley and Gerry Halls and the Kiewit Computation Center.

Just finishing a major addition to the Thayer School of Engineering, the firm of Venturi, Scott Brown & Associates considered the possibilities for the hospital property. Denise Scott Brown said that acquiring the hospital property "was as if the lake dried up in Chicago," and her 1989 portfolio of options led the school to select a bold and purposeful plan in 1994.[1] The selected scheme proposed to create a novel narrow quadrangular space in the ravine between two parallel rows of relatively high buildings that would focus on a pair of gateway buildings to the north. The plan would leave the existing houses around the edges of the block and still provide considerable academic space at the heart of campus in seven or more new buildings. Scott Brown acknowledged that all plans are modified or abandoned, however, and this one met the same fate as Dartmouth's last experiment with a "quadrangle" a century before north of the Green.

After taking the strong initial steps of erecting one building at either end of the proposed ravine quadrangle, the school succumbed to long-held and well-founded doubts about the scale and density of the plan and abandoned it. A 2001

Berry Library's main corridor to Baker Library

competition to redesign the ravine produced a modestly practical proposal by Moore Ruble Yudell that reflexively sliced the Scott Brown double row along its length. The resulting one-sided east-facing figure, called Berry Row, is analogous to Dartmouth Row. A landscape design by Richard Burck Associates (2007) cemented the informal pedestrian routes that ran the block and established an axial central path focused on an arc-shaped series of stone-walled terraces at the near end. Although much of the zone is more notable for its potential than for what has been built on it, the work so far already makes difficult to imagine how the campus could have neglected this place so near its center for so long.

74. Berry Library and Carson Hall

Berry Library
Venturi, Scott Brown & Associates with Shepley Bulfinch Richardson & Abbott, 1998–2000
Carson Hall
Venturi, Scott Brown & Associates, 2001–2002

Berry Library is a major addition that finally put a face on the back of Baker Library, reorienting the building toward the new academic precinct that was emerging to its rear. The original unpolished rear facade of Baker was the place where its designer expected expansion to take place, and the old library's last major addition

Berry Library colonnade

Berry Library, with Baker behind

was a flat-roofed and factory-like rear range that Jens Larson designed in 1941. The school traded some distant sports fields to the Town in return for permission to close Elm Street, which ran behind the library, and by the summer of 1997 the stage was set for the long-awaited expansion of the library.

The release of the designs for Berry Library provided Dartmouth with its biggest aesthetic controversy since the revelation of the preliminary images of the Hopkins Center thirty-five years earlier. This time it was not alumni who were particularly vocal but faculty members. The college's architectural establishment inside and outside its Design Review Committee attacked many aspects of the building, especially what seemed to be the architect's claim that he had based the design of Berry Library on the idea of the New England mill.

Venturi had written for years about noble buildings whose relatively dull exteriors, relieved by simple fanfares of decoration applied at their openings, indicated their simple and unitary natures—stacks of long and narrow open-plan spaces divided by partitions, like the nineteenth-century buildings of Dartmouth Row. Invoking the general typological ideas of "the mill," "the loft," or "the factory" signaled a conservative argument for flexible timelessness, an appreciation for a building's total cost of ownership over time; it was also meant as a criticism of the self-involved artist who is more concerned with originality than practicality. Dartmouth's library collection had occupied two of the generic academic lofts of Dartmouth Row before it moved to a purpose-built structure, Wilson Hall, whose very specialization reduced the

Carson Hall classroom

building's utility for the inevitable succeeding functions. Of course Venturi's mention of "the mill" did not refer specifically to the rugged Italianate mills of Lebanon or Manchester, and those exemplars of the Enlightenment ending up unfairly losing out in the whole debate.

The trustees declined to ask the architect to change his design, and the result, while imperfect, is far from the terrible pile that some predicted. If Berry is bulky and out of scale with its neighbors, the blame lies with its program, which required that much space because the school simply had that many books. Berry Library extends Baker directly to the rear, where it meets a crossbar that is angled to face toward the anticipated quadrangle in the ravine. The middle levels of the building project outward, and as the firm's Thayer School addition predicted, the library's recessed upper level terminates in a close-cropped side-gabled roof. Even the metal-framed glass box of the bridge leading back to Baker's seventh level had an ancestor in the clerestory of Venturi's Thayer School project.

Berry's front facade is relatively mundane. Horizontal limestone bands stretch across the building's fourth story, and a vertical stripe of stone marks a bend in the building. White-painted metal mullions divide the building's rectangular windows, giving an overall feeling of thinness. It is a background building. The one spark of mannerist invention is the freestanding sculptural colonnade that runs the full width of the long main facade, a primitive limestone-faced double-decker henge that screens the building's lower levels. Ostensibly a routemarker for cross-campus pedestrians, its main purpose as communicated through the presentation drawings seemed to be to indulge Venturi's love of supergraphic Sixties pop art by providing

Carson Hall Main Street entrance

a place for the names of the great authors, in fine *bibliotheque* tradition. As built, however, the entablature bears only the last name of the chief donor, John W. Berry ('44). Berry led the company that his father established in 1910 to print the timetables for interurban trains in Dayton, Ohio; the L.M. Berry Company later went on to create the Yellow Pages. George W. Berry ('66), who studied under Kemeny and went on to develop software, also is a namesake.

Berry's white and gray interior, accented with wood tones, is slightly more whimsical than its exterior. Lighted signs feature typography that imitates the letterforms of the dot-matrix printer, advertising all of the libraries on campus. A dashed center line divides the floor of the skylit main corridor, a route that the architects called "the street through the building" and a place where each major library service has some street frontage. Along with holding about forty percent of the library's books, the building took on functions that had outgrown Baker, from the Jones Media Center to the Map Room. Novel spaces include a set of classrooms, a large lecture hall, and the ground-level Novack Café, which must substitute for a great collegiate reading room in the Age of Espresso.

The short end of the building's main range is actually a slightly later wing known as Carson Hall, after the Carson family and Judy and Russell Carson ('65), a trustee and private investment firm cofounder. The decision not to bring Carson Hall's gable end to Main Street initially seemed odd, but the composition works superbly now that adjacent buildings have sprung up to provide a frame for it. Carson was built for the history department, although its floors are reinforced to hold book stacks. Amphitheater classrooms occupy the basement, and the ground level is the home of the Kiewit Computation Center, which carried on President Kemeny's goal of providing universal access to computing. Kiewit managed the pioneering Dartmouth Time-Sharing System (1964–99), helped install the campus-wide data network (1983–84), produced the influential email program that became a mainstay of campus life (BlitzMail, 1988–2004), supplied students with Macintosh computers before and after the school made them mandatory (1991), and created the school's integrated data-phone-television wireless network (2001–2006).

Gallery joining Haldeman and Kemeny   *Kemeny Hall stair*

75. Kemeny Hall and the Haldeman Center
Moore Ruble Yudell with Bruner/Cott & Associates, 2004–2006

The most interesting building designed by Moore Ruble Yudell on campus is the
product of a demanding site. Several disparate waves of development preceded
it on the corner of Main and Elm, starting with the houses of a nineteenth-century
neighborhood and continuing during the late 1920s with a formal ensemble of
Choate House, Webster Cottage, and the Clement Greenhouse. The two houses
moved across the street to make way for Bradley and Gerry Halls (Edgar H. and
Margaret K. Hunter, 1961; demolished 2007), a pair of International Style towers
designed by the town's pioneering Modernists. Bradley and Gerry had rock-
faced granite end walls that provided excellent climbing, but their front facades
featured large panels of blue, green, and white that encouraged the nickname
of "the Shower Towers." Bradley in particular was notable because it housed
the mathematics department's GE-235 and Datanet-30 computers, with which
professors John G. Kemeny and Thomas E. Kurtz and their students developed the
pioneering computer language BASIC in 1964. On the corner stood the bunkerlike
one-story concrete-roofed Kiewit Computation Center (1966–67, Skidmore
Owings & Merrill; demolished 2000). These experiences with Modernism prompted

Main Street entrances of Kemeny and Haldeman

a stylistic reaction in Kemeny/ Haldeman and also shaped its footprint.

The personality of Kemeny/ Haldeman is split along urbanistic lines as much as programmatic ones. Main Street's prevailing domestic iconography mandates a height of two levels above a basement on the building's west facade, topped by a conventional side-gabled roof clad in copper. Here, the building's shallow C-shaped footprint features a giant-scale distylar portico on each arm, marking the entrances of Kemeny Hall on the north and the Haldeman Center on the south. Several of the building's spandrels display decorative brick patterns arranged in the Fibonacci Sequence.

Things change around the back of the building, where the ground slopes away into Berry Row. The wings are of unequal lengths here, each featuring a short octagonal tower engaged at its gable end—a form with a local precedent in Rollins Chapel. The ground-level lounge in the base of Kemeny's tower is the kind of space that was particularly important to the mathematics department, which was split among a trio of buildings for years. The shallower Haldeman Center wing was built to host a trio of college institutes focused on multidisciplinary activities: the Ethics Institute (1981), the John Dickey Center for International Understanding (1982), and the Fannie and Alan Leslie '30 Center for the Humanities (1999). The Center is named for Barbara and Charles E. Haldeman, Jr., '70, a trustee and Putnam Investments head.

76. Moore Hall
Robert A.M. Stern & Associates, 1997–99

The headquarters of the psychology department speaks to the creative possibilities of the early 1990s, when the school was examining a variety of ways to build on the hospital property. Denise Scott Brown specified that the quadrangular mall south of Maynard Street should be lined with five-level academic halls, each with a stepped-back top level terminating in a side-gabled roof. The school gave the larger but later

Moore Hall, Berry Row entrance

Berry Library project to Scott Brown's firm and asked Stern's firm to design the first building on the quadrangle. The L-shaped Moore Hall began as "a contextual building awaiting its context," according to Stern's firm. The plan for the interior of the block changed almost as soon as Moore opened, and the building was left to face Raven Home, instead of an expected counterpart of similar scale.

Although its program required a large volume, Moore remains a member of Dartmouth's architectural family by adopting its simple palette of substantial materials, mainly granite, red brick, limestone, and copper. Its more elaborate street facade follows the Classical base-middle-top disposition, with spandrel panels allowing the middle levels to read as a single story. The entrance facade on Berry Row focuses on a shallow two-level stone temple-front of almost Egyptian mystery. Above is a round-arched opening whose traditional Georgian tracery has been pushed out to create a projecting beacon for the building's library. A replacement for Filene Auditorium, which originally connected Bradley and Gerry Halls, lies beneath Moore's plaza; the building also contains the school's Center for Cognitive Neuroscience and the Brain Imaging Laboratory. The building memorializes Florence Bennett Moore and Lansing Porter Moore of the class of 1937.

77. Raven and Parker Houses

Raven House
Jens Fredrick Larson, 1945–47
Parker House
1917; ca. 1985

Now an academic department headquarters, the building originally built as the Winifred Raven Convalescent Home was given to the hospital by Anton Adolph Raven, a hospital trustee and long-time English professor, in memory of his wife. Raven Home's twenty-nine beds were for patients who needed assistance short of full hospital care, and the building also had an apartment for a caretaker couple. A connecting element joined the building to what is now Sudikoff, while on the west a colonnade joined it to Fowler House (1896; demolished 1992). The college intended to put a mathematics building in Raven's place as an answer to Moore Hall, but the revision of the Berry Row master plan gave Raven a reprieve and allowed the college to renovate the building during 2003 as the first freestanding home of the Education Department. Federal Education Secretary Rod Paige called Raven "an inspiration, a citadel of learning," and the building's robust hospital-era elevator tower does give it something of the literal appearance of a fortress. With its gable end to the street, the long, two-level red-brick building continues to hold up its side of the gateway to Berry Row.

The first building to face into Dartmouth's twenty-first century campus space does so unwittingly, having arrived while the ravine still contained only parking lots. Dr. George H. Parker D.M.S ('95) originally built the traditional two-level clapboard house on College Street where Bildner Hall now stands, part of a small row of houses that eventually would make way for the hospital and the Medical School. The hospital bought the house during the mid-1960s to rent to employees and moved it in the mid-1980s to expand the hospital parking lot. By planting the building near the Mental Health Center (now Sudikoff Hall), the hospital could use the house for psychiatrists' offices, and the college continued its office function after acquiring it.

78. Sudikoff Hall

Ellerbe Architects, 1968–69; R.M. Kliment & Frances Halsband, 1993;
Fleck & Lewis, 2003–2004

The red-brick Sudikoff Laboratory for the Computer Sciences began as the Dartmouth Mental Health Center, invested by the hospital with a kind of miniature urbanism to create a self-contained three-level hill town. A variety of recesses and projections, monitors and ridges provide the L-shaped building with visual

Sudikoff Hall, Berry Row entrance

interest, while the occasional white marble spandrels were meant to communicate with the architects' Faulkner House across the street, which had similar panels of green marble. The Mental Health Center focused on providing homelike spaces of an unthreatening scale for up to twenty-eight resident patients, with doctors and nurses expected to wear everyday clothing. The hospital also installed a novel closed-circuit television network for counseling patients in their home towns. The resulting building was more humane than the projects the college was erecting at the time.

The 1989 hospital acquisition obviated Dartmouth's need to build a curving computer science addition that Kliment & Halsband had designed in 1987 for Bradley Hall, and the architects turned their attention here. Their extensive renovation of the mental health center sought to wrest the building from one campus and to place it in another. While the original entrance still faces north, a flat-roofed quadristylar portico of square columns clad in granite shelters a new entrance on the ravine, facing Berry Row. The designers applied a frank and slightly whimsical high-tech Modernism to revive the building's interior, reveling in overhead cable channels and utilitarian wall sconces, making the first freestanding home of the computer science department.

A decade after the renovation, the department expanded its space by half in order finally to rescue the last of its members from Bradley Hall. The contrasting white clapboard traditionalism of the ell attached to the building's south end is a nod to the nineteenth-century houses of College Street and the adjacent White Church. The building and its addition carry the name of Joyce and Jeffrey Sudikoff ('77), a communications mogul and hockey team owner.

79. The Old Hospital

1 Rope Ferry Road (formerly the Hitchcock Clinic)
Jens Fredrick Larson, 1938; F.P.O., 1993
3 Rope Ferry Road (formerly the Mary Hitchcock Memorial Hospital Women's Ward)
Rand & Taylor, 1889–93; 1913; 1937; F.P.O., 1995
5 Rope Ferry Road (formerly the Hitchcock Wards)
John A. Fox, 1912–13; F.P.O., 1993

Plaque on wall of 3 Rope Ferry Road

The row of connected buildings along Rope Ferry Road is a remnant of the Mary Hitchcock Memorial Hospital, which opened in 1893 and grew almost continually afterward. It attracted a variety of related institutions with functional and architectural links, including a contemporary nurses' school, the college infirmary, an independent physicians' clinic, and the Medical School's new campus of the 1950s. Dartmouth bought the whole complex and demolished most of it in 1995.

Hiram Hitchcock was a New Hampshireman who joined with a pair of partners to establish the Fifth Avenue Hotel in New York City in 1859. Within about thirteen years, Hitchcock was able to retire with his wife Mary Maynard Hitchcock to Professor Fairbanks's Main Street estate, with its flamboyant Victorian mansion. The couple traveled while Hiram pursued his interests in exploration and archeology, also becoming a bank president, state legislator, and trustee of Dartmouth and the state college. Mary died in 1887, and two years later Hiram Hitchcock donated a hospital complex to the town's fledgling hospital organization.

The Mary Hitchcock Memorial Hospital originally comprised four distinct pavilions, each built to house a different function. The use of the pavilion form by a hospital emerged most directly from the model of the influential Johns Hopkins Hospital in Baltimore (1877–85), an institution whose director declared—while at the Fifth Avenue Hotel—that "[t]he clinical unit of a hospital is the exact counterpart of one of the subdivisions of any great hotel."[2] The Boston architects of the M.H.M.H. had designed similar institutions in the northeast, including the Bancroft

Former hospital buildings, 3 and 5 Rope Ferry Road

Building "for Lady Patients" at the Concord State Insane Asylum and the large State Asylum for the Insane in Waterbury, Vermont. They focused their domestic complex in Hanover on a three-level central administration block containing a mosaic-floored entrance rotunda as well as the hospital dining room and nurses' quarters. Arcaded corridors to the east and west led to domed pavilions for male and female patients, respectively. Behind the men's ward, a conservatory led to a grandly domed surgical theater that featured a special side entrance for students, oriented toward the Medical School. Of the elements of this original complex, only the western or women's ward survives.

The pace of the hospital's expansion through the twentieth century foreshadowed its departure from Hanover. By 1907, the hospital was having to put tents on its lawn to house patients. More beds became available in the Hitchcock Wards, which mirrored the position of the surgical theater. Expansion during the late 1920s and early 1930s created a need for extensive master plans by Curtin & Riley and Jens Fredrick Larson during the mid-1940s, which led in turn to a 1947 gift in memory of Edward Daniels Faulkner. The broad Modernist tower of Faulkner House (Ellerbe Architects, 1950–52, 1967–72; demolished 1995) occupied the entire front lawn of the old hospital, creating an eight-level palisade on Maynard Street. Although modulated and stepped back, the building was more alien to the prevailing scale of the town than anything ever built in Hanover. After expanding into buildings across Maynard Street, the hospital built its last major addition, the Norris Cotton Cancer Center (1973), adjoining Faulkner House. Planners were pointing to the problems of traffic and parking, and the renamed Dartmouth-Hitchcock Medical

Center (1973) took its last patient in 1991 before it moved to the suburbs.

Early on, the hospital had a difficult time retaining physicians in Hanover, especially after the Medical School dropped clinical training from its curriculum in 1914. Dr. John Bowler ('15), D.M.S ('17) joined the hospital's other four physicians in 1927 to create a pioneering mostly-rural group practice called the Hitchcock Clinic. Instead of practicing out of their home offices, the doctors shared space in the hospital. Uniquely, the clinic formed not only the exclusive physician contingent of the hospital but also the teaching staff of the Medical School and the staff of the college infirmary. The organization is credited with reversing the drain on talent and eventually became successful enough to have the college architect design a headquarters adjoining the hospital. Now numbered 1 Rope Ferry Road, the building mainly held offices and reception rooms, since the X-ray machines and other pieces of equipment the clinic shared were located in the hospital. The clinic expanded into Faulkner House when it opened in 1952, and it was the Hanover Planning Board's 1982 denial of permission to build a new clinic building north of the Medical School that eventually prompted the entire D.H.M.C. to leave town. As the Dartmouth-Hitchcock Clinic (1999), the group remains one of the country's oldest and largest multispecialty group practices and has opened more than a half-dozen branches around Vermont and New Hampshire. Its old building now houses offices.

The ten-bed women's ward of the old hospital, now known as 5 Rope Ferry Road, is the only part of the 1893 building remaining. Despite the architects' concern for scientific rationalism, they gave the hospital a domestic appearance that seemed appropriate for its function. At the time, hospitals were still competing against the home as the appropriate place to convalesce. The designers modulated the building's scale and massing of the large complex to fit it into the village with a stylish Renaissance note. This flanking ward, like its mirror-image counterpart on the east side of the hospital, adopted the footprint of an attenuated octagonal figure with a rectangular service block behind it. Like the rest of the hospital, the wing was built of yellow-gray Pompeiian bricks and topped with a Guastavino-domed roof originally clad in light-red Spanish tiles. Terra-cotta ornament made a significant appearance in the form of pilasters, capitals, and other elements. A plaque of Vermont marble from the demolished Faulkner House now occupies a prominent wall on the building's exterior, relating a history of the hospital. Following the demolition of the rest of the hospital, the building became the office of the dean of the Medical School and the school's admissions office. Comfortable leather chairs have replaced the iron-framed hospital beds that once encircled the ward's central fireplace beneath the dome.

Hiram's cousin Dawn L. Hitchcock expanded the hospital's capacity by more than half when she gave a building behind the women's ward, now 5 Rope Ferry Road. Boston architect John A. Fox designed the building as part of his extensive

Dick's House

hospital-design practice, originally specifying a small ward for men on the ground level, children's and maternity wards on the second level, and a dining room in the basement. During 1955, renovations in accordance with the ideas of hospital surgeon Dr. William T. Mosenthal created a "special care unit" to segregate patients on the basis of their need for acute care rather than their particular ailments, thus creating arguably the nation's first intensive care unit. The unit influenced many others and carries on its operation in the replacement hospital, still one of the country's only multidisciplinary ICUs. After the college acquired the building, it installed offices for Dick's House and studios for the Facilities Planning Office (later the Office of Planning, Design & Construction), the design house that created the two-and-a-half level stucco-finished connector that joins the Hitchcock Wards to the infirmary.

80. Dick's House
Jens Fredrick Larson, 1926–27; Fleck & Lewis, 2001

During the late-1920s golden age of building that culminated in Baker Library, no building received more attention per square foot than the college infirmary, Dick Hall's House. Richard Drew Hall of the class of 1927, the son of trustee and AT&T executive Edward Kimball Hall ('92), was a sophomore when he died of polio during 1924. His parents proposed an infirmary as a memorial, with Jens Larson drawing up the plans and the college buying land for the building between the nurses' school and the hospital. Dick's classmates laid the cornerstone during the fall of their junior year.

The school had long needed an infirmary. After the College Mills on Mink Brook served as pest houses during smallpox outbreaks of the eighteenth century, the one-time agricultural dormitory of Allen Hall, behind New Hampshire Hall, was similarly meant to isolate illness more than to cure it. Edward Hall himself had a broken nose set by a doctor he met walking down the street after a football game, since there was no infirmary at the time. Even after the Mary Hitchcock Memorial Hospital opened, it was not seen as an appropriate place for ordinary student illnesses or injuries.

The goal that drove the building was that of presenting an impression that was domestic rather than medical or even merely institutional. "It is our hope that the boys will come to feel that 'going up to Dick's house' is the next best thing to going to their own homes," wrote Edward Hall.[3] To convey the atmosphere of a home, the patrons banished white paint, white furniture, the use of room numbers, or the name "the Infirmary." In their place would be varied color palettes, idiosyncratic Colonial Revival furnishings, and rooms named for presidents or friends of the college. A raft of objects loaded with sentiment greeted anyone who entered the building between its welcoming arms. The doorstep, inscribed "1784," came from the original Dartmouth Hall; the eagle door knocker (1805) allegedly came from a lamppost in the Place de L'Étoile in Paris; the "Scenic America" wallpaper in the reception hall depicted idealized scenes of the 1840s. The student living room at the heart to the building featured a portrait of Dick and a desk donated by the Jack-O-Lantern humor magazine. Admiral Byrd gave a small flag flown at the South Pole, while family and friends gave the books in the library, each with a bookplate from Dick's House and a donor's inscription. Along with the forty upstairs infirmary beds, the building contained rooms for parents, nurses, and the house mother, whose job it was to act as hostess and maintain the cheery atmosphere. Just in case, a ground-level passage joined the building to the Hitchcock Wards next door.

After Edward Hall retired, the family moved to the nearby house at 35 Rope Ferry Road (Adden, Parker, Clinch & Crimp, 1930) and maintained an interest in Dick's House. The hospital's departure allowed the college to expand its infirmary into the former Hitchcock Ward. Dick's House still deals with students' medical complaints and retains much of the atmosphere of the idealized Colonial "home" as it was imagined during the 1920s.

81. The Old Nursing School

11 Rope Ferry Road (formerly the Billings–Lee Nurses' Home)
Larson & Wells, 1920–1921
37 Dewey Field Road (formerly the '37 Building)
Jens Fredrick Larson, 1936–37
50 Dewey Field Road (formerly the '50 Building)
Curtin & Riley, 1949–50

The hospital's Training School for Nurses, a Hiram Hitchcock benefaction that started operating in 1893, initially housed its students inside the hospital as well as in the houses of the patients whom the students served. After expanding its program from two to three years during 1905 and shifting its curriculum to emphasize academic training over apprenticeship, the school started renting and buying houses near the corner of College and Maynard Streets. The school also built three buildings of its own, beginning with a three-level white clapboard dormitory erected with gifts from the Billings and Lee families. The thirty-seven-bed building is the first part of the medical complex to face west and has much in common with its smart and domestic Rope Ferry Road neighbors. Yet the building's simple rectangular footprint, flat roof, and regular fenestration indicate unmistakably that its origins are institutional. A two hundred-foot tunnel connected the building to the hospital complex behind it.

A large fundraising drive during the mid-1930s expanded the hospital in several directions and placed an addition behind Billings-Lee. Forty-eight nursing students moved into the '37 Building, helping expand the school's enrollment. The T-shaped brick building substitutes heavy masonry walls for the frame construction of the school's first building, its sloping site allowing it to stand three levels above a basement. When it opened, the hall contained novel social spaces such as a men's lounge and a sunbathing deck.

The Modernist brick addition to the '37 Building gave up trying to appear Georgian, although it still features a roof parapet and divided-light windows. Along with living quarters and social spaces, the four-level '50 Building finally brought classrooms and offices to the school's campus. The nurses' school closed in 1980, and today its buildings contain college offices.

82. The McLaughlin Cluster

Berry, Bildner, and Rauner Halls
Moore Ruble Yudell with Bruner/Cott & Associates, 2004–2006
Byrne II, Goldstein, and Thomas Halls
Moore Ruble Yudell with Bruner/Cott & Associates, 2004–2006
The Class of '53 Commons

*Moore Ruble Yudell with Bruner/
Cott & Associates, 2007–2009*

Bildner Hall, with Rauner Hall on left

Architect Charles Moore reintroduced the idea of a campus as a kind of town to American architecture before he established the firm of Moore Ruble Yudell in Santa Monica during the mid-1970s. Although Moore left for Texas in 1984, the firm continued to explore city planning as well as architecture, and Dartmouth selected the firm's entry in a 2001 competition to redesign Berry Row and beyond. The firm's dormitory group north of Maynard Street was the concluding flourish in the Student Life Initiative that President Wright pushed during the late 1990s as a way to recommit the school to its support of students' activities outside the classroom, in this case by handling part of the housing crunch that plagued the school at the time. The college named the group for the late David T. McLaughlin ('54), Tu ('55), whose presidency of Dartmouth from 1981 to 1987 was shorter than any since the 1820s but exhibited stellar fundraising and a construction boom of its own. Businessman McLaughlin was criticized for displaying the leadership style of a CEO, but that is what he was: after Dartmouth, he would go on to run everything from Toro Manufacturing to the Red Cross to the Aspen Institute.

The eminently inhabitable dormitory cluster comprises two building trios that adopt C-shaped footprints, rather like casual versions of the Gold Coast of the late 1920s, and frame a grassy multifaceted urban space between them. The buildings' gabled roofs feature off-center ridges marked by stocky ventilators as well as partially-glazed brick end "chimneys." Careful limits rule the choice of materials: patterned brick clads the main block of each building, while the multilevel connectors and other subsidiary elements are rendered in white. Granite appears in alternating rock-faced and smooth-faced square columns at the entrances. Without recalling any particular local building, the group's Classicism and its insistence on fostering a sense of community make it a better fit than any dormitory built here in

The McLaughlin Cluster, with Sudikoff Hall and Baker Tower in the distance

sixty-five years or more.

The eastern group differs in its inclusion of an apartment for a programming director. Its three buildings are named for John W. Berry Sr. ('44); Joan and Allen Bildner ('47) Tu ('48), a supermarket executive; and Diana M. and Bruce V. Rauner ('78). The western trio contains an apartment for a graduate assistant and features the cluster's projecting social room, a memorial to Samson Occom. These buildings bear the names of Debbie and Jack Thomas ('74), the C.E.O. of firms that produce money-handling equipment; Dorothy and Jerome Goldstein ('54), an investment banker; and Dorothy and John J. Byrne, Jr.

The Class of 1953 Dining Commons terminates the axis of Berry Row to the south with its glassy central tower. This is the first dining hall the college has ever built more than a few yards from the Green. A flat-roofed colonnaded portico and an off-center entrance face the Burck-designed lawn in front of the building, a space that had been the site of Faulkner House and, before that, the lawn of the

Rendering of '53 Commons, with Thomas Hall at right

nineteenth-century hospital. The latitudinal main dining room at the front of the building is overlooked by a novel social space for graduate students at the second level. When it opened, the building also contained an upstairs headquarters for the Office of Residential Life, a bureau originally established in the basement of Parkhurst Hall during the early 1980s to make dormitories friendlier to coeducation and implement the Cluster system.

1. Denise Scott Brown, quoted in Grace Shackman, "Master Architects/Master Plan," *Michigan Today* (Spring 1998), available at http://www.umich.edu/~newsinfo/MT/98/Spr98/mt12s98.html (viewed August 14, 2007).
2. Dr. William Oster, quoted in Sherry H. Olson, *Baltimore: The Building of an American City* (Baltimore, Md.:Johns Hopkins University Press, 1997), 237.
3. Edward K. Hall, quoted in Eugene F. Clark, "Dick's House," *Dartmouth Alumni Magazine* 20, No. 1 (November 1927), 20.

Occom Commons in Goldstein Hall

WALK EIGHT: THE TOWN

TUCK DRIVE

DARTMOUTH CEMETERY

WEST WHEELOCK STREET

WEST STREET

SCHOOL STREET

COLLEGE PARK

THE GREEN

WHEELOCK STREET

CROSBY STREET

SOUTH PARK STREET

LEBANON STREET

CURRIER PLACE

SOUTH STREET

SUMMER STREET

91

90

90

90

90

92

92

93

93

93

94

92

Hanover, New Hampshire

Sometimes described as an ideal college town, Hanover lacks enough used bookstores or coffeehouses to fit the image of the typical seat of an American college. With about 6,000 people spread over a relatively wide area, Hanover is comparable in population to the enrollment of the college and its associated schools, which would be about 5,600 if everyone were on campus at once. Dartmouth and Hanover have been intertwined since they originated in the same educational settlement, and town-gown tensions now revolve around the omnipresent need for parking or the occasional neighborhood zoning spat.

Dartmouth carefully distinguishes its campus from whatever other property it owns in Hanover. In town, it builds regular commercial buildings in traditionally townlike forms, although the Hopkins Center is a partial exception. Outside of Hanover, much of Dartmouth's development focuses on the Centerra Resource Park, a nearby but suburban development that sprawls over the town line in Lebanon. It has commercial labs and technology incubators, office buildings and restaurants, a grocery store, a courthouse, and even the college's development office. The passage of time is helping to enliven Centerra, and the town has considered designating it as a growth area worthy of higher densities and functional desegregation. Near Centerra along Route 120 are the school's storage facilities, mostly preengineered steel buildings serving as the University Press of New England Warehouse (1973–74), the Remote Storage Library (1981), the Remote Data Storage Center (2007), and the Hood Museum Remote Storage building (2008). The behemoth of the eastern suburbs is the Dartmouth-Hitchcock Medical Center, the state's largest employer and a thrumming engine of growth.

The medical center's original multilevel Main Mall (Shepley Bulfinch Richardson & Abbott, 1985–91) really does draw on the model of the shopping center, placing hospital departments next to chain restaurants to become, at its best moments, a skylit and genuinely friendly Main Street. Architecture critic Donald Maurice Kreis points out that the later East Mall (Shepley Bulfinch Richardson & Abbott, 2002–2006), in contrast, downplays the influence of the mall in favor of the contemporary airport terminal, pleasing in its efficiency. The home-away-from-home of David's House (Randall T. Mudge & Associates, 1994) also is affiliated with the hospital, as is the Medical School's adjoining collection of buildings.

Leaving Hanover to the south takes one past Sachem Village, a largely prefabricated outpost of graduate student housing a mile from the Green. It has been expanding regularly since the school first planted it here in 1958. Its first buildings came from an earlier iteration of Sachem Village, a temporary housing development erected on the Hanover High sports field in 1946.

North of town, the land beyond the golf course features the most interesting suburbs in the region, a brace of disparate developments that neatly occupies a row of former farms along the riverbank. About a mile and a half north of town is the Cold Regions Research and Engineering Laboratory (1961), run by the Corps of Engineers as the only United States Army installation in the state. Then comes the college's 170-acre Rivercrest housing development (1958), whose master plan (Wolff Lyon Architects, 2004) proposes a total reworking along New Urbanist lines. Next is Kendal at Hanover, the Quaker-affiliated retirement community (Ewing, Cole, Cherry & Parsky with Fleck & Lewis, 1989–91; Perkins Eastman Architects, 2001–2002). Next, about three miles up, is a dairy farm that stopped production in 1973 and became the Dartmouth Organic Farm in 1996 as the result of several student proposals. Although part of the property is a dedicated circus ground and much of it is returning to forest, providing a fine maple sugar wood, the bulk of the farm supplies food to the campus. The College Child Care Center also occupies this region north of town, near the rugby clubhouse and the Institute for Security Technology Studies.

83. The Casque & Gauntlet House

1823; 1905; Fred Wesley Wentworth, 1915; Randall T. Mudge & Associates, 1995; Smith & Vansant Architects, 2001–2002

The Casque and Gauntlet House

This student clubhouse persists in the commercial heart of town, anchoring two gateways to the college behind the building's small but extravagantly uncommercial lawn. The earnest, upright red-brick Federal house, with its tall windows and four tall chimneys, was historic before the society acquired it. When Dr. Samuel Alden built the house, the eighteenth-century tavern where he lived stood in front of it, facing Main Street. Alden dragged the old building down Wheelock Street and established the present lawn in its place. In 1888, the house became Purmort's Club, a student eating club with an ideal location; meanwhile the Casque & Gauntlet society (1887) was renting rooms next door. The society bought the house in 1893, designating its "Castle on the Corner" in reference to the Arthurian legend that was the society's mythical model of choice. The purchase made C&G the first of many societies at Dartmouth to adopt a domestic form for its meeting space, and the presence of living quarters probably restrained the group's secrecy in comparison to contemporary societies, which have built halls that contain no living spaces.

Casque & Gauntlet installed a replacement gabled entrance portico (1905) with tripled Tuscan Doric columns and added a cross-gabled rear ell (1915) to the designs of founding member Fred Wesley Wentworth. Although the college took over the building as a "Hostess House" to welcome wives visiting sailors and marines in the nation's largest Navy V-12 Unit (a proto-R.O.T.C.) during World War II, the society did not decide to admit women until 1978. More recently, an exterior ramp and an interior renovation have allowed the house to continue as the oldest and longest-occupied building of a Dartmouth society.

84. The Wheelock Mansion House
Hezekiah Davenport, 1773; 1838; 1846; Charles Alonzo Rich, 1899–1900; Curtis William Bixby, 1914–15

The executive mansion of Dartmouth's founding president is the oldest building in Hanover and the first substantial building of the college, although it has been in private hands for most of its existence. Philanthropic London evangelist John Thornton, the treasurer of the English fund supporting Moor's Charity School, gave £250 of his own money to Eleazar Wheelock to build an official presidential residence. The town carpenter led a team of fourteen men to complete the building on a site overlooking the Green, where Reed Hall now stands. George Ticknor ('07) described the mansion house around 1803 as a comparatively primitive building, and medical student William Tully wrote in 1808 that it was "neat, not elegant."[1] Yet the building was one of the first in the town with any pretension to style, and it formally represented the authority behind the institution. Next to the house stood Wheelock's original cabin of 1770, which became a slave quarter. Despite Wheelock's wish that the "hutt of loggs" be preserved as a relic, it did not last more than a dozen years.

Following Eleazar, presidents John Wheelock ('71), William Allen (of Dartmouth University), Bennett Tyler (of the college again), and Nathan Lord occupied the house as the school's executive mansion up to 1830. Their occupancy was largely reflexive, since Wheelock's descendants remained the owners of the building. When Dartmouth planned to erect Reed Hall, it bought the house in 1838 and sold it for removal. Its new owner dragged the house to its present site on West Wheelock Street, where later alterations would replace the original gambrel with the current gabled roof.

Local philanthropist Emily Howe lived in the house for forty-five years before her friend Hiram Hitchcock suggested she donate it to the town as a library—which she did during 1899, making Hitchcock the first chairman of the library corporation. The new Howe Library hired the college architect to remodel the house into a public building. Howe wanted to perpetuate associations with Colonial history,

The Wheelock Mansion House

and the remodeling—dedicated on Washington's Birthday in 1900—added a flat-roofed portico resting on a robust trio of Composite columns at its outer corners. A new front door and surrounding decorative elements were copies of Colonial designs from elsewhere in New England, and the removal of a pair of Victorian bay windows from the front facade completed the twentieth century's portrayal of the year 1770. On the interior, workers reconnected the two halves of what had become a duplex, making the building's central hall into a book delivery corridor with reading rooms alongside. The library rented out the dormlike suites upstairs to young faculty, including future art professor Homer Eaton Keyes, future antiquarian Alice Van Leer Carrick and her husband, Professor Prescott Orde Skinner, and future president Ernest Martin Hopkins.

Emily Howe married Hiram Hitchcock after the library opened in 1900, and she inherited her husband's fortune following his death a few months later. Emily Howe's library was the main beneficiary of her wealth after she died in 1912, allowing the library to add a reticent two-level brick ell for book stacks. Eventually, the town began funding the institution, and in 1973 it took over the whole operating budget. The library moved to a new building on East South Street and sold the Mansion House for commercial use. The tiny Anne Frey Park next to the building occupies the site of Storrs' Tavern (1772, demolished 1973), which housed the Delta Kappa Epsilon fraternity (1853) from 1908 to 1970.

85. St. Thomas Episcopal Church

Frederick Clarke Withers, 1873–76; 1887; Orcutt & Marston, 1953; Frank J. Barrett, Sr., 1959; Richard Monahon with Haynes & Garthwaite, 2002–2003

St. Thomas Episcopal Church

Despite some nineteenth-century hostility from the Congregational college, St. Thomas is the nearest church to the campus. In 1835, for example, Dartmouth abolished the chemistry professorship of Rev. Dr. Benjamin Hale after he began leading the local Episcopal congregation. When Dartmouth bought a particular lot at the south end of the Green in 1842, it was allegedly to prevent an Episcopal church from being built there. Nevertheless, the congregation acquired a church on Lebanon Street around 1850, and it officially became a parish in 1855.

Declining to build alongside its chapel and rectory on Main Street, the congregation acquired the present Wheelock Street site and began raising funds in Northeastern cities during the late 1860s. Prominent English-born architect Frederick Clarke Withers, a master of the High Victorian Gothic, designed the new building and illustrated it in his 1873 book Church Architecture. The published engravings indicate an entrance tower topped by a tall spire standing at the building's west end, but because Withers intended the construction to proceed in stages, he made the tower optional, and the congregation has not gotten around to building it. Uncluttered walls of granite rubble laid in courses gave the exterior its Gothic solidity, while extensive decorative work designed by the architect and donated by a New York family that summered in nearby Lebanon originally elaborated the interior of the church's east end. A great limestone arch separates the chancel's arched ribs of cherry from the church's nave, with its steeply pitched roof supported by pine trusses. Architect Ralph Adams Cram named the building one of the milestones in the development of good architecture in 1905.

The 1950s saw the church renovate its basement and add an office ell (Milham House) behind the west end, while Winifred Raven gave the narthex of Concord granite and Indiana limestone that mirrors the original eastern porch. Extensive work at the beginning of the next century altered the chancel extensively and replaced Milham House with a full-length clapboard ell containing the timber-framed St. Thomas Hall and an expanded basement. A blond timber porch at the east end, looking like the porches that Withers included in engravings of other churches, provides access to the addition.

86. West Wheelock Street

Hanover's oddest building was built too late to explain as an example of the region's postwar Modernist flowering, for all its affinity with Le Corbusier's Villa Savoye. The Banwell Building (Banwell Architects, 1971, 1984) is a monument to the importance of the car in the late twentieth century, since its form is dictated by its occupancy of the airspace over an eight-car parking lot owned by the Town. Six steel pilotis support the cantilevered one-level flat-roofed studio building, while copper panels sheathe its side façades. The ceiling of the parking lot is an irregular grid of white-painted steel I-beams infilled with painted cedar boards, while a board-sided stair-and-utility tower provides life support to the building from the earth below. Architect Roy Banwell, who carried on the postwar firm of Edgar H. and Margaret K. Hunter when they moved to North Carolina in 1966, designed the building as his firm's office; he also would pick up Edgar Hunter's post as Dartmouth's architectural instructor and continue to teach until 1989. The firm expanded its building slightly in 1984 and moved to West Lebanon in 1995, when a bookstore moved in.

Down the street stands the house of Sigma Delta (Wells, Hudson & Granger, 1936–37). The Phi Gamma Delta fraternity (1901) built it to replace the 1840s house that occupied this site when the society acquired the property in 1909. The group first advertised a design by Little & Russell in its fundraising, but the side-gabled Georgian house with the ground-level brick arcading, one of the last buildings in the wave of brick society houses, follows the designs of Hanover architect Alfred T. Granger. The basement originally contained a ski room, a period feature of fraternities. After the student government banned affiliations with discriminatory national fraternities during the nineteen-fifties, the group went local as Phoenix in 1965 before moving out and then folding in 1971. The college acquired the house and in 1981 began renting it to the Sigma Kappa sorority (1977). That society has experienced more success than its predecessor in the building since it too became a local group (1988).

The ghosts of former wall openings hint at the long institutional past of the simple one-level brick First Church of Christ, Scientist on School Street (1839; Frank J. Barrett, Sr., 1975). The Village of Hanover, apparently influenced by Dartmouth students voting as a bloc, erected the building as a schoolhouse on the site of a predecessor school. Theodosia Stockbridge operated a Sunday school here from 1855 to 1867, helping out the "rough boys" of the village so thoroughly that President Tucker called her "a saint of Hanover" and businessman Dorrance

Psi Upsilon house

B. Currier wrote that "she unwittingly taught us to fear God and to worship Miss Stockbridge."[2] An 1894 boys' club that met here adopted the name of the Stockbridge Association in her honor, purchasing the building in 1909 and officially naming it Stockbridge Hall. The Christian Science Society began renting the hall in 1954 and bought it in 1960 before adding a frame reading room with a square-columned portico to the south.

For about forty years, the rooms of Theta Delta Chi were unique because they overlooked the Green— the group occupied the upper level of the mansarded bank that stood south of today's Robinson Hall. In 1908, the fraternity (1869) bought an 1827 frame house on Wheelock Street, remodeling and expanding it in 1909. A 1924 fire became a reason to join the postwar building boom, and the group demolished its old house and replaced it with the three-level brick building that now stands, facing toward the college instead of the street (Putnam & Chandler, 1926). Its Georgian detailing on this house includes a molded brick watertable and a parapet-end lunette that gives the expansive wall planes an appearance of solidity; the rooftop balcony is a later addition by the group.

Students formed ephemeral or long-lived clubs during the eighteenth century, but Dartmouth did not have a permanent Greek-letter fraternity until a group of students formed Psi Upsilon in 1841 with a charter from an outside organization.

The club met in students' rooms and rented space in the upper levels of the Tontine, a downtown commercial block . Around 1860, the club joined the trend of carving a monumental meeting hall out of two levels in the Tontine. Professor Edwin Julius Bartlett ('72) described the "high and dignified room extending from front to rear of the building and provided with ante-room and 'guard-room'" where "we gathered to supplement the meager curriculum with debates, 'conversations,' book reviews, essays and the reading of plays....And once a year, at the initiation feast, came forth the unwonted cigar to be cautiously burned perhaps near an open window."[3] Leading the societal shift to domestic architecture in 1900, Psi Upsilon acquired a site on West Wheelock Street about a hundred yards from its hall and built its present Dutch cottage (Fred Wesley Wentworth, 1908; 1940; 2006). The building sought to impress not by height or symmetry but by coziness, presenting a two-and-a-half level clapboard form of slightly irregular arrangement. The second-level jetty, topped by a steeply-pitched side-gabled roof with flared eaves, advertises a warm hearth and good fellowship within, where mahogany and mission oak "in the German club style" lined the social rooms, according to The Dartmouth. Homer Eaton Keyes and R.L. Taylor designed a relatively extensive landscaping program, orienting the house toward the college rather than the town. The architect of the building, a society alumnus, had designed a fancifully towered stone fraternity house as a class project during his senior year of 1886–1887, and he would go on to create a country-clubbish 1890s headquarters for the National Rifle Association (he also designed the country's first theater exclusively for cinema, Jacob Fabian's 1914 Regent Theater in Paterson, N.J.). The fraternity added the large but sympathetic north ell to its building in 1940, reorienting the building's entrance southward.

87. The Connecticut River

The longest river in New England forms the western edge of the college campus, the town, and the state. Although the first college on the Connecticut River is deprived of a river view by its location high above the bank, Dartmouth's history is bound up with the history of this essential American thoroughfare. Governor Wentworth followed his help in planting the college with a royal charter that granted the school a monopoly on ferry rights along Hanover's entire bank in 1772. The college licensed one private ferry operation at the mouth of the Vale of Tempe, where Rope Ferry Road terminated, and licensed another at a landing located near today's bridge. That landing also served commercial flatboats poling between towns, but the river's most remarkable commercial activity was the annual log drive that occurred as early as 1761 and enjoyed a heyday from 1869 to 1909. Engaged in some of the longest drives in the United States, the lumbermen would tie up their sixty-foot-wide spruce rafts at the Ledyard bridge to spend the night; students would come down to watch with envy as the men cooked pork and beans over an open fire.

The northernmost of an early sequence of six navigation canals on the Connecticut River lay just below Hanover, at Olcott Falls. Dartmouth treasurer and trustee Mills Olcott ('90) and his partners had obtained a charter to dam the river in 1810 and by the 1820s they were taking boats around the dam through a set of locks and a canal on the New Hampshire side. That canal failed to make the passenger steamboat John Ledyard profitable during the 1830s, but it served flatboats until the railroad put it out of business. The Wilder Brothers' paper company bought the rights to the falls and built a new dam and pulp mill (1882–83), to which the International Paper Company, the successor owner, added two electric powerhouses (1910). Paper declined, the mill closed in 1927, and the dam shifted exclusively to producing electricity. The fifty-nine-foot-high Wilder Dam of 1948 to 1950 flooded the old dam and the valley beyond, impounding water for forty-six miles. The river rose at Hanover by about eighteen feet.

The rising water did not alter the state border, which had followed the waterline on the Vermont side since the Supreme Court mandated that it do so in 1934, also requiring the two states' attorneys general to perambulate the boundary every seven years. With the border under water at Hanover, its location is marked by an incised granite block on the Ledyard Bridge, near the center of the span.

The first bridge to span the river here (Rufus Graves, 1792–96) was one of the longest spans in New England, a single arch of timber that operated as a toll bridge until it collapsed in 1804. The replacement (1806; 1839; burned 1854) introduced a central stone pier. A covered timber lattice truss bridge (1859) was the first free bridge anywhere on the Connecticut River and became iconic: however stinky and old-fashioned the Ledyard Free Bridge was, it symbolized the town and served as a familiar gateway for generations of students. The New Hampshire Highway Department replaced it with a federal public-works project, a dual-span steel-arched concrete deck bridge with Art Deco touches (1934–1935; demolished 1997).

Higher, longer, and wider than its predecessors, the latest Ledyard Bridge (1996–99) is the first to require two river piers, and its scale and appearance caused controversy. Partway into the design, the state department of transportation brought in the Concord architectural firm of C.N. Carley Associates to design the Classical superstructure with its rusticated concrete abutments. The main feature of the award-winning bridge is its use of gigantic concrete gateway globes at each end to form celebratory entrances to the two towns and a proud interruption in the green fringe of the river.

When the dam drowned the canoe club's three islands and their cabins in 1950, the New England Power Company let the group use the rocky Gilman Island,

Ledyard Bridge from the Vermont side

just downstream from the bridge. The island had been part of an African-American neighborhood during the nineteenth century, when it was easier to reach, but by now it was uninhabited, a wooded world unto itself. The power company helped the Ledyard Canoe Club build Titcomb Cabin on the island in 1952 as a memorial to Capt. Jack Abbott Titcomb ('32), who was killed in the Battle of Luzon during 1945.

On the other side of the bridge is Lewiston, Vermont, a ghost town within the township of Norwich. The township's central village of Norwich proper thrives farther up the hill, where it served as the home of Norwich University (1820–25, 1830–66) before the military school moved to Northfield, Vermont. Down here along the riverbank, however, stood a distinct village where the Passumpsic & Connecticut Railroad laid its tracks during 1848 and built the area's first station. As a stop on the Boston & Maine, the station provided a first impression of college for thousands of freshmen over the years. Legendary coachmen would hang around the station, waiting to haul the new arrivals across the bridge and up Depot Hill (West Wheelock Street) to dump them at the inn. Recruiters for fraternities and eating clubs also waited at the station to compete for fresh members. The building was important enough to the college that Jens Larson included it somewhat imperialistically in his 1920 master plan for Dartmouth, suggesting that a new bridge should terminate at a formal "Station Square" here.

Lewiston's economy declined during the 1920s. Much of Hanover's rail traffic had shifted southward to White River Junction, Vermont. Some prostitution and bootlegging took place in Lewiston, with the Buckets of Blood speakeasy operating during Prohibition. The water rising behind the dam engulfed much of

The Connecticut River

the town during the early 1950s, and the remaining residents left in 1967 ahead of the bulldozers that turned part of the town into an interchange for Interstate 91. The college owns most of the town, including a metal-sided warehouse, a few dwellings, and a rotting coal trestle. The railroad station (1884, 1975), home of an area fraternal organization called the X Club, also survives. The main outpost of the college here is the pre-1870 brick house and shoe shop that the school's Davidson Pottery Studio has occupied since the 1980s. These faded remnants of the village enjoy an enviable view of the river and stand but several minutes' walk from the center of Hanover, suggesting that Lewiston is ripe for a careful rebirth.

88. Buildings West of Main Street

The Episcopal Student Center at 14 School Street (1960, Frank J. Barrett, Sr.) is named Edgerton House for long-time college treasurer Halsey C. Edgerton ('06), who donated the building with his family to the school's Anglican Fellowship. Also known as "the Edge," the brick building continues to house St. Christopher's Chapel and the campus ministry of St. Thomas Episcopal Church up the street. Next door at 12 School Street is an 1815 house that the church has used as a rectory since the late 1920s.

Hanover's best Greek Revival house is Panarchy, at 9 School Street (1835; 1923). As a clapboarded domestic contemporary of Reed Hall, the house features both a giant-scale quadristylar Doric temple front and an octagonal cupola—products of the original construction for Stephen Brown. The succession of individual owners, mostly reverends and professors, concluded at the turn of the twentieth century with Dr. William T. Smith, who occupied the place with his coachman and domestic servant. Smith's estate sold the house to the Phi Kappa Psi fraternity (1895) during 1902. Instead of replacing the house in brick during the 1920s, the fraternity added a Doric wing with a Mount Vernon portico to the north. Among the building's multiple basements is a Tomb Room meeting hall that is lined with concrete seats and focused on a central concrete sarcophagus. Most of the group's recent changes have been strictly organizational, as the fraternity protested the racist policies of its national organization by becoming the local group Phi Sigma Psi during 1967. Following Dartmouth's coeducation in 1972, the fraternity admitted women as members and began using the name Panarchy, finally dropping the Greek letters during 1990.

The conventional clapboard Foley House at 20 West Street (1912) hosts the least orthodox branch of the college's official housing system. The house served for many years as a rooming house, originally occupied by women of the Stickney and Daggett families. Ruby Eames Daggett, a long-time bookkeeper at the Dartmouth Bookstore, lived in the house for more than forty years, renting rooms to clerks and professors and maintaining a literary connection to the college (she eventually donated a collection of books to Baker Library). The college acquired the house and preserved the family atmosphere by renting it beginning during 1984 to the independent fraternity called Foley House (1920). The group had spent its first forty years as a chapter of the national Delta Upsilon fraternity before seceding in 1966 and renaming itself for a favorite advisor and original chapter member, Professor Emeritus Allen R. Foley ('20). Inducting two transfer students during 1969 made Foley the first Dartmouth fraternity to admit women, and by the early 1970s the group had taken on a communal bent, focused on sharing meals and occasionally housing "thru-hikers" on the Appalachian Trail. As an officially recognized "cooking cooperative," Foley remains a nonexclusive affinity group centered on preparing and eating meals as a community, housing up to ten members in its building.

89. Main Street

The long, flat-roofed New England commercial blocks that have formed the commercial heart of Hanover since the turn of the twentieth century lack much beauty, but they are highly flexible and timelessly effective as a backdrop for civic life. Near the top of the street, the upper (1903) and lower (1893) halves of the Davison Block have housed several student societies apiece, along with many other tenants. With a projecting bay at each end, the Bridgman Block (Louis Sheldon Newton, 1907; U.K. Architects, 2002) bears the initials of the Odd Fellows, since

Panarchy

its original owner had helped establish the group's local branch and provided a meeting hall here. The Dartmouth Co-Op occupies a part of the building, independent since it began in 1918 and once a leading national ski store. In the Gitsis Building (1929) is the Dartmouth Bookstore, the archetypal college shop since it was established by a student during the late nineteenth century.

Below the practical Allen Street, Frank Abbott Musgrove '99 commissioned the finely articulated Musgrove Building (1915) around a set of printing presses standing on the site, survivors of a fire that destroyed the predecessor building. Both buildings housed Musgrove's ancient printing company, which was producing The Dartmouth and other local papers at the time. The quiet Municipal Building (Larson & Wells, 1928) was built as a combination firehouse and town office, with space to park a half-dozen fire trucks on what is now a landscaped forecourt. The low Bishop Block to the south dates to the mid-1920s and features a leaded-glass shopfront transom.

The Bridgman Block

On the east side of Main Street is the small but varied Lang Building (Jens Fredrick Larson, 1937), a college-owned commercial building that carries the name of the early Hanover merchant Richard Language. It was planned in part by James Campion, whose clothing store occupied it for decades, dealing in green ties, traditional blazers, and the like.

The Currier Block (1887) replaces a building lost during the Main Street Fire of 1887, as does the attached Church Block (1887), whose upper level bears the vestige of an unusual molded-brick gable and a circular window opening. This was the site of the first commercial block in town, "a curious old ark" of brick once owned by the college and known as the Tontine Building (1815; destroyed 1887). As the 1887 fire moved south, it was stopped by the Lebanon Fire Engine and Company before it could destroy the Whitcomb Building, now the last frame building on the street (1867; Randall T. Mudge & Associates, 1990). The Italianate clapboard structure housed the town's hardware store during much of the twentieth century until the Ledyard National Bank renovated it and moved in.

Finally, the kernel of the Dartmouth Bank Building (Hutchins & French, 1913; 1959; 1977) was built on the Lebanon Street corner for the Dartmouth Savings Bank (1860) as the bank's old building on the Green made way for Robinson Hall. Here too the bank shared its lobby with the commercial Dartmouth National Bank (1865). The northern bays and upper levels of this building are later additions.

The Hanover Municipal Building

South of Lebanon Street is the brick Post Office (1930–31; 1964) with its giant-scale quadristylar Temple of the Winds portico of limestone. Writer Bill Bryson described how the familiar but too-small building "even smells nice–a combination of gum adhesive and old central heating turned up a little too high."[4]

   Opposite Lebanon Street is the Nugget Arcade (Frank J. Barrett, Sr., 1970), a tripartite commercial building fronting an office block that was built to adjoin the modest Palladian villa of the Nugget Theater (Orcutt & Marston, 1950–51). The Nugget's owner, uniquely, is the nonprofit Hanover Improvement Society (1922), which received the theater's original and legendarily uncouth building on West Wheelock Street as a gift. After that building burned in 1944, the society replaced it with this flat-roofed temple-fronted building on Main Street. Pianist Bill Cunningham ('19), who originated the idea of the theater, returned to play for the same Chaplin silent he had accompanied at the original opening of 1916. In contrast to the Nugget's reserved massing and polite siting, the vast brick building at 63 South Main Street (Kenneth F. Parry & Associates, 1974) fairly glowers over the entire corner. Built for the Dartmouth National Bank and known as the Fleet Building, it is owned in part by the college, which moved some offices here during

Clement Hall

2002 to join the bank of the moment. A shopfront addition (Banwell Architects, 2003) moderates the building's relation to the street, and a slightly earlier forest of brick piers alongside it locates the stairs that carry visitors up the slope to the building and its neighbors.

90. Lebanon Street

Lebanon Street is the junior partner in commerce to Main Street, a transitional zone whose businesses have been occupying houses and then replacing them since around World War I. Light industrial operations here have included the auto dealership of Rogers Garage (1914) and the 7 Lebanon Street lumberyard of the Trumbull-Nelson Company, practically the construction arm of Dartmouth since it was founded in 1917. Both firms have since moved to more spacious sites east of town on Route 120. The pre-World War II factory of Dartmouth Skis also has vanished from Lebanon Street, along with headquarters of *Ski Magazine* and the mid-1920s Hanover Diner, which departed from the site of the present Hanover Park retail building in 1962. (Allen Street's Streamliner Diner, a Worcester Lunch Car of 1938, left in 1958 and now serves students at the Savannah College of Art and Design in Georgia.) The commerce of Lebanon Street ends abruptly at the bend in front of St. Denis Roman Catholic Church.

For an emblem of a new era, the college-owned commercial block at 7 Lebanon Street and its linked Town-owned parking garage (Childs Bertman Tseckares,

Passage through 7 Lebanon Street

1999–2000) is unassuming. The building avoids showiness in favor of the plain and dignified brick-faced form of the traditional three-level New England commercial block, throwing in a kink where it meets its next-door neighbor. A passage leads through the building to a courtyard with a pagoda that marks the stair down to the four-level parking deck, which also is articulated as a commercial building. The two buildings of the joint project represent the first major construction downtown since the advent of the New Urbanism, the postmodern planning movement that emphasizes the spatial and civic lessons of the historic built environment. Thus 7 Lebanon Street, unlike its neighbor of the 1980s, is built up to the street line and features shop-front windows and actual entrances. The building also marks the first major step down town by Dartmouth's entrepreneurial real estate arm, which shifted its focus from the suburban Centerra development to explicitly recognize the long-term importance of Hanover's civic qualities to Dartmouth College.

The Robert C. Strong Memorial Building of the Hanover League of New Hampshire Craftsmen (David Robert Campbell, 1959; Smith & Vansant Architects, 2000) shows the North Country regionalist version of Modernist architecture that flowered here during the late 1940s and the 1950s. Craft-shop owners originally

St. Denis Roman Catholic Church

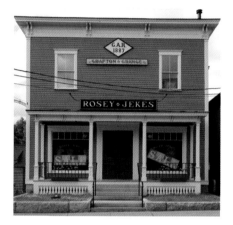

The Grange

started the state's League of Arts & Crafts during the 1920s and obtained state backing in 1932 to promote home industries by teaching craft techniques and selling works. One early state director was Edward Keen, who had apprenticed with Arts & Crafts figures in England before World War I and executed several carvings at Dartmouth. Dartmouth's Dean of Freshmen and Director of Admissions Robert Chamberlain Strong ('14), a friend and student of Keen and the advisor to Dartmouth's student workshops, helped establish Hanover's chapter in 1940. The group borrowed a frame building on Lebanon Street from the college in 1952, and when the Hopkins Center needed the site, the group erected this permanent headquarters. The architect was the long-time state league director David Campbell, author of a number of Modernist houses around the state as well as the Museum of Contemporary Crafts in Manhattan. This modestly scaled one-level building is a planar composition, its glass front playing against an honest wall of bare brick to suggest how local traditions could tame the cold reductivism of the International Style. As one of the state League's ten facilities, the Strong Building continues to house the Hanover League's gallery and education department. A later rear facade takes advantage of the building's new visibility from the 7 Lebanon Street garage.

The local chapter of the Grand Army of the Republic, the organization for U.S. Army veterans of the Civil War, erected its meeting hall in 1887. It rented out the ground level to other societies, including the Odd Fellows and the Grafton Star Grange (1875–79, 1886), the local chapter of the state agricultural society. Although the G.A.R. naturally faded, the Grange continued to meet in the building, which it acquired. An extensive renovation raised the building above a granite foundation and basement café, inserting an antique stair and set of columns from other buildings into the commercial space in the building's ground level (B.L. Benn Architects, 1990).

Hanover High School

A better example than the Blunt Alumni Center of the way Modernist architecture could deal with pressure to acknowledge its context, David McIntire's design for the brick Serry's Building features not only a Bauhaus ribbon window but also a paradoxical stack of quoins that marches up the opposite side of the facade (the Architectural Studio, 1986; 2005). The Zappala family built the three-level commercial building to replace their house, where since 1954 they had operated the tailoring business that Pasquale Serafini founded in 1907 as the Dartmouth Clothing Co. After the family closed Serry's in 2004, the college installed a more conventional ground-level rental space by replacing the original stuttered arcade with granite panels.

The majority of the block southeast of Lebanon and Currier Streets came into the hands of the college as part of a package with the South Street block. The first building to fall in the ensuing redevelopment was not one of the new acquisitions but a college-built motel that Dartmouth had been using as a dormitory since the early 1970s: the Hanover Inn Motor Lodge (W. Brooke Fleck, 1961; demolished 2007). The town's master plan suggested that commercial buildings should occupy this blockfront, and the school has held to its policy to stop at the Hop rather than to expand the campus beyond Lebanon Street.

St. Denis Roman Catholic Church is one of Jens Larson's rare Gothic forays, a substantial and thick-walled pile characterized by its variegated, uncoursed, uncut stone (Larson & Wells, 1924–25). A square-planned flat-roofed tower telescopes three stories at the building's northeast corner, alongside the entrance to the nave.

Hanover High School continues to occupy the building erected for it here (Wells, Hudson & Granger, 1935; 1957) as well as its earlier neighbor to the west, the Frances C. Richmond Middle School (Larson & Wells, 1924–26; 1951). The older building, originally built as a grade school, adopts the form of a cross-gabled mass engulfed by a huddle of lower additions, predicting Larson's design for Bucknell University's library of twenty-five years later. The high school's students come from both sides of the river as a result of an interstate compact that created the Dresden School District in 1963, the first interstate district in the nation. The district decided during the early twenty-first century to preserve the high school in town instead of trading it to Dartmouth for a suburban building site, and it then revamped the complex (Banwell Architects, 2006).

91. The Visual Arts Center
Machado & Silvetti, 2008–10

Millennial master plans for the town and the arts center confirmed Dartmouth's woeful underuse of its Lebanon Street parking lots and the insufficiency of its spaces for studio art, whether the Hopkins Center or Clement Hall. Clement was a concrete-framed arched-roofed mill building that originated as the Reo automobile dealership of Heating Plant Engineer Samuel C. Rogers (1914; 1925; Wells & Hudson, 1931). It stood back from the street and formed a pleasant courtyard for student sculpture, and its replacement would be of an utterly different scale, a neo-Modernist Visual Arts Center. The center terminates in a traditional saw-toothed roof, as at the Hop, but in this case the roof shelters a unique stacking of interior floors, mezzanines, and ramps that surround a central atrium. The building creates a new relation between the college and Lebanon Street, presenting a public facade that rebukes the blankness of the Hop next door. The Loew Auditorium moved to the center from the Hood Museum, finally enjoying a truly public entrance, and at the top of the building, glazed studios for senior majors face the street. By demolishing Brewster Hall, a dormitory originally built for Inn employees (Jens Fredrick Larson, 1938), the architects created a museum forecourt alongside the center, allowing pedestrians in town to experience a direct view of Charles Moor's Hood Museum for the first time.

92. Summer and South Park Streets

Unlike most religious societies in town, the Chapel of Our Savior Lutheran Church and Student Center at 5 Summer Street began as a student ministry (1955), with the local congregation emerging later. The group worshiped in a chapel designed by E.H. & M.K. Hunter in the second level of the Musgrove Building before erecting a Hunter chapel on this site (1958–61). The Hunters' successor firm, Banwell Architects, designed the current church in 1974 and turned the old church into the Parish Hall. Banwell's 2003 expansion of the complex created a Sunday school and a new narthex.

The little collision of a house on the corner at 13 Summer Street (1888–92) is the meeting hall of Cobra, the first women's senior society to occupy a building at Dartmouth. The white-painted clapboard building is contemporary with Summer Street, which was laid out before the turn of the century and anchored a neighborhood of farmers and farm laborers. Several college employees in succession occupied the house during the early twentieth century, and by the late 1950s the college was using it as a faculty rental. Following Dartmouth Hillel (1984–98), the school moved in Cobra. Of the half-dozen senior societies at Dartmouth, this was the first exclusively for women, its name chosen at its 1979 founding apparently in reference to the head of the goddess Medusa. (Phoenix, the second women's society, followed in 1984.) In 1980, Cobra unsuccessfully proposed a new verse for the school's alma mater, then known as "Men of Dartmouth," before others reworded the song more subtly to refer to both women and men.

Katherine and Harold Rozelle Bruce, a political science professor, occupied the house at 27 South Park Street (Larson & Wells, 1923) for most of the building's first thirty years, with other faculty following during a period of college rental. Following Hillel (1973–84) was Fire & Skoal, the first new senior society in more than seventy-five years at its founding in 1975. As the only such group at the time that tapped both men and women for membership, the society modeled itself in part on the school's Great Issues program, a mandatory weekly speaking series that had enlightened and bedeviled seniors between 1947 and 1966. By the time Fire & Skoal began, G.I. had shrunk to an annual student-run Senior Symposium (1966–2001), but it still inspired members to focus on more than socializing. The name of Fire & Skoal, on the other hand, is all about fellowship, since it refers to perhaps the greatest song ever written about winter and the fireplace, the "Hanover Winter Song" (1898).

The song's author was Richard Hovey ('85), Dartmouth's poet laureate and the author of its alma mater around 1893. The bearded bohemian was mourned as one of the greats when he died at thirty-six, although today he is forgotten as even a minor melodramatist everywhere but in this town. Carlos Baker ('32) called him "the presiding genius in forming that part of the myth of Dartmouth which has since been shared by all her graduates," a myth that Professor Allan Macdonald described as standing "any assault of reality, a pagan, Anglo-Saxon myth of primitive living and comradeship."[5] And who could avoid wrapping the sleigh blanket a little tighter while hearing the "Hanover Winter Song" sung to Frederick Field Bullard's melody of clambering minor-key menace?

> Ho, a song by the fire! Pass the pipes, with a skoal!
> For the wolf-wind is wailing at the doorways,
> And the snow drifts deep along the road,
> And the ice-gnomes are marching from their Norways,
> And the great white cold walks abroad.[6]

93. The South Block Redevelopment

The college bought a package of nineteen properties comprising most of the block below South Street, as well as the block to the northeast, in 1998. The radical redevelopment of this block by Dartmouth's real estate arm was the first significant construction since the town published its brazenly traditional downtown "vision" plan (Brook McIlroy, 2001). That plan proposed to extend Main Street's vibrant pedestrian life by requiring larger mixed-use buildings on what were then the sites of downtown parking lots and commercial houses. Such a plan comported with the national about-face on the wisdom of segregating downtowns by function and contradicted a 1955 survey, emblematic of the period, that showed most Hanoverians wanting non-business uses "cleaned out" of the downtown. Thus Dartmouth would create leasable commercial space on the ground level of every new building in the redeveloped block while filling the upper levels with office rentals (along Main Street) or apartments (on the side streets). A subterranean interior-block parking garage underpins most of the new buildings. Nine run-down if sometimes historic buildings made way for the project, including an 1887 Catholic church on South Street that had become a fraternity house and then a ramshackle student rental known as the Crack House for its interior fault lines.

The one building that recalls the time before Dartmouth reworked the block is 3 South Street (U.K. Architects, 2007), which adopts the form of a 1785 building that once stood nearby. Its model is the Gates House, which had stood at the corner of Main Street since making way for Wilson Hall in 1884. The dismantling of the old house for the redevelopment supplied a number of architectural elements that found their way into the recreation.

The varied row of four two-and-a-half level domestic buildings at 5–9 South Street and 5 Currier Street (William Rawn Associates, 2006) shows some

9, 7, and 5 South Street

influence of the Arts & Crafts movement. Far larger and bolder is the commercial block at 68–72 South Main Street (Truex Cullins & Partners, 2007–2008), designed to comport with the scale of its surroundings. The openness of the building's single ground-level floor plate is belied by the building's exterior, which is articulated as four distinct structures. A couple are flat-roofed white-corniced commercial buildings reminiscent of the post–Civil War period, while next door stands a shop with a contrastingly broad, cross-gabled roof. The composition is friendly to shopping, and if its frivolity seems forced, like that of a ski resort, that is a small price to pay for the building's avoidance of the disruptive blunders of the 1970s. The college's redevelopment succeeds at its goal of weaving into the fabric of downtown a great amount of new steel and brick while attempting to reinforce the intangible qualities of Hanover's urban energy.

94. The Howe Library
Shepley Bulfinch Richardson & Abbott, 1974, 2004–2005

One of Hanover's vital centers of activity, the Howe originated at the turn of the twentieth century in Emily Howe's creation of the library in the Wheelock Mansion House. This Modernist brick building at the southeast corner of East South and South College Streets features a uniform use of a distinctive tan-painted wooden trim that helps soften the building's lines. The poured concrete causeway and stair leading to its entrance are reminiscent of the Fairchild Center, while the building's steeply pitched shed roofs and high clerestories create opportunities for interior timber framing. Original architect Gerrit Zwart '54 returned to design the expansion, which disposes the building's front façade along South Street nearly symmetrically about the library's central clock. The addition contains several reading rooms, along with the Ledyard Art Gallery.

1. William Tully, journal (1808), reprinted in Oliver S. Haywood and Elizabeth H. Thomson, eds., *The Journal of William Tully, Medical Student at Dartmouth 1808–1809* (New York: Science History Publications, 1977), 23.
2. Dorrance B. Currier, quoted in Francis L. Childs, "Personages and Eccentrics," in Childs, ed., *Hanover, New Hampshire: A Bicentennial Book* (Hanover, N.H.: University of New England, 1961), 143.
3. Edwin Julius Bartlett, *A Dartmouth Book of Remembrance* (Hanover, N.H.: The Webster Press, 1922), 23.
4. Bill Bryson, *I'm a Stranger Here Myself* (New York: Broadway Books, 1999), 5.

ACKNOWLEDGMENTS

People whose generous correspondence or scholarly research is reflected in this book include Jacqueline Baas, Ray Banwell, Frank Barrett, Jr., William Bruning, Christopher Closs, John Cone, Jr., Kenneth Cramer, Raymond Cunningham, Alex Duke, William Flynn, Brandon Fortune, Jason Gaddis, David Harrison, Allen Hodgdon, Dick Hoefnagel, John MacAuliffe, Dick Mackay, Victoria Newhouse, Richard Polton, Nancy Pompian, Sue Reed, Bryant Tolles, and John Wilson. Thanks to Sheila Culbert for her encouragement, and deepest gratitude to Sarah Hartwell of Rauner Library, whose research in the college archives was essential to this project.

Scott Meacham

SELECTED BIBLIOGRAPHY

Barrett, Frank J., Jr. *Hanover, New Hampshire.* Dover, N.H.: Arcadia Publishing, 1997.

Chase, Frederick. *A History of Dartmouth College and the Town of Hanover, New Hampshire (1815).* Edited by John K. Lord. Brattleboro, Vt.: Vermont Printing, 1928.

Childs, Francis L., ed. *Hanover, New Hampshire: A Bicentennial Book.* Hanover, N.H.: Town of Hanover, 1961.

Edgerton, Halsey C., compiler. *Terms of Gifts and Endowments and an Annotated Copy of the Charter of Trustees of Dartmouth College.* Hanover, N.H.: Dartmouth College, 1940.

Hill, Ralph N. *College on the Hill: A Dartmouth Chronicle.* Hanover, N.H.: Dartmouth Publications, 1964.

Hoefnagel, Dick, with Virginia L. Close. *Eleazar Wheelock and the Adventurous Founding of Dartmouth College.* Hanover, N.H.: Durand Press for Hanover Historical Society, 2002.

Lord, John K. *A History of Dartmouth College 1815–1909.* Concord, N.H.: Rumford Press, 1913.

———. *A History of the Town of Hanover, N.H..* Hanover, N.H.: Town of Hanover, 1928.

Richardson, Leon Burr. *History of Dartmouth College.* Hanover, N.H.: Dartmouth College Publications, 1932.

Tobias, Marilyn. *Old Dartmouth on Trial: The Transformation of the Academic Community in Nineteenth-Century America.* New York: New York University Press, 1982.

Tolles, Bryant F., Jr. "The Evolution of a Campus: Dartmouth College Architecture Before 1860." *Historical New Hampshire* 42, no. 4 (Winter 1987): 328–82.

INDEX

(Italics indicate a photograph)